FAMILY CLANS IN THE MIDDLE AGES

Europe in the Middle Ages
Selected Studies

Volume 4

General Editor
RICHARD VAUGHAN
University of Hull

NORTH-HOLLAND PUBLISHING COMPANY – AMSTERDAM · NEW YORK · OXFORD

FAMILY CLANS IN THE MIDDLE AGES

A study of political and social structures in urban areas

By
JACQUES HEERS

Translated by
Barry Herbert

NORTH-HOLLAND PUBLISHING COMPANY–AMSTERDAM · NEW YORK · OXFORD

Library of Congress Catalog Card Number: 76-3505
North-Holland ISBN: 0 7204 9009 X

1st edition: 1977
2nd printing: 1979

Published by:
North-Holland Publishing Company – Amsterdam/New York/Oxford

Distributors for the U.S.A. and Canada:
Elsevier North-Holland, Inc.
52 Vanderbilt Avenue, New York, N.Y. 10017

Library of Congress Cataloging in Publication Data
Heers, Jacques.
Family clans in the Middle Ages.

(Europe in the Middle Ages; 4)
Translation of Le clan familial au Moyen Age.
Includes bibliographical references and index.
1. Clans and clan systems--History. 2. Italy--Nobility--History. 3. Cities and towns--Italy--History. 4. Social history--Medieval, 500–1500. I. Title. II. Series.
HT653.I8H4313 1976 301.44'2 76-3505
ISBN 0-7204-9009-X

This book was originally published in 1974 under the title *Le clan familial au Moyen Age*, éd. P.U.F., Paris

Printed in England

General Editor's preface

With a few minor emendations and the omission of some sub-headings, this version of *Le clan familial au Moyen Age* is an exact replica of the French original, which appeared in 1974, complete with notes. No justification is needed for translating into English a book which revises in so profound a way our knowledge and interpretation of medieval urban structures. Nor indeed for introducing for the first time to the English reading public the work of Professor Jacques Heers of the Sorbonne; already well-known for his penetrating studies of the social and economic history of the later Middle Ages and, in particular, for his book on Genoa in the fifteenth century. The author has himself read, revised and approved Mr Barry Herbert's English translation of his book, the typescript of which was also revised by myself.

October 1976

Richard Vaughan
General Editor

Contents

List of figures

Introduction

The social group in the Middle Ages

'Social' history passed long ago beyond the stage of the simple, more or less anecdotal and superficial description of ways of life, customs, and of mental or religious practices and attitudes. That type of history, more often than not, was content merely to analyse contemporary writings; it was concerned with chronicles and narratives, and it lent great importance to treatises on morality or on domestic life, and to preachers' sermons.

Yet we are well aware that literary works, whatever they may be (for example, chivalric romances, farces and *fabliaux*), give a highly deformed picture of society. They present types invented sometimes from nothing; they show above all the states of mind or the intentions of their authors, or the conventions which regulated some curiosity or other. In this way they seem to be of interest, especially at a remove, and require in any case very close, very critical study. Moreover, 'literary' social types presented in this way evolve very slowly; most frequently they become fixed and perpetuate, for several centuries, in a thoroughly stereotyped and conventional way, invariable patterns which bear only a distant resemblance to reality. Such is the peasant, always described uniformly, without subtlety, as a bumpkin, of repulsive or even monstrous appearance, dirty, poor and coarse.[1] Such, in a completely different sphere, are the clergy, more especially the monks, grasping, gluttonous, lascivious and lazy; this picture of them persists for a very long time. These fixed types are modified, or purely and simply abandoned, only in exceptional circumstances such as an unusual fate or a fashion not easily understood; towards the sixteenth century the shepherd is no longer the bumpkin lost among the other peasants, but the much more delicate, more refined man of the pastorals.[2]

A second class of contemporary documents consists of registers and other 'journals'; these are more authentic, much richer for the study of material society, but remain little known and little used, except for central Italy. In any case they express the perceptions and thoughts of a single social category, normally the clergy or the bourgeoisie.

Finally sermons, a very special literary *genre*, are also in a sense a curiosity; but, being written according to a certain moral ethic, they give only rare spontaneous clues to the realities of everyday life.[3]

Recently, historians have turned to other sources, of exceptional quality. The study of legal proceedings (royal courts, officialities or even seignorial assizes) and of remissions or pardons yields much information, in this case more genuine, about different aspects of everyday life and of mental attitudes, often in greatly differing spheres. It is very desirable that a systematic examination of documents of remission, for example for France, which have hardly begun to be studied historically, should be carried out, so that this mine of information of all types may be used much more, and scientifically.

Beyond these descriptive preoccupations, which are of definite interest if they inspire true historical research rather than the previous more superficial quest for picturesque or archaizing anecdote, social history seeks to define categories, levels, sometimes structures. This structural enquiry has offered us many pictures which, it is claimed, are characteristic of feudal society: the 'feudal' lord, the 'merchant' bourgeois, the peasant 'bound to the soil'. These types, obviously simplified, correspond essentially to different economic spheres, to professional activities. Readers have long accepted crude ideas of them, fixed ideas without subtlety, more dependent on a vivid imagination; they seem to be the product of a historico-literary *genre* which reached the height of its expression in the Romantic era. The relationships and forces linking these different social categories remain, moreover, ill-defined, or are defined very conventionally, in a purely arbitrary and whimsical manner.[4]

Further, a statistical study of levels of wealth, undertaken primarily from tax records, often meets obstacles, such as fraud, privilege, or the difficulty of deciding the exact basis of a tax. Such statistical data, very uncertain or at least approximate, form only one side of the examination of social structures; they do not allow one to reach the human aspect, to understand relationships and solidarity.

It seems therefore that neither a socio-professional classification nor one by wealth can satisfy a study which, becoming more and more demanding, sets itself the goal of showing how men are distributed inside 'medieval' society or societies, and whether they really feel that they belong to a social category. From this comes the more ambitious desire to demonstrate the mechanics of this past society, to delineate and analyse its social 'strata'.[5]

Here the historian can choose between two attitudes; he may attempt to apply to the past, in this case to the Middle Ages, an existing schema, or a schema built up over a period of time and with differing fortunes by some ideological school; or he may try to find out what ideas men had, at the time, of this social distribution.

The former approach, which is nevertheless called 'historical', includes the attitude of those writers who propose a schema based on a more or less authentic, more or less well defined Marxism, which puts at the head of any social analysis the distribution of men into 'classes'. In these class societies the hierarchy is established according to wealth; attention is given principally, and sometimes even exclusively, to the pursuit of economic interests, while religious or sacred factors are ignored. In this case class consciousness and then the class struggle inevitably set those who hold capital and have the monopoly of manufactured goods against those who work for a wage and have no chance, or little chance, of changing their situation.

The existence of social classes as such, which is generally accepted by historians for the industrial civilizations of the recent past, is much more contested for earlier periods. For example, with reference to French society under the Ancien Régime, we have seen the polemic between the supporters of this theory, often united under the colours of Porchnev whose arguments seem in fact very tenuous and fragile, and non-Marxist historians, more especially those who rallied to the point of view of Roland Mousnier.[6]

It seems very significant that where the Middle Ages of the West are concerned, no systematic attempt has been made to apply this schema, at least by non-Russian historians. Nowhere is there any comprehensive study of 'medieval' social structures in terms of class, of class consciousness, or of the class struggle. Such presumptive attitudes are found only in a diffuse, hesitant, sometimes detached way, normally as the dull and unconscious echo of a theory implicitly accepted but not proven, to which it seems good to give, in passing, some small homage. Very many authors speak readily of social 'classes' and even occasionally of 'class struggles', as if the use of such words went without saying, but without properly justifying them. It is often a question of linguistic facility, negligence – or complacency. These formulae have become very commonplace and have thrust themselves into many different works. They are found above all where there is a social conflict to be analysed. But there again, this presumptive history has given no evidence, which would entail a detailed analysis of the origins of social conflicts (political, economic or religious reasons, or personal ambition?) and an admittedly difficult study of the social status of the rebels.

Attempts to explain the numerous heresies of the end of the Middle Ages – for example, the Lollards, Hussites, Albigensians and Waldenses – by opposing rich and poor classes, have long been made by various well-known historians, including some in eastern Europe; these do not satisfy the reader and end in failure. The opinions of E. Werner on these problems are now contradicted by the well-proven fact that heresies, the Albigensian and the Hussite among others, enlisted their adherents from greatly differing social circles through professional activities, social prestige or wealth.

Similarly, so-called 'social' or 'popular' revolts, peasant or urban uprisings, all highly complex events, can surely in no case be reduced to a class struggle. In the absence of precise studies on the true social composition of revolts, historians may conveniently put forward not only opposing economic interests, but also: misery and unemployment, racial or religious hatred, social imbalance caused by massive movements of people from the countryside to uneasy settings in urban societies. One must also note the role of the aristocrats themselves, their ambition, their lust for vengeance.[7] The historian of these social conflicts might also emphasize, for example in Paris, the bitterness of confrontations between the king and craftsmen intent on defending their privileges and monopolies. Finally, he might also see in certain peasant revolts more or less spontaneous surges of regionalism against the royal administration and its taxes; widely in western Europe rural riots followed closely after the institution or increase of royal taxes; the peasants did not rise against their lords but against the revenue officials sent from the capital.

The social class theory neglects in addition one fact which is in my opinion of prime importance: the fluidity of human situations. It is true that the masters did all in their power, inside the art and craft guilds, to block the progress of the journeymen and apprentices. It is not certain that they succeeded, and it would be very ingenuous to accept at face value the many measures decreed to this end which are preserved in the statutes of craft associations; rather, the multiplicity of prohibitions would prove that they were constantly flouted, directly or indirectly. Moreover, to accept the idea of more or less closed classes is to fail totally to appreciate the numerous opportunities for social advancement through the tenure of innumerable royal, princely or municipal posts, through clerkship, the law, or accounting; also through war, or quite simply through marriage.

Generally I think that one must beware, in the present state of research, of such *a priori* theories, and even of such vocabulary which corresponds to nothing certain and seems to be completely subjective. Admittedly the study of forms of commerce and industry in many cities of the West at that time shows techniques and structures which are of a distinctly 'capitalist' nature. But this is not so new, and to try to contrast a thoroughly archaic society of the feudal era with the precapitalist or capitalist society of the fourteenth or fifteenth centuries seems rather illusory. In fact 'capitalist' techniques were spread much earlier and much wider than our history books claim. We may take the example of credit: in many circumstances men openly made loans at interest; the notorious ban on usury seems not to have been respected – rather the reverse. Certain types of land revenues, well known from the eleventh century, testify to the coexistence of these 'capitalist' practices and of ancient social structures founded on relationships other than those of clearly separated and hostile 'classes'. Much later, the triumph of mercantile capitalism, for example in the cloth industry, the journeymen's economic subservience to the leaders of industry, the precarious and miserable condition of many of them, do not *ipso facto* imply class consciousness and social relations regulated solely by class struggles. For these periods class feeling remains to be proven. In the absence of such proof the use, for convenience, involuntarily even, of the word 'class', can only cause regrettable confusion. It is better, depending on each case, to speak of social categories, of levels of wealth, of ways of iife, professional activities and crafts. These expressions are more precise and have at least the merit of being meaningful.

The second course of action open to the historian who wishes to define the strata of medieval society – to see that society through the eyes of people of the time – is in line with real-scientific criteria and gives rise to absolutely rigorous research. Hcrc, thc accent is resolutely placed on Orders. This society of orders – clergy, nobility and third estate – depends no longer on fortunes or means of economic domination, but on honours and dignity; each order includes men whose economic situations differ greatly and who are even found at all levels of the hierarchy of wealth. Moreover, very often these orders are not closed. The composition of political assemblies in various western countries, sometimes from as early as the thirteenth century, definitely shows the existence of these three orders. Numerous contemporary documents of different kinds also emphasize this. Historians have been forced to the view that medieval society was rigorously classified into three well-defined orders.

However, it is far from certain that this classification was felt by the men of the age, or indeed that it regulated all social relationships. Let us not forget that these divisions were, naturally, asserted by the clergy, the doctors of the Church, who often invoked a particular ethic and a divine order; fiscal considerations also contributed, in the minds of princes' officers, to make the distinction between categories sharper and more rigorous than it really was. I believe that we must take these arrangements, which are probably quite abstract, only for what they are really worth; up to a certain point they are merely convenient procedures, or at other times the speculations of intellectuals. In their daily lives men were probably not so keenly conscious of this division.[8] In any case, these political orders and those Estates, which were similarly represented, I think, at quite a high abstract level, were opposed, or at least were capped, by 'social orders', by perfectly constituted, concrete and real 'social groups'. It is the reality of this social group that I wish to discover.

The target is probably much more limited. There is no question of putting forward a schema valid for the whole of a country's society, but merely of seeing what were the frameworks, sometimes on a very reduced scale, of individuals' social lives; of defining the nature of these frameworks, their origins and their inner life (on the political, social, religious or artistic level). I wish also to analyse the composition of these social groups and thus to note precisely the reality of human relations in town or country; and finally, I wish to see how these social bonds may have marked different aspects of our 'medieval' civilization.

It is likely that these groups had a particularly important place in 'medieval' society, in the West and in the East. This is readily explained by the living, ever present heritage of primitive societies which had a tribal, more or less communalistic character; also by the heritage of certain strictly Roman traditions, such as the *gens*, and professional organizations and religious societies of all kinds.

Moreover, the prevalence of sacred and spontaneous demonstrations of religious feeling also shows how our 'medieval' societies were so interested in religious communities, in confessional brotherhoods, often despite differences of situation, wealth and office. Further, these societies seem to have been unsettled: groups and individuals were very mobile, economic fortune and social situation were uncertain. All the most recent serious studies of urban aristocratic families in the West bring out a constant, sometimes rapid renewal or rather enrichment of those families. This mobility does not easily suit too rigid or too narrow a social schema.

Finally, and above all, the strength of the social group counterbalanced the weakness of the state. Throughout the Middle Ages, and probably throughout our past, the deficiency of a monarch's central authority or of a city's local administrative power caused the formation of natural or artificial social groups and increased the strength of those already in being. It has long been a commonplace to link vassalage to the enfeeblement of the king; this enfeeblement also resulted in the consolidation of family or suprafamily clans. Conversely, to institute a solid royal administration was to attack these groups' power. This was a long struggle and its stages, in France for example, emphasized the progress of the monarch and of the state. As early as 1280 Beaumanoir bitterly criticized the peasant communities of the Beauvais region. Yet only at the end of the reign of Louis XV was the family's joint penal liability (recalling or proving the family group's cohesion) suppressed, and only under Louis XVI was the parish's joint fiscal liability discontinued. Attacks on common of pasture, increasing throughout the eighteenth century, bore fruit only in 1791 with the abolition of easements and commonage, the sale of common land, and the right of enclosure granted to every landowner.[9] Thus for centuries the survival of *taisible* ('tacit') communities in the country districts of central France was constantly threatened by the attacks and encroachments of royal legislation which sought to liberate the individual from these communal constraints.[10]

Similarly the Church tried to control the brotherhoods; urban communities, free or seignorial, strove to reduce the power of family clans, to forbid private conflicts and to assert peace and order. This is well borne out in *Romeo and Juliet*.

So the existence of social groups is seen in a particular political context. Without doubt they appear to have been very active, at a time when in large kingdoms the monarch's authority was not yet evenly asserted; when all manner of disturbance, struggles for political influence and even armed conflict inside cities and states naturally caused new feelings of human solidarity.

For all these reasons, in the Middle Ages, social links stand out as numerous, many sided, active in many different areas and, in all, very powerful against the state or the individual. The isolated man, foreign to these groups, suffered; from this the most serious social disorders arose, especially in towns, where populations seemed less stable, where new arrivals, who were not part of solidary groups, were more numerous.

These social groups were not all similar. Some vaunted their loyalty to the family, in the different senses of that word. Their members felt united by close bonds; they bore the same name, and protected and defended the honour of that name; they led their lives more or less in common. In any case, 'family' bonds were strongly reinforced by political or military solidarity, and by neighbourhood links. These family groups differed from each other in their economic systems, which might vary between practically free individual property and total community with the most severe constraints. Above all they differed in their form and composition. Some claimed a single common ancestor and common blood; these consanguineous families – for example, noble lineages of town and country – might spread by numerous admissions and by the amalgamation of several groups. Then they formed what I shall call here vast 'family clans' which were sometimes made up of several hundred individuals.

Other groups, also known as family groups, allowed less importance to a common blood. They were born of more or less artificial unions which brought together not only brothers but also outsiders who wished to live and work together like brothers. In this way, through the practice of *affrairamentum*, were formed small or large communities, brotherhoods or *taisible* communities.

Other groups still arose from links of neighbourhood alone, from the need for security or mutual help, from a shared religion and belief, or again from economic links. The range seems wide, and despite many valuable studies devoted to different kinds and examples of religious or professional groups, it still seems difficult to establish with any certainty the extent of their activities and importance. In the country, the peasant communities of the mountains, associations which were of a politico-economic nature, regulated at first areas for sheep and the use of pasture, then the whole life of a valley. Certain artificial, primarily political brotherhoods bear witness to the desire for self defence, or for the appeasement of conflicts. In southern France they had some of the characteristics of the movement for peace and for brotherhoods of peace which in Languedoc, and more particularly in Auvergne, went back to the 1180s. In Spain, especially in Castile, the *hermandades*, political associations for defence and security, armed themselves against brigands and felons. It is not always easy to distinguish between the strictly religious brotherhoods, whose history, however, is much better known, and organizations for political protection, mutual help, or even professional protection; that is why the study of craft groups should cover ground much wider than the strictly economic sphere – the study of statutes and regulations – to which it has previously, too willingly, been restricted.

Finally we must come to know better the factions which divided between them a whole city, sometimes even a region or a country; for example, in Italy, the Guelphs and the Ghibellines, then the Blacks and the Whites; men have attempted to define their political attitudes, but not their recruitment of members or their inner life.

It is not easy to study these groups. The historian has great difficulty in assembling a 'classical' type of documentation. Usually, written documents do not exist. These social groups, born outside the state, maintained against the state, leave little trace in historiography or even in official texts; royal agents were unaware of them, or only interested in curbing their activities. Therefore there are vast gaps. Very often, too, a group arose spontaneously, was slowly organized, without feeling it necessary to determine written rules; in many countries it was based on ancestral traditions and an unwritten law, transmitted by word of mouth from generation to generation, and known to all; this for the *taisible*, the tacit, communities. Certain associations never decreed their statutes. Those which did often decided to do so only very late, under pressure from royal or municipal authority (especially, here, the crafts and brotherhoods) or in response to legal necessity. So the statutes, the only texts which we can study in quantity at our convenience, are generally concerned only with a certain very restricted category of these groups, and a relatively late phase of their history; whence the danger of a false view, leading to ignorance of many aspects of social life which are not represented in these regulations and more especially, with reference for example to the crafts, of religious and human factors which however are of prime importance, at least in their origins.

The statutes, solemn documents even if frequently modified or complemented, have been religiously kept in associations' chests and thus have defied the passing centuries. But the constantly renewed lists of brethren and the accounts, which lost all interest as soon as they were audited, disappeared, and cannot now satisfy our curiosity. This explains why the history of these brotherhoods and crafts, once attempted, has remained institutional and legal, more than social or economic.

Only those countries where the tradition of written documents was strongly established give a different type of documentation, more authentic and more varied, thanks particularly to deeds drawn up by notaries. Only in these cases is it possible to describe the human composition of a group and the life which was its own.

In the absence of traditional written documents the social group may be approached through the study of external signs of the strength of human solidarity; the study of family names, even toponymy, and especially the study of rural and urban habitats leads one to deduce the existence of family clans or brotherhoods, and occasionally to measure their size and power. Also in this direction the examination of fiscal records, lists of hearths or buildings, provides first-rate information. Moreover, the history of these groups should be based on information obtained from the study of private law: the administration of property, settlements upon spouses or heirs and forms of corporation; marriage settlements or wills testify to the nature of social bonds and to the weight of family or community constraints.

The notion of the family clan and medieval history

Marc Bloch deplored the fact that historians of medieval societies took little interest in the family; since then, only the studies of G. Duby on the seignorial family in the feudal period[11] have enriched a record which otherwise in France has been poor.

Yet the idea of the family itself deserves attention. First from the sociological point of view, for the study of the group itself and of its evolution; also from the economic point of view, for family solidarity was often a great burden and left its mark on many aspects of material civilization; finally, from the demographic point of view, for only when we know the size of the family group can we use fiscal records more certainly and more profitably and obtain a better quantitative approach in this area. Specialists in medieval demography have been quick to ponder what factors they should apply to the numbers of hearths or houses in order to find the approximate level of population. But for a long time they have been concerned with proposing mean factors valid for the whole of the western world rather than with providing a more limited history, a sound study of hearths and dwellings in different areas. They have understood that hearths were only administrative and fiscal abstractions and they have attempted, sometimes without success and in a very uncertain manner, to distinguish between real hearths and composite hearths. The fiscal hearth is of course a quite abstract and artificial notion, having only a tenuous link with reality; its value may change suddenly: towards 1426 an ordinance of the duke of Brittany declared the fiscal hearth to be thenceforth equivalent to three heads of family, where previously it had meant one.[12] But this difficulty aside, authors have generally accepted that real hearths were everywhere the same, whatever the place or time. J. Glénisson and E. Carpentier[13] have shown the need for caution by affirming that the hearth was only an imaginary notion and the search for the average hearth a 'false problem', and similarly R.H. Bautier's study of the population of Carpentras[14] has shown that inside one town the hearth varied according to social and ethnic conditions and from year to year. These studies have called this approach into question, yet the idea of a single constant notion of the hearth is still shared, sometimes unconsciously, by many authors. This is to fail to recognize the extreme diversity of social structures in the 'medieval' world and to project onto the still obscure past our own modern certainties;[15] above all, it is to bring the size of the family group down in all cases to its lowest level and to deny the existence of very large families, much bigger than the conjugal family, consisting of a great number of people.

My research in the Genoese archives has allowed me to verify very readily the considerable importance, in all areas, and the often exceptional size of family or rather, suprafamily, groups, of associations of individuals who all bore the same name. This veritable family clan, called here the *albergo*, consisted of between several dozen and several hundred souls. It is relatively easy to study it, thanks to the abundance of deeds drawn up by notaries concerning its structure or its inner life; thanks also to the fact that the Genoese *albergo* became an institution of an official character, one of the normal frameworks of political life. This situation is without doubt quite exceptional; Genoa probably presents the most obvious example of the role of family groups inside the medieval city.

However, this exemplary structure is not unique. I have investigated institutions close to the Genoese *albergo* in other urban and even rural milieux in the western world, most especially in the fourteenth and fifteenth centuries. In this I have nowhere had at my disposal such an abundant, original and authentic documentation: far from it. Indeed, written sources seem *a priori* much less accessible, rarer and more widely dispersed in the case of other cities; only frequent visits over a period of years and a deep knowledge of the resources of all kinds of archives would make it possible to use this documentation profitably for every city. I have therefore restricted myself to the study of published documents and I have also used individual works, often very old, on some aspect, or offering some evidence, of the existence of the family group: for example, on family names, on private law, on the history of vendettas or on the urban habitat. So this study, which I believe is reasonably exhaustive as far as the Genoese example is concerned, is presented, for other milieux at different points in time and space, as an essay, the statement of a general line of enquiry; it is open to considerable expansion from much future research.

It was relatively easy to establish the connection between the different family groups of the Tuscan towns, *consorterie* or *consorzi*, and the Genoese *albergo*. Here the use of a special word is very helpful; and the word *gente* is also used for a family group or clan. This ease does not apply to other Italian towns, especially in the north: in Milan and Venice, for example; but everything points to the existence of large and even very large groups of families or clans, not only in the commercial towns of Italy but also in the south of Italy, in certain cities of the Spanish Levant and Catalonia, and in the south of France. So at first sight one might think of the Roman heritage or of a certain unity of Mediterranean civilization, in East and West, which would explain the survival of the very large family clans, not to say, as in Islamic countries, of tribes.

However, other studies or simple indications attest, often admittedly timidly and imperfectly but nevertheless very clearly, the existence of large family groups in many towns of northern Europe. Almost everywhere they were called *lineages*, a word from the period or a word freely, sometimes abusively, used by historians: in Metz they were *paraiges*;[16] in Alsace the family clan retained the ancient name of *Geschlecht.*[17] These lineages, far from the Roman heritage, played a decisive economic and political role in the Hanse towns.[18] In Germany, as in the Netherlands and Belgium, they monopolized all power for their own benefit. When the prince recognized their power and shared the urban judicial appointments among them, their existence and their political life show clearly in official texts. That is why the northern lineage is unfortunately almost always revealed to us only in the context of its political action; the human side and the social composition of these groups are much more difficult to approach.

Despite the disproportion of sources and studies it seems to me artificial to distinguish *a priori* between the towns of the north and those of the south. Even if a more precise geographical study of the extent of these structures led us to isolate certain regions, the phenomenon must be taken as a whole and the family clan deserves a synthesizing picture.

Notes

[1]Blankerberg, W., *Der Vilain in der Schiedernung der altfranzösischen Fabliaux*, Dissert. Greifwald, Julius Abel, 1902; and Arland, M., *Les paysans français à travers la littérature*, Paris, 1941; Guitard, D., "Les paysans dans la satire bourgeoise", unpublished dissertation, University of Paris X, 1970.

[2]Kaiser, M.T., *Le berger en France à la fin du Moyen Age*, Paris, 1974.

[3]Langlois, C.V., *La société au Moyen Age d'après quelques moralistes du temps*, Paris, 1908; Langfors, A., *La société française vers 1330 vue par un frère prêcheur*, Helsinki, 1918.

[4]There is much that could be said on a great deal of 'romantic' literature about rural societies and the relationships between peasants and lords. These ideas about social structures and relationships in the rural world, uncritically accepted, have had great repercussions at every level of historical popularization; they inspired all the novels and plays of the late nineteenth century, they led to pseudo-historical works such as an extraordinary book by C. Fellens entitled, very significantly, *Les droits du seigneur sous la féodalité. Peuple et noblesse.* Even today, although these ideas have been totally contradicted by recent research, they are widely found in school text books. This blind attitude explains how studies in rural history have paid much more attention to the lords than to the peasant communities themselves.

[5]Here the choice of words meets insurmountable obstacles because of the great confusion which has increasingly grown between the word when it is taken in its widest sense and when it is used by such and such an ideological or sociological school. Historians have constantly wavered between these two attitudes: the word in general, or the word charged with a specific meaning. The word 'stratum', which has the advantage of remaining free of any *a priori* meaning, has been used by R. Mousnier in several

works: *Problèmes de stratification sociale. Actes du Colloque international (1966)*, Paris, 1968; and *Les hiérarchies sociales*, Paris, 1969.

[6]The latest works on this are: Porchnev, B., *Les soulèvements populaires en France au XVIIe siècle*, Paris, 1972; and Mousnier, R., "Les concepts d''ordres', d''états', de 'fidélité' et de "monarchie absolue" en France, de la fin du XVe siècle à la fin du XVIIIe siècle", in *Revue historique*, No. 502, 1972, 289–312. It seems that the ideas of some historians on 'classes' have recently changed, at least with respect to the Middle Ages; some writers have accepted that class conflict is not the whole truth; see, for example, Rutenburg, V., "Révoltes ou révolutions en Europe aux XIVe et XVe siècles", in *Annales: Économies, Sociétés, Civilisations*, 1972, 678–683 (a critical account of Mollat, M. and Wolff, P., *Ongles bleus, Jacques et Ciompi. Les révolutions populaires en Europe aux XIVe et XVe siècles*, Paris, 1970). V. Rutenburg states very pertinently that "In feudal society there were neither classes nor class consciousness, pure and simple, especially during the period of that society's development in the fourteenth and fifteenth centuries", and "No analysis of all the nuances of the class structure and class consciousness of any given period . . . can be successful if it depends on fixed formulae and schemata" (p. 682); but it is difficult to understand how society in the fourteenth and fifteenth centuries remained 'feudal'. Moreover, Rutenburg, even after his more nuanced analysis, still asserts the existence, *a priori*, of classes and of class conflict (pp. 682–683). It is unfortunate that these genuine nuances may take a considerable time to filter through to the works of generalization or popularization which, especially in France, hold to these fixed formulae and schemata.

[7]See below, pp. 115 ff.

[8]Nobility was not easily defined at the end of the Middle Ages. Every detailed study shows that noble status, for example in northern France, although linked to the family, was acquired in many different ways; it depended on reputation and prestige rather than being an easily recognized legal status. In his recent study of rural life in Hainault, G. Sivery concludes his examination of the nobility with the following statements: "There is no decisive criterion to determine membership of the Hainault nobility at the end of the Middle Ages", and "The fact that the word hardly appears in everyday documents, especially in records of fiefs, shows at the very least indecision and vacillation . . . It was no longer really sure who was noble and who was not" (*Structures agraires et vie rurale dans le Hainaut à la fin du Moyen Age*, Lille, 1974.)

[9]Gaudemet, J., *Les communautés familiales*, Paris, 1963, 181–185.

[10]See, for example, Dussourd, H., *Au même pot et au même feu*, Moulins, 1962.

[11]Duby, G., "Structure de parenté et noblesse, France du Nord (XIe–XIIe siècles)", in *Miscellanea J. F. Niermeyer*, Groningen, 1967, 149–165.

[12]Le Guay, J.P., *La Bretagne aux XIVe et XVe siècles*; *Documents sur l'histoire de la Bretagne*, Coll. Univers de la France, Toulouse, 1971, 129–130. Hearth tax (1428–1440?), 129, note 38.

[13]"La démographie médiévale", in *Annales E.S.C.*, 1962.

[14]"Feux populaires et structures sociales au milieu du XVe siècle: l'exemple de Carpentras", in *Annales E.S.C.*, 1959, 225–268.

[15]Heers, J., "Les limites des méthodes statistiques pour les recherches de démographie médiévale", in *Annales de démographie historique*, 1968, 43–72.

[16]Schneider, J., *La ville de Metz aux XIIIe et XIVe siècles*, Nancy, 1950.

[17]Weill, G., "Origine du patriciat strasbourgeois aux XIIIe et XIVe siècles". Les lignages Zorn et Mullenheim, in *Bulletin philologique et historique du Comité des Travaux historiques et scientifiques*, i, 1969, 257–302.

[18]Dollinger, P., *The German Hansa*, London, 1970, especially 132–136; Bruns, P., "Der Lübecker Rat. Zusammensetzung, Ergänzung und Geschäftsführung", in *Zeitschrift des Vereins für lübeckische Geschichte und Altertumskunde*, 1951; and Schildhauer, J., "Das Sozialstruktur der Hansestadt Rostock", in *Hansische Studien*, 1961.

CHAPTER 1

Family clans in the countryside

Rural origins of the urban aristocracy

In Italy and Germany at the end of the Middle Ages powerful family groups belonged to the urban aristocracy. These families took the wall side of the pavement and either through the workings of institutions or through pure and simple monopoly they governed their cities. In most cases they claimed to have noble status. In Genoa, every person described as 'noble' was obligatorily a member of one of the *alberghi*. The family clans made up of men of the 'people', formed much later, seem to have been only imitations.

This evident link between the vast family group and the 'nobility' deserves consideration. Many authors have thought that the urban clan, the Genoese *albergo*, for example, asserted itself, only in the fourteenth century and even later, as a reaction against the rise to power of the *popolani*, in the wish to unite the powers of the great families, to ensure numerous dependents and to oppose the power of the crafts.[1] This theory finds support in the fact that, again in Genoa, the institution of *alberghi* becomes obvious only at this period, and that in other towns or regions documents concerning them appear to become more numerous at this time.

Yet I believe this hypothesis to be untenable. The increasing quantity of written evidence at the end of the Middle Ages is a general phenomenon from which no conclusion may be drawn. Above all, this theory prevents consideration of the links between the urban aristocracy and the fiefs of the countryside or of the immediate vicinity. In fact, this theory looks back to the now superseded thesis that the merchants and the urban aristocracy had a new, original, in a way revolutionary, character.

On the contrary, throughout Europe the great merchants were very often of rural origin and the 'nobles' played a very important part in the establishment of city governments.[2] We know, appositely, that in Italy the first communities thought of as 'mercantile' were controlled, like great commercial enterprises, by *compagne*, associations of great noble families.[3] In Pisa such families were very early rooted in the city.[4] In Orvieto, still in the fourteenth century, the nobles built imposing fortified palaces inside the city, but they lived more often in their country castles on their fiefs, from which they drew the greater part of their revenue and power. The Filippeschi, still at this time, possessed vast territories in the north of the *contado*, whereas the principal castles of their rivals the Monaldeschi stood in the south, in the Bolsena region.[5] R.S. Lopez has perfectly demonstrated the decisive role of warlike nobles possessing fiefs, in the first economic fortunes and the first military adventures of Genoa.[6] Therefore, we must seek the origins of the urban family clan in the very structure of rural, of 'feudal' nobility, and even of much more ancient times. Then we must see, by regions, at much later times, whether these structures were retained and reinforced.

Social structures of the feudal nobility

The medieval noble family is still, on the whole, little known. The group's size still escapes us, and with it, above all, the differences between social structures inside the western world. However, the vocabulary of contemporary authors, the habitual use of the word *lineage* and a little less frequently of the word *parentele*, the enormous evidence of the lineage's cohesion and solidarity in combat, certain forms of daily life and of the military art, all this information leads us to think that the holders of fiefs, or more generally the nobles, gathered together into large families which were much greater in size than the conjugal family in the modern sense.

The theses of L. Génicot,[7] L. Verriest[8] and K.F. Werner[9] emphasize well that medieval nobility was independent of chivalry. The noble looked not to his power, nor to his fortune, nor even to the profession of arms, but to his forebears. What counted was ancestry, membership of a vast clan whose ancestors were well known and honoured. The first concern was to draw up a list of one's forebears. Thus, contrary to theories which asserted that there was a break between the aristocracy of Carolingian times and the feudal nobility of castle owners and of knights, it seems likely that Carolingian, or Frankish, nobility was passed down for centuries through direct lines of descent; G. Duby states, with reference to the Mâcon region, that "the aristocracy of 1100 is a society of heirs".[10]

The theses of these Belgian and German historians are confirmed for a quite different region by the recent study of Mme Nortier on the aristocracy of the province of Narbonne in the early Middle Ages. The upper aristocracy numbered only three families of counts solidly rooted in the district: that of Toulouse, the so-called 'gothic' family of Carcassonne, and that of the counts of Melgueil Guillerma. A careful examination of relationships, of Christian names and of places of residence makes it possible to reconstitute the genealogy of all the lineages from the middle of the ninth century to about 1020–1030; these three families certainly belonged to a hereditary nobility and two of them were without question of Frankish, Carolingian, origin. The other dynasty, that of the counts of Carcassonne, was put there by the Carolingians, and when they died out the descendants of Arnaud, probably of Pyrenean origin, made matrimonial alliances with the Raimondine Carolingian family of Toulouse. Mme Nortier also thinks that the vicecomital lineages of Rouergue, Narbonne, Béziers, Lodève, Nîmes and Toulouse itself were of Frankish and Carolingian origin.[11]

According to L. Verriest noble descent was exclusively or essentially through the female up to a very late period (early thirteenth century).[12] This thesis, put forward rather intransigently and based on very unusual arguments and on uncertain facts, is nonetheless very attractive and cannot be rejected outright. It is possible that in this the German tribes were the heirs of very ancient traditions stemming from oriental civilizations.[13] In any case great families where succession is through the female can be found among the kings and nobles of Celtic peoples, in Ireland and Scotland; for example, the queen of the Picts transmitted the blood royal through her own marriage.[14] These traditions remained sometimes until a very late date in these countries.[15]

With regard to Germanic societies and therefore to 'Frankish' nobility, the studies of G. Tellenbach[16] and of K. Schmid[17] make it possible to modify the highly categorical assertions of L. Verriest. It seems that the Frankish nobility consisted of two types of great family; the break, or rather the evolution from one to the other, would have taken place about the year 1000. At first the *Sippe* was merely a rather vague and uncertain group of allies; it knew neither fixed domicile, nor manor, but many temporary resting places;[18] family names were absent; baptismal names were all taken from the maternal line and daughters shared in the inheritance of land; wealth was therefore greatly dispersed, moving and changing according to different unions. K. Schmid tells us that this family clan corresponded to a political society in which the only way to make one's fortune was to join the king's household and live among those 'kept' there.[19] So this domestic nobility, this *Hausadel*, could not organize itself into individual households.[20] Afterwards, at different times according to regions, later for the countries of the Empire and their western marches, such as the Namur region, Franche-Comté or even Champagne, the nobles, beginning with the powerful families of counts, left the king's household and established a very different kind of family group called a *Geschlecht*. This was a dynasty which brought together all those men who claimed a common ancestor. Wealth and authority were now handed down through the male. This very complex group possessed land and a house, which was the cradle of the line, and from which it took its name. Traditions exalted martial virtues and made a veritable symbol of the sword.

In the absence of sufficient detailed studies on this point, this schema, which probably applies more to the Germanic countries than to others, may be an acceptable hypothesis. L. Génicot, examining the whole of north-western Europe, acknowledges that the noble tradition was long handed down through the female; then, with the development of chivalry, in the twelfth century, descent through the male prevailed.[21]

Genealogies of lineages from these regions demonstrate clearly this interest in descent through the male line. Thus, for example, the genealogy written precisely in the twelfth century by Lambert de Watrelos, canon of Cambrai, who belonged to a relatively modest noble family of Flanders, which he traces back to 1050. Out of seventy-three people mentioned, in three generations, fifty-four are men. The man alone gave nobility. The rich women of great nobility did not give this to their children who remained, like their fathers, knights. This dynasty especially valued its martial virtues: *habuit . . . fratres, et decem ex illis in una die ab hostibus suis in pugna prostrati sunt. Unde apud nostrates de illis adhuc elegi versus per cantilenam mimorum recitantur.*[22]

However, the evolution of mental attitudes and of customs in these same countries may not always be so easily defined, at least for certain areas. Here, the valuable information given by J. Schneider about the Metz aristocracy adds some confusion. In this town the social and family clans, the *paraiges*, were certainly based on blood links, but the maternal family seems to have been as important, or nearly as important, as the father's; this, moreover, at a very late date. Texts constantly mention "relatives and friends through the mother". During the years 1209–1215 many members of 'patrician' lineages bore the surnames, not of their fathers or grandfathers, but of their fathers-in-law. Much later, the new patricians were often men who entered the *paraiges* of their wives, and the ordinance of 1367 which regulated such adoptions into the clans preserved the choice between the paternal line and the maternal family.[23] Finally, towards 1400, widows were permitted to take part in the political assemblies of lineages.[24] In fact these 'patricians' were always rich land-owners, controlling estates and privileges; they were often the descendants of knights who came early to the towns and were admitted to the *paraiges* through alliances with other notables. Should we see in this very late preservation of the prestige of maternal descent an archaism preserved by an unusual way of life – that of knights more concerned, in the framework of the episcopal *familia*, with administration than with war? Or should we believe, on the contrary, that from this point of view Metz is an absolutely rare and unique case?

So, *Sippe* or *Geschlecht*, descent through the female or the male line, the family clan of nobles brought together a great number of relatives; for centuries, but very unevenly, it has marked the nobility of western countries. This is especially clear in the East where Germanic traditions were more firmly asserted. They seem also to have been particularly strong in central and northern Italy where this Germanic heritage would have been strengthened by the arrival, later, of the Lombards. Despite Charlemagne's conquest, despite some Frankish colonization, the Italian feudal system kept alive certain unusual elements which historians readily attribute to the Lombard heritage.[25] According to the *jus Langobardum*, in contrast to the *jus Francorum*, fiefs were held by all brothers making up a *fraterna* or more frequently a *consorzio* which, in the name of all, exercised all seignorial rights. All brothers inherited jointly and therefore remained united; inheritance by daughters was not excluded.

Lombard influence seems above all to have been very strong in Tuscany, where peculiarities were evened out very late. L. Chiapelli's most suggestive study brings out the problem of the *Lombardi*, groups of men settled in country districts, whom chronicles show were hostile to the establishment of communes; various texts, dating from between about 950 and 1350,[26] prove their existence. These *Lombardi* were not to be found in all areas of Tuscany, but only in the valleys of the Arno and the Era and around Volterra and Maremma; they were also encountered further afield, as far as the districts of Orvieto and even Viterbo. They seem to have established themselves in preference away from towns, and their colonies were more numerous in the region of Pistoia, where they stretched as far as the eastern quarters of the city. L. Chiapelli affirms their ethnic originality and, in any case, their particularism.[27] Some of their Germanic traditions survived until a very late date: even after 1400 marriages were celebrated in Pistoia according to German rites.[28] Above all, family clans, *consorterie* of nobles, seemed in that city to be particularly cohesive. Here, collective ownership of lands and privileges was maintained at least up to about the fourteenth century, as is proved by many estates called *gentilize*. This same structure is found, although doubtless less conspicuously, in the Lucca and Arezzo regions and in the Arno valley. For Pistoia, L. Chiapelli can cite more than 110 *terrae* which in the twelfth century belonged to fifty family groups of Lombard origin. In the fourteenth century estates remained under the co-ownership of several families who were no longer linked by obvious kinship, but who still held their portion of a common heritage.[29]

The 'popular' nobility

However, in the whole of the western world, total coparcenery and equality between coparceners could not be indefinitely maintained. Barbarian, or rather, Germanic traditions grew weaker during the last centuries of the Middle Ages, at which time they suffered the consequences of the development, more or less close at hand, of princely authority, and the repercussions of the evolution of political structures and of the triumph of the market economy. As a result wealth and power finished by being concentrated in the hands of a few. Thus many individuals risked being ejected from the lineage and losing their noble status.

This derogation, even for the poorest, was not inevitable. Where powerful, coherent family groups, which brought together many men bearing the same name and claiming a common ancestor, asserted themselves, clan solidarity was sufficient to keep the least fortunate members in the nobility, or in a sort of lesser nobility. In this case, of course, the social composition of the clan appears very varied. In the same lineage a few men had at their disposal vast estates, military power and authority; the others, although they still claimed a 'noble' quality, common blood and a common ancestor, were reduced to a much lower position, from the political and the economic points of view.

Historians of western countries have hitherto omitted to study this particular form of nobility, which is characterized by the considerable size of the lineages and by the inequality of power and wealth within them. The existence of a popular nobility is scarcely known, save in those countries where it lasted for a long time, until well after the Middle Ages. This is true of the northern provinces of Old Castile and still more of Poland, where noble clans play a very important part throughout the 'modern' period. In both cases the social structure of the country is marked by a high proportion of noble individuals: one in ten in Asturia, one in twelve in Navarre and half the inhabitants of Biscay, according to W. Zaniewicki, who admittedly looks to the nineteenth century and gives no precise references.[30] In Poland estimates for the sixteenth to the eighteenth centuries give the figure of about 10 per cent of the country's population,[31] and between 16 and 20 per cent of the catholic population, Jews excluded.[32] In each case also the political and social conditions of the nobles differed greatly.

Polish nobles made up the social category known as *szlachta* – an indubitable borrowing from the German word *Geschlecht* (race, family) whose meaning we have already noted. The noble was distinguished by possessing a coat of arms and a motto. Each coat of arms was common to several families grouped together into a kind of heraldic clan; survival perhaps of very ancient totemic clans of freemen. The mottoes, which first appeared towards 1200, were originally only war cries, delivered in combat;[33] most consisted of a single word, the name or soubriquet of an ancestor, or the name of a castle, of a lake or a river.

The size and complexity of Polish noble clans are proved by:

(i) the small number of these clans: towards 1430 a heraldic treatise describes only seventy-one devices for the whole of Poland.

(ii) the extent of their territorial roots and the dispersal of their wealth. One eleventh-century lineage in particular which W. Semkovicz studied had a home, a fortified area to the south of Poznan, where it also founded a Benedictine abbey, but also chains of villages along the roads leading to the principal administrative centres; these villages allowed the members of the clan to break their journey on their own estates.

(iii) the great variety of conditions of power and wealth. Small nobles bore the same devices, belonged to the same clans, as the great; the Polish adage says: "a noble in a cottage is the equal of a noble in a palace". Beneath the heads of lineages lived those nobles who owned lands which they farmed themselves, aided by two families or even a single family of serfs. Other nobles had no land and they settled as tenant farmers on the property of a well-endowed landowner. This is the explanation of villages inhabited entirely by noble peasants, called *zascianek* in Lithuania, in contrast to the *wies*, a village where only serfs live. At the beginning of the nineteenth century Mickiewicz could still describe one of the noble villages, Dobrzin, in Lithuania: "The Dobrzinski . . . are forced to work to live, like peasants, yet they do not wear the peasant dress, but white capotes with black stripes". Their womenfolk reaped with gloved hands. These are very interesting indications of the benefit of a real, well-directed sociological study of costume.

Then W. Zaniewicki also points out the existence of numerous domestic servants called "nobles in attendance" employed by other, rich nobles; these 'paid nobles' made up a very useful kind of political dependency; finally, W. Zaniewicki even counts the artisan nobles living in towns.

Among all the regions of Castile, the Basque country seems to present a particularly clear example of popular nobility and large heterogeneous lineages.[34] The nobility of Biscay lived apart from the rest of the kingdom: no Basque had any interests outside his own country and no stranger had any possessions in Biscay. This is the probable reason for certain archaic structures and very marked peculiarities.

Medieval Basque society was characterized by the strength of the lineage, by its cohesion, attributed by all Spanish historians, throughout the peninsula moreover, to these peoples' Germanic origin. Nearly 150 lineages have been counted in Biscay for the period around 1470. Three quarters of these lived in the country and made their living, directly or indirectly, from the land. From this time however a small number of these groups entered the *villae*, of which there were few, where they managed municipal life: this is another example of the gradual movement of the noble aristocracy from the country to the towns and of the influence of rural structures on municipal ones.

These Basque lineages, which inspired aristocratic pride in all their members, were in fact made up of two quite distinct categories of nobles in very different circumstances. There were on the one side those known as *parentes mayores*, who claimed direct descent from their ancestors through the male line. They were the military leaders, they lived in houses shaped like fortified towers and they alone called the lineage to war. As spiritual leaders they were patrons of churches or hermitages and presided over devotional brotherhoods. They possessed great wealth. Finally, they watched over the purity of the clan by authorizing or forbidding the bearing of the lineage's device. All the other men of the clan, of whom there were many, formed the popular nobility of *parentes minores*, a sort of dependency for the service of the leaders in whose interest it was to protect the greatest possible number of families. Among these dependants were many bastards, born of concubines. They had different names, indiscriminately it would seem: *escuderos* (those who had coats of arms), *caballeros* (who fought on horseback), *hidalgos* or rather *fijosdalgo* (*hijos de algo*) and *infanzones*. They owned a single house and farmed the land, and thus led lives very close to those of the peasants. They were in fact peasant-nobles. But they paid no taxes.

In short, in Biscay all real freemen were noble and belonged to a lineage. These lineages were often federated into solid, widespread clans, and formed two resolutely hostile parties: the *bandos*.[35]

The *infanzones* are found in all the northern provinces of Old Castile, especially in Navarre and in the Labourd region;[36] they were second-class nobles, of modest estate, more numerous and obedient to the others. In Navarre the *Hijos-dalgos de linaje*, noble in origin and blood, who claimed to descend from the *repartidores y pobladores de la tierra*, were certainly the masters among the nobility. The *infanzones de carta* formed a completely different nobility which appeared as a concession by the king only in the twelfth century. These royal privileges increased and 300 years later ennoblements still seem to have been very numerous: for example in 1435 John II granted *hidalguía* to 110 common households of the Alberque region. The *infanzones de carta*, still paying quit-rent to the king, really lived peasants' lives; they were also known as *infanzones de abarca*, recalling the sandals worn by the country people. So in all these provinces there was a very numerous popular and peasant nobility, but here the internal structure of the family clans does not, in the present state of our knowledge, appear as clearly as in the Basque country.

In the other regions of the kingdom of Castile the nobles also banded together into powerful lineages possessing vast estates throughout the country. These lineages founded, then reinforced, their political power and landed wealth following the reconquest of the southern provinces of Castile, then of Andalusia, with the help of the civil wars and the evolution of certain factors of economic life. Unfortunately for our present concern the formation of the noble lineage in Castile and its territorial establishment are much better known[37] than its inner life and structure, the study of which has not yet aroused much interest.[38]

Great noble lineages, probably identical or very similar, are found in the Basque country north of the Pyrenees.[39] In another connection P. Tucoo-Chala notes, in the mountains of Béarn under Gaston Phoebus, the existence of family clans called *casalères*, grouping freemen from several villages in the valleys: for example the Sacaze clan in the Ossau valley, which included men from ten different villages.[40]

The most striking example of clannish societies which survived the centuries despite or in opposition to feudality is of course that of Scotland. Although the Scottish clan is better known in its origins or in the 'modern' period than in 'medieval' times, and authors have emphasized the clan's political or military aspects[41] rather than the truly social side, it is certain that the Scottish clan proves the astonishing persistence of the power of family groups, which is, at least for the aristocracy, the basis of any social structure.

A complete work would be necessary in order to present a full discussion of both the origins and the principal characteristics of the Scottish clans. We shall note, for comparison, only a few precise features, the best known. The clan probably descended from the tribe and its totemic characteristics asserted themselves for a long time. The survival of descent through the female is a very old tradition inherited from peoples who practised it widely in the early Middle Ages: out of the names of the first twenty-two Pictish kings given by chroniclers, twenty are linked to their mothers' names. Moreover, the widely spread settlements, the lands and castles scattered over several parts of Scotland, the existence of many b anches, all show that we are concerned with real federations of clans; the use of the word *mac* (son of . . .), the admission of strangers or dependants, show the desire at once to broaden the clan and to keep for it a certain family aspect. Finally, the clan has its war cry and its colours – the tartan – normally different for war, hunting or parade. These same conclusions would probably apply to the less well-known Irish clans[42] and also to the northern counties of England where clan structures long resisted the establishment of feudal institutions.[43] Thus Poland, the Celtic countries of the British Isles and certain Iberian regions on the borders of Castile present very unusual social structures which seem to be inherited from the earliest times of nobility. The permanence in all three cases may be explained by geographical isolation, imposed by position or relief, and by strong ethnic originality. Other marginal countries not yet so closely studied from this point of view probably then showed similar structures.

The internal stratification, in the Middle Ages, of the Breton nobility, its ways of life and the levels of its wealth are still little known. There is no doubt here of the existence of a great number of petty nobles, and even of poor nobles, without property. Hearth lists in the lands of the Vannes diocese on the orders of the count of Brittany show clearly that many nobles had neither estate nor fief, nor any other landed property. Some lived on others' land; others pursued different sorts of trades, and in particular sold beverages. The parishes allowed these noble tavern-keepers to enjoy their previous fiscal privileges and to retain their way of life: the unreformed hearth list for the village of Brest mentions, in 1427, one Olivier Dreianou, "a nobleman who keeps a hostelry, who goes to war";[45] but the ducal *Chambre des comptes* insisted on payment, exempting only nobles who really were owners of fiefs. An ordinance of the duke, in 1456, states clearly that men referred to as "of noble lineage" sold goods wholesale and retail, kept taverns, engaged in the service of others and kept cattle on other men's lands.[46]

This practice of poor nobles, devoid of lands, of engaging in a trade probably explains a noble custom characteristic of Brittany, which is found practically nowhere else in France: that of 'dormant nobility', whereby the noble state was never completely lost through trade. Derogation was not irreversible; one had merely to abandon one's trade in order to re-establish one's noble status.[47] Thus sons of nobles without fiefs, who led quite different lives, were not completely excluded from the family clan.

In any case the 'noble plebs' remained very numerous in Brittany, at least until the beginning of the eighteenth century. J. Meyer notes that in 1710 about one third of the nobility of the present department of the Côtes-du-Nord consisted of men "devoid of all property and unable to pay" taxes; some were even reduced to beggary. Still in 1710, in the diocese of Tréguier, 77 per cent of the nobles were destitute and 13 per cent completely destitute; for the diocese of Saint-Malo the figures are 55 and 8 per cent respectively.[48] This poverty, this destitution, obviously explains the considerable number of peasant-nobles and this dispersal of wealth, these greatly differing styles of life, certainly imply a 'popular' nobility such as in Poland or Castile.

These inequalities, certainly, do not necessarily imply the existence and survival of noble clans, family-based, cohesive and highly structured; but we are obviously tempted to see in these poor relations, who still claimed nobility and never willingly gave up their status and privileges, allies or dependants, more or less subservient to the masters, yet still bearing the principal family name. In Brittany the diversity of names inside one family often concealed a common descent and membership of the same clan; it was not necessarily an indication of the real fragmentation of a group but merely of the diversity of lands shared among the cadets. Moreover, it is significant that regions with poor nobles were also those where the greatest noble fortunes were established;[49] evidently, a few very rich and powerful leaders coexisted with a noble plebs. One thinks of dependencies.

Has the family clan, more or less vast in size, bringing together nobles of different circumstances and dependencies, lasted in the West in the less marginal countries where social structures were deeply marked by the action of a strong state?

In truth, historians have given little attention to these aspects of social life in the Middle Ages and generally we can only note indirect evidence or external signs which are not always obvious.[50] Here as in the countries already mentioned, the number, large or small, of nobles compared with the rest of the population seems a valuable indication. Where nobles were very numerous, as in Poland and the Basque country, many of them were necessarily completely reduced to a peasant way of life and limited wealth. In Brittany, at the beginning of the eighteenth century, 56 per cent of the nobility still lived on only 20 per cent of the land, all round the bay of Saint-Brieuc, precisely where destitute nobles were the most numerous.[51] Thus a high proportion of nobles implies in all likelihood the presence of a 'popular' nobility and therefore of dependencies and of greater cohesion in groups or family clans. In fact we can imagine that the firm maintenance of lineal links beyond the narrow family framework may have played a decisive role here; these links permitted the poorest relatives to consider themselves still as nobles, gave them a proper group consciousness and for a long time prevented them from falling into the status of commoners among the simple peasants whose activities, life styles and economic fate, however, they shared.

It even seems that in certain countries the less favoured descendants of noble families might lose their real nobility, in the contemporary sense, while not falling to the rank of peasants; in that case they kept a special status and a group consciousness, which is conveyed by a special word. This seems to me to be one of the conclusions of a study by L. Génicot called, precisely, *De la noblesse au lignage*, based on the case of the Boneffe family, lords of a small village in the east of the Namur region.[52] This family, still powerful around 1260, including many knights at that time, disappeared from the nobility in the fourteenth century. This was the result of sharing out their allodial lands, for custom allowed the cadets their portion, and daughters were not excluded from these apportionments. L. Génicot notes that if nobility was hereditary (although the method of transmission cannot be defined here) and was passed down to all the heirs whatever their wealth might be, the prestige and title of *milites* did not, in the years 1280–1300, go to the poorest; these were now no longer mentioned among the nobles; but often despite their lack of economic power they remained *hommes de loy* or, in a very significant expression, *hommes de lignage*. The idea of the clan and of solidarity comes out once more.

L. Génicot, in a more general and more dogmatic study, extends this conclusion to the whole of north-west Europe. He asserts plainly that noble status was above all hereditary. For example, military service was not sufficient; in Friesland, in Sweden and even in Spain military service, and in France the dubbing of knights, certainly conferred privileges such as exemption from tallage and other fiscal advantages. However in certain regions such as around Namur the new knight had the title of noble but those of his descendants who were not knights, who had not been dubbed, kept their title only for a few generations; moreover, this knight, who was not of noble origin, "failed to merge into the noble sphere".[53] Only blood and descent gave definite nobility to all generations; this nobility was linked neither to office nor to wealth. That is why, according to L. Génicot, "the Middle Ages, in these regions, knew no derogation" and "whatever you did and however you behaved, if you had noble blood and if you owned an allodium or a fief, however small, where you gave sentence and above all justice, you were noble and were treated as such".[54] However, as with the Boneffe family, poor nobles without fiefs and, more importantly, without jurisdiction, benefited only from the privileges, and not from the prestige of nobility; "he was no longer called a noble, but, for example, a gentleman".[55]

For a long time this distinction between *nobility* and *gentry* affected social structures and relationships in England. It was not as clear in France, where vocabulary seems more uncertain, where a prince, a king even, can be called *gentilhomme*, where the words *gentillesse* and *noblesse* are often confused. Here too, however, texts often show the difference between *gentilshommes* or *simples gentilshommes* on the one hand and *seigneurs* or *grands seigneurs* on the other.[56]

Thus, in many countries, the force of heredity and the cohesion of the family group maintained very many small nobles in the ranks of the nobility, sometimes admittedly with a lower status emphasized by different epithets (for example, *men of lineage*, or *gentlemen*), while their economic position was akin to that of many common people.

In Normandy, or more precisely in the Cotentin district, after the troubles of war and the English occupation, all kinds of disturbance certainly aggravated the social contrasts within noble families. Men living 'nobly' were few and represented only a minority of the 'nobility'; a real noble, be he a rich landowner or a mere squireen, "counts among his brothers or cousins serjeants, merchants and peasants".[57]

Generally, even in different French regions, trade did not *ipso facto* bring derogation; a document of the fourteenth century says: "There are some, noble through their fathers, who live and have long lived as cloth, corn, wine or other merchants, or as craftsmen: furriers, cobblers, tailors".[58] This idea of linking derogation to trade or to manual work was first laid down by jurists, then it spread in fact, slowly and quite late, throughout the fifteenth century. The idea which men had of derogation and the rigour with which it was applied certainly varied greatly according to the regions, and to the cohesion of lineages which remained more or less united, in solidarity with their poor relatives. That is why the varying number of 'noble' or elsewhere, 'gentle', heads of families, is a good indication of the size and strength of family clans. It is a clear sign that the less fortunate descendants were still part of the lineage.

Several historians have counted noble hearths in different regions of

France, and have attempted to establish the proportion of nobles liable to this tax in the total of taxpayers. In my opinion these figures remain subject to caution, for they show only the relationship between the number of noble lineages and the number of non-noble hearths, the composition of which is certainly not the same, and may vary according to time and place. Remembering these restrictions, we may establish that in the years 1270–1360 this percentage appears distinctly higher in the county of Provence (3.7 per cent; 6 per cent for the rural population) than in the centre (1.4 per cent for the Clermont-Ferrand region) or the north of France (1.3 per cent for the bailiwick of Amiens).[59] We can therefore assume a zone of 'high noble density': Brittany, Anjou, Maine, compared with a zone of 'low density': Berry, the Nevers region, and parts of Burgundy and Champagne.[60]

It seems that authors have readily neglected or underestimated this poor nobility in all western countries; for example, entries in the hearth-books relating to nobles who were destitute and therefore exempt from taxes were interpreted rather as proofs of fraud or abuse. Such entries are quite frequently found, and we should see in them signs of a nobility whose levels of wealth varied greatly, and of greater cohesion in the family group. These poor nobles are found in this way, for example, in regions as distant and as economically distinct as Provence and Burgundy. G. Sivery notes, also, that in Hainault the standard of living of certain descendants of good noble families was lower than that of the most well-to-do peasants: and this in many villages of the county.[61]

Cohesion and structure of noble clans

Apart from these external signs, the historian can also obtain information regarding the strength and permanence of the links themselves, which are economic or even psychological. Thus, the study of the maintenance of family links necessarily complements the study of rights and customs of inheritance on the one hand, and of collective mentalities on the other.

It seems that the nobles rejected family obligations much later than did the commoners. Here, solidarity clung to obvious economic necessities: inheritances should not be excessively divided or curtailed. So the lineage remained a large and cohesive group. There are many indications of this: for example the maintenance of indivisible fief' or 'communal fief' still obtained, wills of nobles often alluded to a the nobles seem, around 1260, to have abandoned the division of fiefs and adopted coparcenary fiefs to stop their erosion. In 1267 ten coparceners rendered homage to the count of Rodez for the fief of Saint-Christophe and again, in 1287, ten men did homage to the bishop of Clermont for the castle of Murat de Barrès; it should be noted that daughters were not excluded.[62]

In Franche-Comté at the end of the Middle Ages, when the 'shared fief' or 'communal fief' still obtained, wills of nobles often alluded to a group of relatives and friends, members of the lineage, who formed a sort of family council, to which constant reference was made, entrusted with the tutelage of daughters in their nonage and with the choice of their husbands. These daughters must marry "according to the counsel of their friends". Jean d'Avilley, although only a simple esquire, preparing to leave on a pilgrimage to the Holy Land, declared that he did so "by the counsel and advice of many of my relatives and kindred friends".[63]

This cohesion was also reinforced by a common way of life, in the castle and at war, and G. Duby has shown[64] that this group consciousness set great store by a common education which, through stories of historic deeds (*Maurice and the Theban Legion*, *Arthur of Brittany*), eventually created a real mental identity common to the whole clan. In any case chivalric literature, in all the *Chansons de geste*, seems very attached to the clan idea and constantly exalts it. Studying the *Siege of Barbastre*, a chronicle in the cycle of Garcin de Montglane, A. Micha asserts that the solidarity of the lineage is one of the leading ideas of the work; its author tells of "the exploits of Aymeri", of King Aymeri and of the family of the Aymerids. A particularly important scene shows the six sons accompanying their father; another describes with satisfaction a family meal.[65]

Even later, feudal vocabulary still showed this solidarity of the lineage and the strength of these collective attitudes. J.M. Turlan's masterly and extremely precise study of the use of the words *amis* and *amis charnels* ('friends' and 'kindred friends') right through the feudal period, then in the fourteenth century, especially in the records of the *Parlement* of Paris, provides much new information and shows fully the permanence of the lineage.[66] These kindred friends, so often mentioned in law as witnesses or counsellors of plaintiffs or defendants, were taken from the very large group of blood relatives; for the

Parlement they represented a real institution; their extent was known and was regulated by certain rules of kinship, often very strict, and constantly examined. They were numerous: in 1342 an affair called into question the barony of Séverac in Rouergue, and sixteen *amis charnels* were referred to by name.[67] These relatives came above all to protect minors and therefore paternal power, to agree to betrothal and marriage or the taking of the veil; they also intervened with many 'good offices' and to secure the group's internal peace; often they were seen to show their solidarity in lawsuits and even more in private wars: no peace might be agreed between two opposing lineages without their consent. To pay for these settlements, men spoke of 'the friends' fine' and each paid his share according to his degree of kinship.[68]

We have already seen that this economic and mental cohesion could obviously not maintain equality between people's positions. Thus was formed a dependency of poor nobles, of cousins established in the castle as officials or servants, nobles without fiefs, adventurers and crusaders, spinsters without dowries. Sometimes the lineage had difficulty in supporting this dependency, which amounted to a kind of dependent proletariat, which was more or less confused and dangerous; but the lineage relied on it in difficult times, making it into a powerful tool. On other occasions, even, the most influential clans created suprafamily links and gathered about themselves a vast, more artificial dependency of many allies and friends. Such alliances were often ephemeral and, through the lack of first-hand texts, they almost always elude the historian.

The origin and structure of one of these noble clans, in northern France, are fully elucidated in a very interesting study by J.B. Ross, based on the chronicle of Galbert of Bruges.[69] I shall simply take from that work the points which are most significant for my purpose; it concerns the Erembald clan of Bruges, which gained a sad fame in assassinating the count of Flanders, Charles the Good, on 2 March 1127, while he was praying in his castle chapel.

Their ancestor was probably Erembald of Veurne who had married the daughter of the castellan of Bruges. Subsequently, the head of the clan was not the son who inherited the post of castellan but another son, Bertulf, who usurped the provostship of St Donatian's, Bruges, and became receiver-general of the revenues of the count's lands. At the heart of the clan Bertulf controlled a solid group made up of his twelve nephews: the chronicle constantly refers to "the provost and his twelve nephews", emphasizing that the ties of blood between uncle and nephew were more important than those between father and son or between brothers. Most of the nephews were alive at the time of the count's death and each had his armed followers. In addition Bertulf had constantly with him numerous relatives, friends and vassals, whom he threw into private wars with his neighbours; for example, against the rival clan of Thincmar of Straten. Even beyond the immediate faithful, the clan could count on all kinds of solid alliance. After the murder the leaders fled; about thirty men, who had sought refuge in the castle and were besieged by the count's men, were hurled from the top of the great tower. The other allies were prosecuted after the execution of four of Erembald's five sons. These prosecutions, according to Galbert of Bruges, affected 125 people in Bruges itself and twenty-seven in Aardenburg who were with Lambert, the son who was spared. The text of the enquiry held by the new count in September 1127 shows, for its part, 115 living people under accusation.[70] These figures clearly show the size of this clan of relatives and friends.

So the fortunes of the Erembald clan depended on:

(i) military power: the post of castellan, and a group of knights trained for war;

(ii) the variety of their revenues: the posts of Bertulf who, moreover, endowed all his nephews with the canonical prebends of the chapter of St Donatian's;

(iii) limited regional recruitment, and therefore the strength of neighbourhood ties: the members of the clan were essentially from the Veurne country, in the coastal plain to the south of the Yser, cradle of the original family; and

(iv) a very close communal way of life. Bertulf lived in a private house inside the castle walls; this house was quite comparable to the count's. In a great beamed hall, seated on a *cathedra*, he presided over the assembly of his relatives. He 'kept' them and after the victory over Thincmar, he received his 'proud and happy' relatives in the canons' cloister and refectory.

It is difficult to say whether other family, or even suprafamily, clans in the countryside, bringing together a large dependency, could for long have any effect on the political destiny of such and such a county. But we can certainly accept that blood ties were maintained to a very late date, in very different regions.

Transfer of the noble lineage from the country to the town

Family cohesion is found to be especially strong in northern and central Italy. I believe that the constant emphasis of historians on the economic rise of the 'mercantile' towns and on their somewhat original political institutions has greatly contributed to the neglect of Italy's real social structures. The erroneous idea, which is linked to an obvious abuse of vocabulary, of a typically 'bourgeois' Italian town, has been generally accepted, and has falsified our whole outlook. We may, however, recall that all recent studies, although they are few, already lead to the same conclusions: that these 'mercantile' towns were governed by 'noble' aristocracies. In order to delineate precisely the evolution of urban society, we need to have a much better knowledge of the life which was peculiar to the mountains, often close by, with their threatening human potential, where 'feudal order' long reigned. Mountain regions remain the great unknown of Italy's economic and social history.

In central Italy, in the whole of that zone which separates Tuscany from the plains of Bologna, from Modena or from Parma, large family clans, bringing together many nobles, laid down their own laws. The 'merchants' of the town were not unaware of their power and G. Villani is startled by the strength of the Cancellieri: "(There was) a lineage of noble and influential people called the Cancellieri, not however very long established . . . and numerous sons and nephews were produced by them so that at that time they comprised more than a hundred rich, powerful and influential men-at-arms".[71] This information is unfortunately highly generalized, but quite significant.

The peculiar structure of one of these groups is very precisely brought out in a study by G. Santini,[72] whose intentions are particularly original, and whose conclusions are especially interesting; he is one of few writers who have concerned themselves recently with Italian mountain areas. His work shows first of all the importance, in many areas of Italy, of those *aggregati soprafamiliari* whose basis was nevertheless strictly the family. These groups, which were very large, were governed and kept in internal peace through the election of a head who often bore the name *podestà*, as well as through an assembly of all heads of families, who drew up rules for behaviour. The author studies more particularly one mountain canton or *pagus* in the Apennines, the Frignano, to the south of Modena. In the eleventh century a great noble family, referred to in texts as the *domus Fregnanensium*, communally held a fief from the bishop and various administrative offices which they had from their lords, the marquesses of Canossa. Subsequently, the increase in the number of members and internal disagreements caused the group to divide into several families, or *domus*, which took their names from the different castles where they became established. One of these families remained noticeably superior and retained ownership of the central part of the fief; the others had other, neighbouring fiefs, portions or *sortes* of the original fief; these were the *consortes.* Ten different branches all maintained a common family origin, referring constantly to the *progenia* of the *Fregnanenses.* They also retained a certain right (*podere*) over the first fief, which remained indivisible. All this constituted a *consorzio* of *militi e capitanei,* ruled by a college of *rectores* who were elected at large common assemblies; the first mention of the election of such rectors goes back to 1156, but it seems that the group was solidly formed from 1130.

G. Santini sees in this *consorzio* primarily a military power: it was a *compagna* of knights, a veritable *commune militum,* renewed by a voluntary pact every ten years. Those who remained outside found themselves excluded from the family 'peace' and, in the case of any conflict with one of the members, had to contend with the whole group together. This *consorzio* was strong enough to exert considerable pressure on the two great city communities nearby, Modena and Bologna. Subsequently, it developed into a much vaster and more complex group through the recruitment of new primary families and through the intervention in the government of this aristocratic community of knights (*capitanei*), of the consent of the 'people', appointed by the *vicini.*[73]

The same political structures were certainly to be found in many other country districts, on the mainland and in the islands: thus, in Lunigiana,[74] in Gafargnana and Versilia,[75] and in Corsica.[76]

In the case of Tuscany, the reinforcement or the very consolidation of these collective noble structures is brought out in the highly convincing statistical research undertaken by D. Herlihy, and presented by him in a brief article.[77] He shows firstly that the *consorzii* or family groups are easily identifiable when their properties are referred to by the word *terra,* followed by the family name; for example, *terra Gherardinga* or *terra Chunimandinga*; such references appear, around Lucca, only in the last quarter of the tenth century, and later elsewhere. These family groups also recognized each other – but doubtless with less certainty – through their use, in lists of proprietors, of the expressions 'son of...' or 'heirs of...'.[78] The proportion of these collective lands is 15 per cent for the period 976–1000 and 22 per cent a century later (1076–1100). D. Herlihy believes that throughout the eleventh century rural lords strengthened these bonds of solidarity; very large noble families, *consorzii* whose lands were held indivisibly, would have been better equipped than the simpler 'nuclear' families to defend their own interests.

The studies of F. Niccolai, P. Torelli and E. Nasalli Rocca[79] have shown the importance and the essential role of these clans in northern Italy: in highland cantons of the Alps and of the Ligurian Apennines, and even in certain districts of the Po valley. Studying the development of emancipation among the peasants of Montferrat, a primarily agrarian, thickly wooded county which had remained apart from the great mercantile towns, and where even local trade seems to have been very poor, A. Bozzola emphasizes the permanence of the great *consortili* of noble families, each *consortile* descended from the same ancestral stock, each claiming the same blood.[80] These *consortili* governed themselves in a way comparable to that of a rural commune, with statutes, council and *podestà*.[81] But this was a completely aristocratic commune of noblemen; dependants, being very small merchants, tenants or agricultural labourers, were excluded from it and must submit to all seignorial rights, to taxes and personal labour services. These noble communes of Montferrat are merely the institutional side of the large noble family group; they are exactly reminiscent of the Frignano commune studied by G. Santini.

In the Ligurian Apennines too, above Genoa, the Spinola di Luccoli family held their fiefs in common; as late as 1467 Eliano Spinola, the most powerful of all, in citing the list of his domains, always prefixed the name of each fief with the expression *ex condominis*; so did Batista Spinola; all these fiefs were held in common by different members of a vast family clan.[82]

Despite the small number and the often very individual character of studies on this question, it seems certain that in many regions of the West, and especially in Italy, powerful lineages or clans of nobles survived in country areas; this is most clear in the more isolated districts. These clans nearly always claimed a common ancestor and loudly affirmed their membership of a single tribe, but they went far beyond the confines of one family – even, sometimes, those of a very large family. In fact, they were made up of different branches.

In these districts there is no doubt about the existence of these clans in the eleventh and twelfth centuries. At this time, and increasingly since, certain rural communes were merely noble, family associations of this kind. Is it not possible to accept that from this time these social structures survived similarly, under different names, in different areas, during the evolution of urban communes, and in certain towns even up to the end of the Middle Ages? I believe that the so-called 'mercantile' towns, especially in Italy, most certainly inherited the social structures of neighbouring country districts; at the very least, these towns were deeply affected by their mutual proximity.

In any case, it seems certain that the men who abandoned their lands at the beginning of the urban expansion to move to the cities, were not only fugitive serfs, adventurers or the poor; on the contrary, most of these migrants were men of good rank, owners of land, that is, of realizable capital, who were attracted, not by an indefinable liberty, but by the hope of good business and ecclesiastical careers. These notables, who are referred to in Milanese texts of the eleventh century as *boni homines* or *estimatores*, maintained very close ties with the country districts of their birth.[83] The nobles of the *contado* definitely underwent the same process of transfer; so they joined those whose own origins were in the city.

Thus it seems very likely that the noble family clans which I propose to study in the urban environment came from the countryside. In fact the urban commune, in central and northern Italy, included nobles owning fiefs inside the town and in its outlying parts, as well as in the immediate vicinity; later, the same city commune would try to subordinate, or rather to incorporate, the more distant family clans of the *contado*. The permanence of this transfer of social structures is clearly evident in Tuscany and in Liguria.

In Pisa, nearly all the great noble *consorterie* were established inside the town at an early date; E. Cristiani wondered about the origins of these clans, and showed clearly that the historian is forced to accept the hypothesis of a transference from the nearby countryside. From 1197, the Emperor Henry VI conceded to Buonaccorso di Cicogna the right to build in the town of Pisa houses with "windows, shops, access, stairs, galleries and gutters". In their turn, shortly afterwards, came the Nobili di Caprona, Cattana di Valdera, di Porcari, di Corvara, di Cassiano and di Buriano families; although these *consorti* were economically assimilated into the city, they attempted to preserve their cohesion in the face of the other inhabitants – the *popolani.* In 1188 an oath of unity was sworn by a thousand citizens of

Pisa, who undertook to fight together against Genoa, but fifty-four heads of families made their declarations quite separately; they bore the names of the city's great *consorterie*, especially Visconti, Upezinghi, Capronesi and Ripafratta. These were the nobles whom contemporary texts often call *selvatici*, those who came from the countryside, who owned at least one large *selva*.[84] These nobles did not live apart, far from business life; rather, they established themselves in the Kinzica, Fuoriporta and Ponte quarters, where economic life was concentrated, and they dominated commerce and industry.[85]

So in Pisa the great *consorterie* were at once urban and rural. The Orlandi owned the Selva Palatina, a vast stretch of wooded hills between the sea, the lower reaches of the Serchio and the heights which dominate Lucca.[86] Towards 1260, this *consorteria* split into two branches, Orlandi and Pellari, but both still claimed a common ancestor and retained a solidly structured family organization; a text speaks of the *capitaneus dominorum filiorum Orlandi* which acts *capitanie nomine pro omnibus de domo filiorum Rolandi et pro omnibus suis consortibus et universitate iam dicte domus filiorum Orlandi.* Similarly with the Pellari: these nobles kept, indivisibly, pastures which they rented to rural communities.[87]

The move to the town is even more clearly seen from the study of other *consorterie* in Pisa. Since 970, the Ripafratta family, through concessions, at first from the bishop of Lucca, then from the emperors, had acquired large estates in the Serchio and Ozzeri valleys: *corti* with lands, fields and vines; *selve* and three *monti*; serfs, together with civil and criminal jurisdiction. They took their name from their original castle which stood on the very bank (Rippa) of the Serchio; some possessed only a very small portion of the common patrimony: one head of a family had only a fortieth of the castle; but the clan's solidarity was maintained without any split. Their wealth was administered jointly by those who called themselves *consortes de Ripafratta*; each member acted before a notary, only *pro se et aliis consortibus de Ripafratta*, and texts speaking of this wealth normally emphasize *in quibus comune podere consueti sunt habere*; this, in the thirteenth century, was a powerful, numerous, cohesive family clan.

They had at first been the allies, then the enemies, of the Luccans; then they came into the orbit of Pisa. They had surrendered a third of their castle to the commune which, in 1162, made extensive repairs to it, whilst leaving it in their custody. Some *consortes* remained at

Ripafratta, while others went to Pisa, where they established houses and towers.[88] So in the thirteenth century the Ripafratta family still had a strongly fortified castle holding a strategically important crossroads, controlled a large household, a veritable dependency,[89] and at the same period resided in Pisa, where they took part in all the activities of the city and its government. It seems certain that in the second half of this century the Ripafratta family busied themselves in ensuring for themselves another, large, dependency in the town itself, opening up entry to their *consorteria*, probably by various adoptions, to people of middle rank, to *livellari*, their tenants or leaseholders.

The noble Corvaia and Vallechia *consorteria* is another example, but relatively late; in 1253 the commune allowed them citizenship; most of the fiefs of these nobles were about a hundred kilometres north of Pisa.[90]

Links between town and country family clans are even more evident, much later, in Liguria. The main *alberghi* of Genoa were of rural origin; they were noble lineages which had moved at a more or less early date into the city, subsequently becoming open to other social categories. The specifically urban clans appear to have come into existence much later, at a different time, under the pressure of various circumstances, including increasing disturbances. Some, but admittedly few, did not even claim noble status.

This process of the clan's transfer and its more or less artificial growth would explain the existence and the wealth of some 'noble' *alberghi* which, in fact, were double or triple clans: on the one hand, a real seignorial group, of ancient and rural origin, owning fiefs and having a dependent following of relatives and allies; on the other hand, a specifically urban group, probably of plebeian stock, made up of newly rich merchants and a much more restricted clientele. The fusion of such different clans may have taken place at a quite late period, even in the Quattrocento, most frequently through a simple legal instrument. We have only rare examples of this.[91] However, the compound names of certain *alberghi* point to this, and show that such amalgamation was by no means rare: witness the Grimaldi and the Grimaldi di Oliva; the Fieschi di Carignano and the Fieschi di Canetto. The Fieschi did not come from Genoa, but from the Riviera di Levante; these counts of Lavagna still held their fiefs more or less indivisibly: they had a great number of relatives and their relationships formed inextricably tangled webs. They maintained fortresses, armies of mountain dwellers and several manorial residences; in Lavagna, Pontremolo or

Varese, in the 1460s, Giovanni Ludovico Fieschi, the head of the clan, held court surrounded by a large dependency. In 1459, when two ladies of the family, both widows of powerful members of the lineage, left Genoa in order to return to their house in outlying Albaro, and subsequently to their estates of Montoggio and the eastern Riviera, they departed with a retinue of 150 people. The noble Fieschi family possessed in Genoa a considerable number of houses, including several palaces: in Carignano, on the hill overlooking the port and the town to the east, they had two large manorial estates – land, vineyards and houses; in the old town around San Donato and round the Piazza San Lorenzo, nearer the business quarter, they also had other houses and palaces.[92] They lived in Carignano, that is, outside the city, and rented out their houses in the centre. The other Fieschi were of the di Canetto *contrada*, based in the old, popular part of the city; but they were very different.

In the absence of well-established and powerful urban alliances, some *alberghi* of rural nobles played a large part in the political life of Genoa. Such, in the fifteenth century, were the Adorni, one of the two families from which the doges were at this time chosen.[93] They were rarely to be found in the city and took no part in matters of trade. Between 1402 and 1408 the head of the lineage, Teramo, living at Castelletto d'Orba on the Riviera di Ponante, oversaw his nearby fiefs, especially those of Castelnuovo Bormida and Grimaldi. His accounts show that at least forty people were directly dependent upon him: nine very close and eight more distant relatives, and twenty-three servants. They all bore the name of Adorno.[94] There is no doubt that these families of the doges held faithfully to the old structures and, I believe, also to the old ways of life.

In any case, the *albergo*, as far as we can understand it, certainly seems to have been the real and quite fundamental structure of a very large number of families of the Ligurian Rivieras, where, anyway, indivision of fiefs and even of estates was very often maintained, even at a very late date. On 16 February 1465 four lords of Cogorno (on the eastern Riviera) designated two other members of the family to swear allegiance to the commune of Genoa before the governor of Chiávari; they declared that they acted in their own names and *vice omnium de albergo nobilium de Concurno.*[95]

In Sestri Levante, a large township on the same Genoese Riviera, families who possessed lands in the area called themselves *alberghi*, and were referred to thus by notaries. The word may describe family groups of varying size: in 1467 one lawyer used the term *albergo* for, on the one hand, a veritable clan which had twelve heads of family registered in the year's cadastre, and, on the other hand, one household, represented on the same document by a single named person. Much evidence of this sort shows clearly that at this date the word *albergo* was still commonly used, necessarily so when referring to a great family or its residue, over the whole of the essentially rural territory of Sestri.[96]

A statistical study of the number of *domus*, primary families which were themselves more or less widely spread, but which were contained within the group, serves as reliable confirmation of this conclusion. The cadastre of 1467 notes 1,069 heads of families, yet cites only 286 different names. These are distributed thus: sixty-four isolated heads of families (each name is found once only); 135 names of groups, each consisting of between two and five heads of families; and eighty-seven names of groups consisting of more than five heads of families.

The last figure deserves attention, especially as some groups contain more than ten registered heads of family – thirteen, sixteen, and even twenty-three in the case of the largest group; and as those who own no land are obviously excluded from the document. Thus it seems certain that "a considerable proportion, even the majority of the population, therefore belong to one of these groups, which were solidly rooted in the country areas".[97]

This social study of a Ligurian township thus gives a sure picture of the origins of the *albergo* in this region. The *albergo*, the family clan, certainly appears to be the fundamental framework, the very basis of social structures in the Ligurian countryside. It was, doubtless, a specifically rural heritage which the semi-urban township picked up. Originally, some if not all of these clans were noble. But more, even than in Genoa, political and social evolution led to the disappearance of all traces of nobility. Sestri was free from any seignorial tutelage; its land suffered no burdens other than rents; men paid only their taxes and the Genoese impost; apart from the Church, all landowners were men of the township or of the nearby villages and hamlets. This is a striking example of a rural and noble structure – the lineage – which was handed down to a society of small burgesses and free peasants. The latter were the heirs of the widely spread group containing several families with the same name, or who adopted that name.

This survival and the strength of family ties are further asserted, still at the same period, in other, much less well-known cantons of the

Riviera. Castagnola was a very small village, perched on a mountain but not far from the sea, above Framura, near Levanto, that is, to the east of Genoa. In 1458, one Sunday evening, at about the hour of vespers, thirteen members of the Pinu clan met in the great hall of the house of one of them.[98] These people did not call themselves noble, but they all claimed, together with one who was absent, whom they represented, to belong to the name or *cognomen*, *parentela* and *albergo* of the Pinu. The clan was probably much larger, for according to the notary, only those Pinu "residing at Castagnola" were assembled there. Other key members of the clan must have been residing in other parts of the eastern Riviera.[99] They invoked the unity of "this strain, born of common ancestors", and decided to elect each year two governors to keep their peace.

The hypothesis of the transference of the family clan from the countryside to the town, which seems to me to be readily acceptable in the cases of Tuscany and Liguria, can probably not be completely rejected without deeper consideration with reference to other, even more remote regions. But at this point we lack guidelines, and history is much less clear.

The study of E.N. Rocca on the topographical concentration of great families in the city of Piacenza brings to light a very unusual and highly significant case of the transfer of a seignorial clan from a country district, in this case a very remote area, to the town. The Scotti, who owned the whole south-west part of the city, had apparently come from Ireland or Scotland; in any case, asserts Rocca, they were definitely connected with the Scottish clan of Douglas; later, moreover, they were to take (or revive) the name of Douglas Scotti, which they still use at present. They had retained the memory of those great family clans which were made up of large numbers of people; this clan, of rural origin, was now established, not in a single town, but in several; for the Scotti, who already had power in Piacenza in the twelfth century, had different branches established in other Italian towns.[100]

The social structure of Venetian country districts seems very little known; but it is probable that the great families of the city, who at first were the owners of land in the lagoons, and who long drew the best part of their fortunes from these properties, also retained a very marked cohesion, and administered their estates, then their fiefs, in common. Whatever the case may be, when the Greek islands were colonized these families retained the memory of the clan; together they governed and worked their possessions. The island of Kythera was totally dominated by the Venier family, which chronicles claimed was descended from the *gens* of Aurelia. Venetian assemblies speak only of the Venier brothers and of their island. In August 1363, at the outbreak of the insurrection of the Venier against the metropolis, the insurgents received substantial assistance, and Venice designated those called *omnes de cha Venier* as the commune's worst enemies.[101]

Of course, outside Italy, information is even scarcer, but J. Schneider has emphasized the role of rural families in the development of Metz and of its aristocracy.[102] These family clans–*paraiges* –must surely have come from the country, retaining solid links in the area. In fact, some 'patrician' families of these Metz clans retained, in their patronym, the memory of their origins, the birthplace of their line, the place from which their ancestors had come. Some names might refer to a more or less far-off town (for example Strasbourg, Cologne or Troyes), but most certainly indicated a nearby estate or village.[103] Right through the fourteenth century, and even a little later, the great lineages of Brussels still possessed extensive landed estates in their homelands, remnants of their ancient patrimonies.[104]

Sometimes a clan kept and even strengthened its cohesion when some of its members found themselves settling, albeit temporarily, in town. When the Séverac family were being heard by the Paris *Parlement*, the court finally decided, after fifteen years of set-backs, to summon only those of the "kindred friends" who were in Paris at the time;[105] so the clan could act at once in Paris and in Rodez.

On the subject of this problem of transference from the countryside to the town, M. Tits's study of Louvain advances another argument, which seems to me to be decisive. From 1265–1266 the town had only two lineages, rivals of course, the Van den Blankarden and the Van den Colveren. In, fact, here the word lineage brings a confusing element, or at least needs clarification. Although texts refer to them as *gheslechten* or tribes, they were not only family clans, but also very loose groups, veritable parties; their properties spread into all parts of the town and ties of proximity could not be asserted there. But very significantly, an examination of the geographical situation of families' domains, in each lineage, shows that their property was grouped, that of one side to the north and west, that of the other, to the east and south of the town.[106] So here the proximity of rural domains caused the formation of very large suprafamily groups; subsequently these groups, and their connections, moved into the city.

We accept that we lack enough data to elevate these conclusions into general rules. However, all these indications are reliable pointers to the inheritance received by the town from the countryside. On a new level, they obviously contradict theses which once presented, or still present, towns as new, original worlds. In fact, at least as regards the aristocracy, their social structures often seem to be simply a continuation, or a heritage, of those of the noble lineages.

For our purpose, the study of urban societies, the knowledge of rural family clans, before and during the rise of the towns, could throw much light on this uncertain period and on these obscure aspects of social history. It seems certain that the strength, size and cohesion of these clans must have varied from region to region. The processes of dissolution, of fragmentation or, conversely, of reinforcement, do not have an identical history everywhere, and are not felt at the same periods. I believe that in large measure the social history of towns, or at least of their groupings, is dominated by the greater or lesser cohesion and power of these family clans of rural nobles. The commune, in asserting itself, had to fight these groups; it had only varying degrees of success in its attempt.

Notes

[1]Ascheri, A., *Notizie intorno alla riunione delle famiglie in Albergo in Genova*, Genoa, 1846. I adopted this opinion, which I now consider erroneous, in my book, *Gênes au XVe siècle. Activité économique et problèmes sociaux*, Paris, 1961 (see especially p. 565).

[2]Renouard, Y., *Les villes d'Italie de la fin du Xe siècle au début du XIVe siècle*, Paris, 1969, 147ff.

[3]Renouard, Y., *Les villes d'Italie*, 157.

[4]Cristiani, E., *Nobiltà e popolo nel comune di Pisa. Dalle origini del Podestariato alla Signoria dei Donoratico*, Naples, 1962, 64ff.

[5]Carpentier, E., *Une ville devant la peste. Orvieto et la Peste Noire de 1348*, Paris, 1962, 67.

[6]Lopez, R.S., Aux origines du capitalisme génois, in *Annales E.S.C.*, 1937.

[7]Génicot, L., "La noblesse médiévale dans l'ancienne Francie", in *Annales E.S.C.*, 1962; and "Naissance, fonction et richesse dans l'ordonnance de la société médiévale. Le cas de la noblesse du continent", in Mousnier, R., *Problèmes de stratification sociale, Actes du Colloque international (1966)*, Paris, 1968, 83–92.

[8]Verriest, L., *Noblesse, chevalerie, lignages. Condition des biens et des personnes. Seigneurie, Ministérialité, Bourgeoisie, Échevinage*, Brussels, 1959.

[9]Werner, K. F., "Bedeutende Adelsfamilien im Reich Karls des Grossen", in *Karl der Grosse*, 3rd. edn, Düsseldorf, 1967, i, 83–142. See also Leyser, K., "The German

aristocracy from the ninth to the early twelfth century", in *Past and Present*, 1968, 25–53.

[10]Duby, G., "Lignage, noblesse et chevalerie au XIIe siècle dans la région mâconnaise", in *Annales E.S.C.*, 1972 (803–823), 811.

[11]Nortier, E., *La société laïque et l'église dans la province de Narbonne (zone pyrénéenne) de la fin du VIIIe siècle à la fin du XIe siècle*, Toulouse, 1974.

[12]Verriest, L., *Noblesse, chevalerie, lignages*. On this question see Leyser, K., "Maternal kin in early medieval Germany: a reply", in *Past and Present*, 1970, 126–134.

[13]Lambert, J.N., *Aspects de la civilisation à l'âge du fratriarcat; étude d'histoire juridique et religieuse comparée*, Algiers, 1958, links this custom of descent through the female line to the memory of vast family groups which had their women in common, where consanguinity was assured only with reference to the mother, and where succession took place from brother to brother, rather than from father to son (pp. 6–7). Caesar thus described the family and social customs of the Bretons, a race in which this type of succession remained to a very late stage (*Gallic Wars*, v, 14): "Ten or twelve men have between them common wives, especially brothers with brothers and fathers with sons, but the children who are born are held to be those of him whose wife each young virgin first became."

[14]Lambert, J.N., *Aspects de la civilisation*, 34–35. "Thus together went her sceptre and her hand" (eulogy of a queen of the Picts, quoted by Hubert, H., *Les Celtes*, Paris, 1932, ii, 248. On Pictish matriarchy, see Weisweiler, J., "Die Stellung der Frau bei den Kelten und das Problem des 'Keltischen Mutterrechts'", in *Zeitschrift für celtische Philologie*, xxi, 1939.

[15]Especially in some Scottish clans which apparently hesitated for a long time between male and female descent.

[16]Tellenbach, G., "Vom karolingischen Reichsadel zum deutschen Reichsfürstenbund", in *Wege der Forschung*, Darmstadt, ii, 1956, 191–242; and *Studien und Vorarbeiten zur Geschichte des grosfränkischen und frühdeutschen Adels*, Freiburg im Breisgau, 1957.

[17]Schmid, K., "Über die Struktur des Adels im früheren Mittelalter", in *Jahrbuch für fränkische Landesforschung*, xix, 1959, 1–23; "Neue Quellen zum Verständnis des Adels im 10. Jahrhundert", in *Zeitschrift für die Geschichte des Oberrheins*, cviii, 1960, 185–232; and "Zur Problematik von Familie, Sippe und Geschlecht", in the same, civ–cv, 1957.

[18]Every detailed study of the establishment of this first great Frankish aristocracy emphasizes this dispersal of power and wealth; and this not only in the eastern provinces of the Empire, but in Neustria itself. Thus, for example, for Normandy, L. Musset shows that the family of Vaudemir and his wife Ercamberte, established there by the Merovingians, seems, with several others, to lack 'local links'; in the 690s the family owned eleven estates scattered in the future Normandy (one of which was near Évreux, and another in the Vexin region), and several other estates situated in eight *pagi*, from Beauvais to Quercy; see Musset, L., "Gouvernants et gouvernés dans le monde scandinave et le monde normand", in *Recueils de la Société Jean Bodin*, xxii, Brussels, 1968.

[19]Werner, K. F., "Die Nachkommen Karls des Grossen (1–8 Generation)", in *Karl der Grosse*, 3rd edn, Düsseldorf, 1967, iv, 403–482.

[20]Compare the *Reichsaristokratie* studied by G. Tellenbach: groups of related people were scattered throughout the Empire; they were entrusted with the highest offices, gathered to themselves relatives and friends, but received only temporary posts, so that any permanent settlement was denied them. However, the dominant families of regional aristocracies established themselves sooner, especially in the West. On this point see the

works of Werner, K.F., "Untersuchungen zur Frühzeit des französischen Fürstentums (9. bis 10. Jahrhundert)", in *Welt als Geschichte*, xix, 1959, 146–193; xx, 1960, 87–119; and Bedeutende Adelsfamilien", in *Karl der Grosse*, i.

[21]Génicot, L., in Mousnier, R., *Problèmes de stratification sociale*, 85; G. Duby also notes a change in the Mâcon region, between the ninth and eleventh centuries, which "strengthens the power of the husband over a couple's fortune". See Duby, G., *Annales E.S.C.*, 1972.

[22]*Annals of Cambrai, Monumenta Germaniae Historica. Scriptores*, xvi, Hanover, 1859, year 1108, 511–512; quoted and translated by De La Roncière, C. M., Contamine, P., Delort, M., Rouche, M., in *L'Europe au Moyen Age*, ii, Paris, 1969, 182–187.

[23]Schneider, J., *La ville de Metz aux XIIIe et XIVe siècles*, Nancy, 1950, 126f.

[24]Schneider, J., *La ville de Metz*, 147.

[25]Bertolini, O., Ordinamenti militari e strutture sociali dei Longobardi in Italia, in *Settimane di Studio del Centro italiano di Studi sull'alto medio evo*, xv (1) Spoleto, 1968, 429–629.

[26]Chiapelli, L., "L'Età longobarda a Pistoia", in *Archivio storico italiano*, i, 1921, 227–338; for the present point see pp. 285ff.

[27]See note 26 above. In 1219, when the *popolo* of Carignagno swore loyalty to Pistoia, the Lombards swore separately.

[28]Chiapelli, L., *La donna Pistoiese del tempo antico*, Pistoia, 1914; and *I nomi di donna in Pistoia dall'alto medio evo al secolo XIII*, Pistoia, 1920.

[29]Chiapelli, L., *L'Età longobarda*, 281: *Prata, alpis, silvas que et quas habet simul pro indivisio cum consortibus de Tavianis et cum illis de domo Admannatica.*

[30]Zaniewicki, W.H., *La noblesse 'populaire' en Espagne et en Pologne*, Lyons, 1967; the author goes so far as to assert that *all* the inhabitants of Guipuzcoa considered themselves to be nobles (we should perhaps read this as all the free men).

[31]Gorski, K., "Les structures sociales de la noblesse polonaise au Moyen Age", in *Le Moyen Age*, 1967, 74–85.

[32]Zaniewicki, W.H., *La noblesse 'populaire'*, 4.

[33]Simple, non-noble peasants also had their rallying cries, shouted, for example, on the outbreak of a fire; see also Jedlicki, J., *Klejnot i bariery spoleczne* (*Armorial bearings and social barriers*), Warsaw, 1969.

[34]Garcia de Cortazar, J.A., *Viscaya en el siglo XV*, Bilbao, 1966, 314ff.

[35]On the *bandos*, see Garcia de Cortazar, J.A., *Viscaya*, 316. The study of these noble parties should be related to that of the Guelphs and Ghibellines and, especially, of the Blacks and Whites, in central and northern Italy.

[36]Elso, M., "Les infançons de Navarre et du pays de Labourd", in *Eusko Jakintza*, 1949, 272–284.

[37]Mitre Fernandez, E., *Evolución de la nobleza en Castilla bajo Enrique III (1396–1406)*, Valladolid, 1968.

[38]Miss M.C. Gerbet is preparing an important study of the noble lineage and clans in Estremadura. Investigation of these structures will greatly increase knowledge of family clans.

[39]Veyrin, P., *Les Basques de Labourd, de Soule et de basse Navarre, leur histoire et leurs traditions*, Bayonne, 1947.

[40]Tucoo-Chala, P., *Gaston Fébus*, 200, note 124.

[41]Logan, J., *The clans of the Scottish highlands*, Edinburgh, 1843; Bain, R., *The clans*

and tartans of Scotland, London and Glasgow, 1959; and Cunningham, A., *The loyal clans*, Cambridge, 1932.

[42]Nicholls, K., *Gaelic and gaelicised Ireland in the Middle Ages*, Dublin, 1972.

[43]Hodgson, *A history of Northumberland,* Newcastle, 1827.

[44]Laigue, R. de, *La noblesse bretonne au XVe et au XVIe siècle. Réformations et monstres. Évêché de Vannes,* Rennes, 1902.

[45]Laigue, R. de, *La noblesse bretonne,* 105.

[46]Quoted by Contamine, P., "The French nobility and the war", in Fowler, K. (ed.), *The Hundred Years War,* London, 1971 (134–162) 141, note 43.

[47]Meyer, J., *La noblesse bretonne au XVIIIe siècle,* Paris, 1966, ii, 137.

[48]Meyer, J., *La noblesse bretonne,* 14, 21.

[49]Meyer, J., *La noblesse bretonne,* 24–25.

[50]But see Lancaster, L., "Kinship in Anglo-Saxon society", in *British Journal of Society,* 1958, 23–50, 359–377; and Charles-Edwards, T.M., "Kinship, status and the origins of the hide", in *Past and Present,* 1972, 3–33.

[51]Meyer, J., *La noblesse bretonne,* 21.

[52]Génicot, L., "De la noblesse au lignage, le cas des Boneffe", in *Revue Belge de philologie et d'histoire,* 1953, 39–53.

[53]Génicot, L., in Mousnier, R., *Problèmes de stratification sociale,* 90–91; on this point for Spain, and for comparison, see Pescador, C., "La caballeria popular en Leon y Castilla", in *Cuadernos de Hispania,* 1963, 89–198; and Gauthier-Dalché, J., "Sépuldeva à la fin du Moyen Age", in *Le Moyen Age,* 1963.

[54]Génicot, L., in Mousnier, R., *Problèmes de stratification sociale,* 87.

[55]Génicot, L., in Mousnier, R., *Problèmes de stratification sociale,* 88.

[56]Contamine, P., in Fowler, K. (ed.), *The Hundred Years War,* 136–137.

[57]Favier, J., "La tourmente", in Boüard, M. de, *Histoire de la Normandie,* Toulouse, 1970, 249.

[58]Quoted by Cazelles, R., *La société politique et la crise de la royauté française sous Philippe VI de Valois,* Paris, 1958, 290. In Troyes, at the end of the Middle Ages, younger sons of noble families willingly went into the cloth trade (this is true of the Hennequin and de Marizy families). The des Pleurres family numbered several men who took up once more the profession of arms and led a strictly noble life, founding new branches of warriors, after being drapers and even mercers. Examples of this 'dormant nobility', at that time, and in that region, appear very common. See Bibolet, F., *Les assemblées générales des habitants de Troyes aux XIVe et XVe, siècles, la Saint-Barnabé.*

[59]Analyses by Contamine, P., in Fowler, K. (ed.), *The Hundred Years War,* 137–138.

[60]Contamine, P., in Fowler, K. (ed.), *The Hundred Years War,* 139.

[61]Sivery, G., *Structures agraires.*

[62]Monboisse, R., *L'ordre féodal des 'Montagnes d'Auvergne' du XIIe au XVe siècle.*

[63]For this, see Pernot, A., *La noblesse franc-comtoise d'après les testaments (1350–1500),* unpublished dissertation, University of Paris X, 1969, 36–40.

[64]Duby, G., "Dans la France du Nord-Ouest au XIIe siècle: les jeunes dans la société chevaleresque", in *Annales E.S.C.,* 1964.

[65]Micha, A., Le siège de Barbastre: structure et technique, in *Travaux de linguistique et de littérature publiés par le Centre de Philologie et de Littérature romanes de l' Université de Strasbourg,* vi (2) 1968.

[66]Turlan, J.M., "Amis et amis charnels d'après les actes du Parlement du Paris au XIVe siècle", in *Revue historique de droit français et étranger,* 1969, 645–698.

[67]Turlan, J.M., in *R.H.D.F.E.*, 1969, 667.

[68]In Lille, up to the third remove; see Turlan, J.M., in *R.H.D.F.E.*, 1969, 684.

[69]Ross, J.B., "Rise and fall of a seventeenth-century clan", in *Speculum*, 1959.

[70]Ross, J.B., in *Speculum*, 1959, 385. The enquiry is published in *M.G.H.S.*, xxv, 441–443.

[71]*Uno lignaggio di nobili e possenti che si chimovano i Cancellieri, non pero di grande antichità . . . e di loro nacquero molti figliuoli et nepoti sicchè in questo tempo erano piu di cento uomini d'arme ricchi e possenti e di grande affare*: Villani, G., *Cronica*, cap. 39 (iv, 54), quoted by Herlihy, D., in *Medieval and Renaissance Pistoia: the social history of an Italian town*, New Haven, Yale U.P., 1967, 118.

[72]Santini, G., *I comuni di valle del medioevo. La costituzione federale del 'Frignano' (Dalle origini all'autonomia politica)*, Seminario Giuridico della Università di Bologna, xxii, Milan, 1960; see especially 96–117.

[73]Santini, G., *I comuni di valle del medioevo*: the rest of the work is devoted, particularly, to the development of this *comune di valle*, of noble and feudal origins, and to its transformation into a much more complex political organization.

[74]G. Santini cites studies by De Formentini, but without precise references. Among other things, De Formentini has written: "Turris, il comitato torresano e la contea di Lavagna dai Bizantini ai Franchi", in *Archivio Storico delle Provinzie Parmensi*, nuova seria, xxix, 1929. To this may be added the very interesting essay of Conti, P.M., "Tracee e indizi de una base gentilizia degli istituti limitanei bizantini", in *Memoria accademia lunigianese di Sc. G. Capellini*, xi, 1962, 3–28.

[75]De Stafani, C., "Storia dei comuni de Gafargnana", in *Atti e Memorie della Deputazione di Storia Patria di Modena*, seria VII, ii, 1925.

[76]Emmanueli, P., *La terre du commun, quatre siècles de collectivisme agraire en Corse (1358–1768)*, Aix-en-Provence, 1957.

[77]Herlihy, D., "Family solidarity in medieval Italian history", in *Economy, society and government in medieval Italy. Essays in memory of Robert L. Reynolds*, The Kent State U.P., 1969, 173–194.

[78]On this method, see Herlihy, D., "Church property on the European continent; (700–1200)", in *Speculum*, 1961, 81–105.

[79]Niccolai, F., "I consorzi nobiliari ed il comune nell'alta e media Italia", in *Rivista storica del diritto Italiano*, 1940, 116–147, 292–341, 397–477; Torelli, P., *Lezioni di storia del diritto privato. La famiglia*, Milan, 1947 (cap. 1, *Gli aggregati soprafamigliari, i consorzi gentili medioevali*, 1–10); Rocca, E. Nasalli, "Il consorzio gentilizio dei Fontanesi, signori della Val Tidone", in *Archivio Storico delle Provinzie Parmense*, 1964, 195–218.

[80]Bozzola, A., "Appunti sulla vita economica, sulle classe sociali e sull'ordinamento administrativo del Monferrato nei secoli XIV–XV", in *Bolletino storico-bibliografico subalpino*, 1923, 210–261.

[81]See, for example, Durando, E., "Statuti di Montiglio", in *Bolletino storico-bibliografico subalpino*, 1907.

[82]*Archivio di Stato di Genova*, Notaio de Recco Giacomo, filza 1 (2), No. 123.

[83]Rossetti, G., *Società e istituzioni nel contado lombardo durante il medioevo. Cologne Monzese, i: Secoli VIII–X*, Milan, 1968.

[84]For comparison, see Bowsky, W. M., "Cives Silvestres: sylvan citizenship and the Sienese commune (1287–1353)", in *Bolletino senese di storia patria*, 1965, 1–13.

[85]Cristiani, E., *Nobiltà e popolo*, 33; from 1153, the Visconti family, one of the most

powerful in the city, formed a *consorteria* there; a text says: *Alberto Vicecomiti maiori, suisque filiis, et Gottifredo nepoti, ceterisque suis consortibus Vicecomitibus*... (34, note 39).

[86]Lupo Gentile, M., "Sulla consorteria feudale dei nobili di Ripafratta", in *Giornale storico e letterario della Liguria,* vi, 1905, Nos. 1–5, 22–23.

[87]Cristiani, E., *Nobiltà e popolo,* 108.

[88]Lupo Gentile, M., in *Giornale storico e letterario della Liguria,* 1905, 1–23.

[89]Cristinai, E., *Nobiltà e popolo,* 126–127; they continue *comune et homines regere et suis reformare videlicet notariis, camerariis, nunciis, guardianis, arbitris et cafadiaris et aliis afficialibus consuetis.*

[90]Cristiani, E., *Nobiltà e popolo,* 58. On this *consorteria,* see "Memorie de Guido da Corvaia", in *Rerum Italicarum Scriptores,* xxiv, col. 673f.

[91]See below pp. 79–80.

[92]Heers, J., *Gênes au XVe siècle,* 536–537.

[93]On these families and their role in the city, see Heers, J., *Gênes au XVe siècle,* 601–605.

[94]Day, J., *I conti privati della famiglia Adorno (1402–1408),* Università di Genova, Istituto di Storia Medievale e Moderna, Fonti e Studi, i, 1958, 45–120.

[95]*A.S.G.*, Paesi, 6/346, Cogorno No. 1.

[96]Robin, F., "Sestri Levante, bourg de la Rivière génoise (vers. 1450–vers 1500)", unpublished thesis, University of Paris X, 1972, 172–173 (to be published by the University of Genoa).

[97]Robin, F., "Sestri Levante", 165–166. These figures should be compared with those given in 1571 in a cadastre of the village of Garéoult (Var Département, near Brignoles); here, out of 114 heads of family paying the *cens,* 35 bore the same name: Grisolle (work in progress of Mme P. Leclercq).

[98]*A.S.G.*, Notaio Oberto Foglietta giugniore, 17 Sept. 1458. For the provisions of this pact, see below, 106.

[99]Indeed, we find some of the Pinu family, now treated as noble, in Sestri Levante; see Robin, F., "Sestri Levante", 171.

[100]Rocca, E. Nasalli, "Palazzi e torri gentilizie nei quartieri della città medievale: l'"esemplo' di Piacenza", in *Raccolta di studi in memoria di Giovanni Soranzo,* Milan, 1968, 308, and "Le origini della famiglia Scotti", in *Scure,* Piacenza, 1933. Another example of the geographical diffusion of a large family clan through the establishment of several branches in different areas or towns is that of the Pessagno *albergo* of Genoa, which D. Hughes is studying (work in progress).

[101]Thiriet, F., "A propos de la seigneurie des Venier sur Cerigo", in *Studi Veneziani,* xii, 1970, 206.

[102]Schneider, J., *La ville de Metz,* 91–93.

[103]Schneider, J., *La ville de Metz,* 335.

[104]Fabresse, P., *L'avènement du régime démocratique à Bruxelles pendant le Moyen Age (1306–1423),* Brussels, 1932, 32–35.

[105]Turlan, J. M., in *R.H.D.F.E.* 1969, 667.

[106]Tits, M., *L'Évolution du patriciat louvaniste,* 34, 41–48, map facing p. 48.

CHAPTER 2

The formation and composition of family clans

Evidence of the clans' existence

Absolute proof of the existence of vast family groups, or of federations of groups, sometimes depends, in certain western cities, on the administrative structures themselves. When the clan remained the basis of political life, its importance and role are perfectly clear. In that case documents abound: statutes or ordinances of an institutional nature, lists of magistrates, notables or members of the different councils, the minutes of these assemblies and fiscal records themselves. This situation is wholly maintained where noble clansmen held total power, or the greater part of the power; this is especially true in the cities of Germany and Flanders, and even more clearly in many other cities of north-west Europe, for example, in Brussels.[1] In the cities of Castile, or at least in Old Castile, power seems to have been similarly monopolized by lineages.[2]

Where nobles had to give up some of their influence, in the institutional changes of the fourteenth century, their family clans could no longer assert themselves as clearly as previously as the frameworks of political life. However, some cities, especially in Italy, retained for a long time a double system of representation, or elected their magistrates or councillors on a topographical basis, in small districts which were more or less subservient to the influence of the great families. In Genoa, throughout the Middle Ages, the nobles were always and everywhere grouped by *alberghi*, especially in fiscal records and for the appointment of members of the councils; the *popolani* themselves voted by districts, by *conestagie* and *compagne*.[3] In Pisa, as late as

1228, a list of 4,000 citizens swearing peace with Siena, Pistoia and Poggibonsi, shows the nobles to be clearly distinguished from the 'people'; at the end of this long list, moreover, is a group of persons described as *maiores pisane civitatis*; in addition, the whole list is drawn up according to districts and *populi.*[4]

Later still, in Tuscany and Lombardy, noble clans disappeared completely from official documents. Then other frameworks, other bases for recruitment and election asserted themselves; these were professional associations, guilds which influenced the people, and thus governed a 'popular' commune. Officially, the family clans no longer had the freedom of the city.

This accounts for the findings of historians who, examining especially urban institutions, and particularly in Italy, observe a kind of political revolution and, from a social viewpoint, the obliteration of the ancient aristocracy. The conclusion of D. Herlihy's article on family solidarity in medieval Italy, which is so new and original in its premises and extent, remains absolutely classic on this point: the 'popular' communes are said by all these authors to have succeeded in breaking the cohesion of the great noble houses, to have upheld against them the liberty of each individual. But D. Herlihy accepts that the troubles of the end of the Middle Ages caused these nobles, at a later stage, to return to ancient practices of collective social life, without, for all that, returning to indivision of property.[5]

This political obliteration of the nobles in the face of the 'people' is not indisputable. Several studies have shown that from the political point of view the nobles, although excluded in principle from power, continued nevertheless to wield power, thanks to their alliances or dependencies, often at the cost of their having to join guilds; we should not be deluded by the words 'people' and 'artisans'.[6] In social life, I think the picture is much clearer; without any doubt blood ties and alliances successfully resisted the civic ordinances. The words *consorteria* or *consorzio* were used in Tuscan cities long after their disappearance from recognized institutions. The Florentine *Liber estimationum*, drawn up in 1268 in order to catalogue properties destroyed when the Guelphs were exiled, indicating the unfortunate proprietors, still sometimes gives the name of the head of the family, followed by different references pointing obviously to the existence of a family clan: *et nepotum*, *et fratri*, *heredes* or even *et consortum*. This last expression, proving that the *consorzio* was felt to be a living reality and a juridical entity, is not found equally in all districts: once only in

San Pancrazio, once too in Porta San Piero and Porta del Duomo, whereas the clerks use it three times for Oltrarno, four times for San Piero Scherraggio, and seven times for Borgo (this out of a list of 31, namely 22 per cent of the total), precisely where the nobles were much more numerous.[7] In all this document alone, which concerns only the property of the Guelphs, mentions sixteen *consorzii* in Florence.

It would certainly be naive to take literally the provisions of any law, and to believe that family clans disappeared the moment they ceased to be a normal part of the institutional framework of political life: whence the need to find other evidence, which will be more indirect, and also more uncertain.

The existence of the clan is often shown in vocabulary. To my knowledge, no semantic study has yet brought sufficient light to bear on this subject; but it is easy to see that chroniclers, official documents, administrative and judicial papers, for example, sometimes notaries' deeds, do not use the word 'family' if they are concerned with nobles, or at least with large and powerful groups. Vocabulary seems almost always imprecise and fickle; it reflects a wide and varied heritage; ruled by usage, it must also evolve according to the time, and according to the author's very intentions, as it also varies according to region.

Despite this, all the words used give the impression of a group which was vaster and more complex than the simple family; in Genoa they used *albergo*, *parentela*, *cognome* (this word has remained in the modern vocabulary); in Tuscany they used *consorzio*, *consorteria* or *gente*. In other towns and in different regions of Italy, we very often find the more ambiguous words *casa* or *casato*, or even *casale*, and *linea*; these words, even the first, all signify a social group which was much wider than the primary family. Let us not forget that all these special words were used for the powerful, the *maiores*.

There are other indications, still rather vague, but nevertheless significant: the use of family names in the plural, and the indication of consanguinity. The use of names in the plural seems reserved, almost everywhere, for rich, aristocratic families, often very long established. Admittedly, this usage seems to have been very uneven from the north to the south of Europe, and tended to weaken in the course of time. It was still found, at least in ordinary speech, in Paris in the fourteenth century: *les* Barbette, *les* Bourbon. Above all, it is indisputable and generalized in the cities of north and central Italy, more especially in Tuscany, where the particles *degli*, *dei*, *de'* or even *negli*... are constantly found. This plural obviously points to the idea of a numerous family group, and possibly even of a group divided into different branches.

The indication of one's father's Christian name, whether he was alive or dead, is further evidence of the numerical size of the clan. The habit of often giving the same names, from one generation to another, makes the need greater. Inside the group too many individuals bore the same first name; they could not have been distinguished without this precaution. Very often, this usage corresponded to a really tribal or clannish structure, as for example in the Arab, then Moslem, civilizations and societies (*ben*), or in the case of the Scots and the Irish (*mac*). In certain Mediterranean countries this practice is still, in our own times, very common, for example in Corsica.

It seems that in the Middle Ages the habit of indicating one's father's Christian name was not followed everywhere with the same thoroughness. Careful study should enable us to perceive here marked developments and differences. We lack such a study, which would be tedious to carry out, and it is possible to offer only a few general remarks. I believe that this usage was much less common in the cities of northern France than in Languedoc or Italy. In Paris, official documents such as those of the *Parlement* do not mention the father; neither do private documents in a number of northern towns; popular usage alone testifies to this custom. In Italy, on the contrary, the name of the father was systematically given whenever a family of high social position was involved; this was so, of course, in the whole of Tuscany, where individuals answered to three names. For the *mediocres* this was no longer true. In Genoa, notarial deeds seem quite significant on this point; despite the notaries' carelessness or the formulae which they increasingly used, the father's Christian name, which was still optional at the end of the fourteenth century,[8] was necessary, half a century later, decisively and without exception, for the powerful, the noble and the rich. Notaries regularly omitted this element in the case of strangers, the people of the Rivieras, and for the modest *popolani*. Here, as in Florence, the indication of consanguinity was a clearly established social sign. That shows well the more numerous membership of the family group.

There is finally other evidence, even more indirect; this bears on ways of life, and more especially on where people lived. It seems probable that the form and capacity of the house were not, as has too often been claimed, linked solely to natural conditions, to relief and climate, but much more to social structures. A large house is a mark of family cohesion: whence the usefulness of establishing the house's importance in every aspect; but this, on condition that such assessments be based on specific studies (for example, archeology, or the study of detailed texts), and not on speculation or on improper generalizations.[9] In the same way, the more or less clear localization, inside the city, of individuals bearing the same name, and their regrouping, also show the greater or lesser solidarity of the family or suprafamily clan.[10]

Nature and composition of clans

These numerous and complex clans evolved. Their structure and internal composition often seem to have been variable and differed greatly according to the town, the social milieu and the era. However, all stressed the idea of the family, whether the members really belonged to a single stock, or merely wished to behave similarly and act together. In every case, they asserted this idea.

Thus the clan appeared, above all, consanguineous. This is why I use the term 'family' even if, as in several Genoese *alberghi*, the group was formed by the amalgamation of several families which were themselves more or less complex and, originally, unconnected. Moreover, on the occasion of such an adoption, the individual was never admitted as an individual, but always as the head of a primary family; the adoption was then valid for him and for his family.[11]

In Genoa the term *familia* is used only once,[12] in many hundreds of documents concerning these groups, whereas the terms *parentela, stirpe, progenia* and even *albergo* (seemingly the equivalent of the *domus* of Tuscan and Lombard texts) show constant reference to the idea of the tribe. In Lucca, as late as the sixteenth century, notaries and men of law still use the word *stirpe* (tribe) with reference to direct descent inside great families.[13]

However, we must certainly note the nature and limits of these families. Their succession was clearly and unequivocally masculine. In Genoa, where this phenomenon may be studied in a great many cases, sons-in-law did not enter the clan; obviously, they remained in their fathers' clans. Married or widowed women did indicate their fathers' surnames and Christian names, but always in addition to their husbands'. Very frequently, the members of a group recalled their common ancestor, veritably worshipping him.

Moreover, this family clan, even if it was extremely large, even when it grouped together many hundreds of individuals, remained strictly exogamous. In Pavia, where texts also spoke of *progenia* in reference to nobles, none contracted marriage within his own *progenia*, for such marriages, up to remote relationships, were forbidden by ancient laws. Rather, families sought alliances with other, quite unconnected families, even with adversaries or enemies, which often favoured peace and the end of old vendettas.[14] In Genoa, similarly, out of thousands of documents and tens of thousands of references which enable us to study marriages, one alone, apparently, notes an alliance within a family group,[15] however large. One did not even marry a girl from another branch of the clan: this for the Spinola, Fieschi and Giustiniani families (the last-named being *popolani*); these federations of families which were rather disparate, and originally quite unconnected, strictly forbade internal marriage. The men all behaved as if there really were ties of blood between them all. The simple fact of bearing the same name prohibited matrimonial alliances.

This bears no comparison with those artificial brotherhoods where, especially in the peasant world, the less fortunate sons-in-law or strangers coming to a village would join a family group, and where sons and daughters very often married within the group in order to avoid the dissipation of wealth.[16]

The urban clans, in contrast, seem to have been natural families or federations of natural families, with masculine succession, exclusively exogamous.

It seems pointless to dwell at length on the strength of the idea of the family in medieval societies. We must however note that this idea is not peculiar only to obscure periods, to rural communities and to the most ancient civilizations. In the commercial towns of Italy, during the time conventionally called the Renaissance, while the different fortunes of commerce and banking imposed hierarchies of greatly varying conditions, men looked to their families and forcefully asserted their respect and affection for their relatives. The merchants themselves (although they were called the new men), who some claim were at the origin of the humanist current of ideas and were champions of a kind of individualism, showed themselves in this realm to have total respect for ancient traditions. Their chronicles and all their writings dwell very frequently on the virtues of the family,[17] almost always in the widest sense of the word. Their *Libri di ricordanze*[18] or *Libri degli affari de casa*,[19] equivalent to the French *Livres de raison*,[20] are veritable family record books which, sometimes for two or three generations, scrupulously set out marriages, births and deaths, sought the origins of the *gente* and asserted great pride in their name. Family letters, much less well-known, also bear witness to the same state of mind and to the group's solidarity: such are the *Lettere di una gentildonna fiorentina del secolo XV ai figliuoli esuli.*[21]

Finally, and above all, the historian of collective attitudes finds deep echoes of these mental reactions in the famous *Libri della famiglia,* treatises in which L.B. Alberti, although one of the fathers of Florentine humanism, a man of letters and a merchant, discusses the advantages and virtues of the *gente* and exalts its power, when it remains united and numerous: *Ben mi duole di voi non pochi giovani Alberti, è quali vi trovate senza eredi, senza avere quanto potresti accresciuta la famiglia e fattolà populosa.*[22]

The members of the clan were obviously placed at different levels. For example, the *gente* or the *albergo* united several primary or nuclear families, in the restricted sense of the word. Often allies and friends joined; so did dependants and protégés.

The numerical size of the family clans of nobles was due, firstly, to a particularly high birth rate. This problem deserves attention, for it has been too willingly accepted that in the Middle Ages, everywhere and in all economic and social milieux, the birth rate reached considerable levels, modified doubtless by a dreadful rate of infantile mortality, and even more generally, by a particularly low life expectation. These excessively comprehensive statements must be modified and subtleties must be shown; as they stand, they cannot be supported by sufficiently substantial and definitive demographic studies.

First, the rates of marriage and even of childbirth varied greatly according to ways of life. In Tuscany, a study of the cadastre of 1427 reveals that there were many more married men in country areas than in towns. For example, in the *contado* of Arezzo, the heads of households who paid taxes were distributed thus:[23]

	Town (%)	*Country (%)*
Married men	57.8	74.0
Widowers	5.2	6.8
Widows	17.6	6.0
Unmarried men and women	0.2	0.8
Status unknown: men	13.8	7.6
Status unknown: women	5.4	4.2

In Florence, in 1427, the percentage of young married men was much lower than in the *contado*, or even in the town, of Pistoia:[24]

Percentages of married or widowed men	*Pistoia* (contado)	*Pistoia* (*city*)	*Florence* (*city*)
13–17 years	0.8	0.0	0.0
18–22 years	25.3	17.6	5.5
23–27 years	70.1	61.1	24.5
28–32 years	77.5	70.1	48.6

The contrast between the town and the country clearly reflects the difference in ways of life and social behaviour. Further, social and family life in Pistoia, from this point of view, seems to have been closer to that of the countryside than to that of a great economic metropolis; levels of wealth were probably more constant there, with no great hope of spectacular success in the space of a single generation.

On the other hand, we note that rich or 'noble' hearths were more important, numbering more souls than others. In Carpentras, on the average, hearths of modest or poor circles counted less than three persons: the corresponding average is 7.7 (more than double!) among the rich, who had 'families' of twenty-five persons.[25]

For the Tuscan countryside, around Pistoia, D. Herlihy, studying the 1427 cadastre, has clearly shown that in the case of the peasants the number of children per household grew regularly with the value of landed property, or at least, of the tax levied. The figures, which here too are very significant, are as follows:[26]

Tax level in livres	*No. of households*	*Children per household*
None	275	1.47
0–50	1,108	1.43
50–100	498	1.85
100–150	274	2.14
150–200	141	2.44
200–250	72	2.46
more than 250	136	3.21

For Florence, the table opposite, drawn up on the basis of figures given in the 1427 cadastre, clearly shows a higher birth rate and more numerous hearths among well-off families.[27]

So the average varies greatly, sometimes by 65 per cent, depending on levels of wealth. D. Herlihy explains the greater number of children in the better-off households on the one hand by the group's greater cohesion and the wish to keep their heritage undivided, and to keep the older children together; on the other hand, by the presence of adopted

	Hearths exempt from taxes	*Hearths liable to taxes*
No. of hearths	3,081	1,946
No. of households	3,286	2,302
No. of people	10,427	10,899
People per hearth	3.39	5.60
People per household	3.18	4.74
Children per 100 women	16.8	21.1
Children per household	0.49	0.77

children and young servants. But he also states that poverty and chronic or temporary economic difficulty appear to have been a decisive restraint on marriage and childbirth.

The clerks of the cadastre give some very interesting specific information, again for the countryside of Pistoia: *Nicholosa, sua figliola d'età 18. Nolla puo maritare perchè è povero* (that is, her father). In other cases girls waited for a good harvest in order to marry; even marriages which were promised, and concluded before a notary, were consummated only upon payment of the dowry. In fact, we may be well informed, thanks to studies of civil law, about women's rights in marriage, and their juridical circumstances; but we are still ignorant of the human, social or economic side of these problems.

In 1425, in Siena and Milan, St Bernardino of Siena spoke of girls who were too poor to take a husband; he gave the figure of 20,000 for Milan. He regretted that so many parents were not able to set up their daughters with large dowries, and *in domo steriles . . . retinent illas, et utinam virgines et pudicas*; others, with three or four daughters, gave dowries to the most beautiful, and abandoned the others, the ugly, the deformed or the blind, to a convent. And, by way of conclusion, he said: *Ex his omnibus manifeste apparet quod cessat generatio filiorum.*[28]

The letters of Alessandra Strozzi, so valuable for knowledge of the manners and attitudes of the Florentine aristocracy of the Quattrocento, provide many indications, sometimes naively, but very spontaneously, of the worries of parents trying to establish their daughters; in 1447 one of her letters related at length, omitting no step, no worry, all the negotiations and financial bargainings which foreshadowed the marriage of her daughter Caterina.[29]

In 1480, again in Florence, two brothers who were living together, Piero and Jacopo Guatterotti, affirmed before the officers charged with establishing the basis of the cadastre that they had sold their property: *n'avemmo i deneri per maritare undici fianciulle . . . vive e sane, e le madri che ne fanno ogn'anno*; for his part Piero laments: *Ho maritato tre figliole e m'anno consumato la sostanze e la persona.*[30] L.B. Alberti believed that all the clan, the whole *gente*, must help the young people to marry by lending or giving them money: *Contribuischi tutta la casa come a comperare l'accresciamento della famiglia....*[31] In Genoa, fathers ensured a measure of financial security, which enabled them to give their children decent dowries, through the use of *moltiplicati* entered on the registers of the *Casa di San Giorgio*; on the birth of a daughter, a father would buy a portion of the public debt, generally 100 *lire di luoghi*; these bonds were frozen, and grew through the accumulation of compound interest, up to the girl's marriage.[32] Often, too, the task of providing dowries for the poor daughters of the clan was left to the *albergo* itself, which would obtain to this end a certain number of *luoghi* or shares in the bank of San Georgio, and distribute the dowries.[33]

In Florence, in February 1425, was instituted the famous *Monte delle doti*, a kind of assurance society for daughters' dowries – and originally, moreover, for sons' dowries as well. A deposit of 100 gold florins yielded a dowry of 250 florins after seven years, and 500 florins after fifteen years; in the event of the girl's death the capital went under the same conditions to the younger sister or, failing this, reverted to the commune.[34] The establishment of such an institution shows clearly the difficulties experienced by burgesses in marrying their daughters, and indicates that poverty or even bare financial sufficiency checked demographic increase. In his will, made in Paris in 1413, Dino Rapondi, a rich Lucchese merchant, bequeathed to his brother Filippo, besides his normal portion of one third of his wealth, 800 Paris francs for Filippo's two daughters, "to help them to marry"; he also gave 160 Paris francs "to help to marry any poor virgins among his relatives".[35]

It appears then to have been a charitable deed to give dowries. It was often the act of a prince. Pope Sixtus IV provided an example when he gave dowries to maidens who processed in the streets of Rome, wearing their bejewelled wedding dresses and accompanied by mules laden with their *trousseaux*.[36] As late as 1581 Michel de Montaigne tells us that in Rome, on Low Sunday, he saw "the ceremony of the maidens' alms". There were 107 of them, processing first in the church of Minerva; the pope, "having blessed them, gives to each, with his own hand, a purse of white damask wherein there is a promise that once they have found a husband, they may each seek thirty-five crowns in alms, in addition to the dress which each has on that day, worth five crowns".[37]

Very often a man, too, delayed the age of marriage for lack of money. On this subject Giovanni Morelli, a Florentine merchant, strongly advises prudence and patience: *Ma abbi riguardo di non disavvantaggiare pero pell'affretarti; vo' dire che se tu pensassi per indugiarti insino in trenta anni avere migliorato tuo stato . . . per modo valerne molto di meglio, indugia . . . .*[38] This was especially true for the cities, where employment seems to have been more difficult, and where opportunities and possibilities for social rising appear more numerous.

Malthusian forces not only delayed marriage, but inside marriage itself affected procreation, causing voluntary restriction of births. First Dante, then St Bernardino of Siena, then in the Quattrocento St Antony of Florence, violently accused their contemporaries, the burgesses of the large towns of Tuscany, of practising contraception in order to limit the number of their children, and thus of surrendering their souls to the devil.[39] The *Chronicle of Pistoia*, written by Ser Luca Dominici, states that in Florence, in 1399, many women had few or no children; but a short time after the plague, which raged cruelly in that year, legacies from the dead swelled the fortunes of the survivors, so that very many women brought children into the world.[40] Such information from a contemporary certainly seems invaluable; it deserves to be supplemented by other information, equally direct, about voluntary birth control. It is absolutely certain that restrictions affected comfortable or rich households much less than others; in these, as we have seen, the birth rate was much higher.

There are other reasons, too, why the rich had more children. D. Herlihy puts forward as further reasons the age of marriage and the practice of remarriage. I refer to Herlihy again here because he is one of the few historians to have taken an interest in these problems. Certainly, among the rich, a man married late, often after the age of thirty; but he would marry a very young woman, often between fourteen and seventeen years old. Thus the woman had her children very early. Numerous confinements, accidents of all kinds and illness[41] meant that very often women died before their husbands, who, again, married younger women. The age difference increased. It was not uncommon for two remarriages to take place;[42] children were all the more numerous for this.

I believe that I may advance two more factors, still from an economic point of view. First, a higher standard of living and better hygiene, which might limit the then considerable infantile mortality, and might subsequently favour greater resistance to illness. The studies of R. Cazelles and M. Mollat show clearly that in the north of France, and more especially in Paris, the Black Death of 1348 struck down the poor much more than the rich; it was above all a "proletarian and infantile" epidemic.[43] Secondly, we must accept that for the rich, for the 'notables' of the towns and for other important burgesses, it was possible to pay wet-nurses, which enabled the womenfolk to have children very soon after each other. There is no study which gives an overall idea of the spread of this practice; but chronicles, letters and accounts generally attest the presence of wet-nurses in rich families. Giovanni Piccamiglio, a Genoese merchant of honest affluence, employed two wet-nurses for at least two years, to feed his two young sons; these women were not slaves (two eastern slaves also lived in the house); they both came from the little town of Ceva, on the borders of Piedmont.[44]

There is again no statistical study of the startling birth rate in rich families of Italian cities, but this is clearly brought out in the *libri de ricordanze*, which scrupulously note the births and baptisms of all the children. In the case of the Chorsini, for example, Matteo, son of Nicolo, married in May 1362, at the age of forty; his wife, whose age is not given, bore him twenty children in twenty-five years; eight years after the birth of the last child, she died; the father died in 1402, at the age of eighty; his last child was born when he was seventy-seven. Of these twenty children, only five reached adulthood; six died very young, at a few months, and five in their first year.[45] Here the rate of births definitely strained the limits of physiological possibility. In the second generation, Matteo's son Giovanni married in 1401, at the age of twenty-two; his first wife died in 1409, having borne him five children in eight years; his second wife, whom he married three years later, had seven children in sixteen years, and five of these survived to adulthood.[46] Finally, in the third generation, in 1434 at the age of seventeen, another Matteo married a Medici who was also seventeen; in twenty-two years she bore him seventeen children, of whom eleven reached adulthood.[47] If we compare the three generations, we can see that births became slightly more spaced out, but this appears very largely to be compensated for by the very noticeable drop in the mortality rate.

Each family was further enlarged by a great number of domestic servants–a large dependency living close to the masters whom they served.

This was obviously a very old tradition, and we know that from the earliest days of their lineages, nobles sheltered beneath their roofs, in their fortified houses of town or country, many men-at-arms and servants, valets and chambermaids. In Franche-Comté, at the end of the Middle Ages, the most successful nobles often mentioned five or six servants in their wills; in all likelihood the great, the most powerful families "possessed a veritable army of servants, who were counted by the dozen".[48] These servants formed a real dependency; originally from the rural estates belonging to the masters' lineage, they served them from father to son.

In Italy it was the *consorti* or the *masnadieri* who made up the *gente*, the *famiglia* or even the *brigata*; Alberti speaks of "the house where your *brigata* is lodged"[49] and to the question: "whom do you call your family?" he replies quite clearly: "my children, my wife and other familiars, domestics and slaves".[50]

Among these dependants, in southern countries, were obviously to be counted the slaves. On this matter, for southern cities, at the end of the Middle Ages, there is apparently a large bibliography;[51] but these works are nearly always on two aspects: the study of the slave trade (origins, transport and price), and that of the juridical situation of slaves (personalities, prohibitions, marriage, the rights of the slave-owner, sanctions). The human condition of the slave is still unknown, and few texts give precise information concerning his place in the society of the time. Judicial rules are unsuitable for such a study: was the law applied? Was it respected? Very often the law was merely repressive, and we cannot reach the realities of everyday life, true human relations within the family group. Only Iris Origo's short essay gives any suggestions and attempts any answers to these problems;[52] unfortunately, her conclusions are valid only for Tuscany, the sole province which she considers.

I shall not attempt to go over the whole record, which in the present state of research would probably be premature and would take a whole book; but it seems possible and useful to pick out some characteristics of medieval slavery.

At the end of the Middle Ages true slavery is found only within quite narrow geographical limits. In the western world it was unknown, save in the countries of the south. There were many slaves in the cities of Italy, sometimes even in the outlying countryside, and we find them too in all the eastern provinces of the Iberian Peninsula and, admittedly in a different way, in certain other regions of Castile and Portugal, more especially in Andalusia. In France, the merchants of Marseilles owned slaves,[53] but fewer than the Italians; it is possible that they sold them in

Avignon and Arles. There were thus no slaves in the whole of northern France, even in Lyons; nor, apparently, in Languedoc. The spread, and the bounds, of slavery deserve some explanation.

Slaves were principally bought and sold in the oriental slave trade. Italian merchants, especially Venetians and Genoese, frequented the markets of the Black Sea coasts. The Catalans, the inhabitants of the Isle of Rhodes or their allies, the knights of St John, those formidable buccaneers, made incursions into the coasts of Turkey and Greece at the time of the Catalan Grand Company in the first years of the fourteenth century. Prisoners of war supplied only a very small market, coming almost exclusively from the borders of the kingdom of Granada, at the time of the raids and excursions launched by the Christians;[54] for a very short time, the capture first of Malaga, then of Granada, gave a new impetus to these sales of prisoners of war. Finally, the discovery and use of sea routes along the western coast of Africa opened up a new black slave trade, undoubtedly greatly inferior to the very ancient and traditional trade which was, and is still, plied across the Sahara towards the Moslem countries of the Mediterranean coast. This new Iberian and Atlantic slave trade scarcely affected Italy, but affected rather the Catalan, Andalusian or Portuguese regions. In Italy, black slaves seem to have been very rare up to the very last years of the Quattrocento, as also do the Guanchos of the Canaries.[55] Black slaves were much more common in the Iberian world, but varied according to the city and the time. In Barcelona, Blacks represented about 21 per cent of the slaves imported in the fourteenth century, 17 per cent between 1400 and 1450, and 32 per cent in the second half of that century; so their importation was still limited. In Valencia, on the other hand, between 1489 and 1500, they represented 70 per cent of the slaves sold in the town (the Canarians made up 17 per cent of sales).[56] To my knowledge, no statistics have been established for Seville or Lisbon, but I am led to believe that black slavery was even more highly developed there. Thus the towns of Italy and Catalonia, throughout the Middle Ages, remained bound to the oriental slave trade and, especially in Italy, opened up only very little to the new black slave trade of the Atlantic. From the human and social point of view this situation was obviously very important.

These differences between Italy and the Iberian world, which are considerable, are again met in the study of the slave's position in western, Christian society. It was in the Moslem countries of the East, and most frequently in Egypt, that Venetian or Genoese merchants sold the men whom they had bought on the Black Sea or in Chios; these men did domestic tasks, rather than work in the fields, where their Moslem masters more normally used Blacks; they also served in the sultan's guard. These Tartars, Russians and Caucasians long formed the Mamluks' powerful bodyguard, which was constantly reinforced through the purchase of oriental captives. To the West, on the other hand, the Italian merchants sent women, who were generally very young.[57] They were sold in Italy and Spain as ordinary domestic slaves, assigned to the everyday tasks of the household. The towns and country areas of Italy knew no other form of slavery: neither agricultural work in *latifundia*, in the old manner, nor even work in mines or factories.

As a contrast, in Spain, slave-masters used, in addition to oriental women for domestic work, a work-force of servile men, mainly Moors but also Blacks. In Majorca and in the kingdom of Valencia some landowners owned several dozen such slaves.[58] Apparently the salt works of Ibiza were at that time manned by captives.[59] In cities, in Barcelona and Valencia, merchants and master craftsmen frequently employed such a work force in a number of mechanical trades.[60] In Catalonia itself, from a study of 254 slave sale contracts, between 1390 and 1462, C. Verlinden has established that the proportion of women to men was as low as three to two.[61]

Thus, in Italy, the slave was almost always a woman, and used in domestic service; she came from the East. We shall give special attention to these domestic slaves because we must define the way in which they were integrated into families. These young women lived in the house; mostly, they were lodged in one of the upper rooms, in the attic; they definitely shared the daily life of the masters, both adults and children. They were baptized, they bore Christian, Italian, baptismal names and they attended their own services and devotions. They were really domestic servants, and their living conditions were probably very little different from those of maid-servants in the cities of the north, at this time and much later, right up to the last century. It appears that domestic slavery, from an economic point of view, compensated for insufficient recruitment from the nearby countryside. In places where the same services could be given by girls from more or less nearby country areas, but more cheaply because this obviated the need to purchase a slave, slavery seems to have been, if not absent, then at least insignificant. This was so in Corsica, in Bonifacio, where a single inhabitant of the town, in his will, liberated nine men and seven women, referred to as *servi* and *ancillae*; here, girls from the hills undertook by contract to serve a master as *serva* or *ancilla* for six or ten years in return for their board and a very small amount of money.[62] In Venice, even, girls *de Sclavonie* undertook similarly *juxtam morem et consuetudinem civitatis venetiarum* to serve their masters for eight or ten years.[63]

Obviously slaves brought from the far-off Orient their own habits, customs, language and religious practices, which may doubtless have influenced certain aspects of urban Italian society. Moreover, the presence of large numbers of young women was bound to change the way of life and structures of the families themselves. In almost every case the master, in his will, released his slaves, who, once they were free, owed only a few years of service to the widow; they had a little money, they might marry. Above all, these 'domestic enemies' often bore the master's children. It would be going too far to speak of polygamy in this matter, in law or in fact, as in Islamic countries; but it is possible that cohabitation and the attitudes of the time led to a tacitly accepted kind of concubinage. There were apparently many births. At least in Genoa, all slaves – the young women, the admittedly few men, the children – bore the master's name. Thus the freedmen and bastards had the same names as the most powerful masters; birth and fate might clearly distinguish them, but these differences obviously became blurred and even sometimes forgotten in succeeding generations.

More generally, N. Tamassia has well shown that at law nearly everywhere in Italy bastards belonged fully to the *casato*: for example, in Tuscany and Umbria.[64] A regulation of Todi, in 1434, speaking of the members of a noble household, specifies: *omnes de domo C. tam legitimi quam bastardi et spurii.*[65]

In the towns of southern Spain and Portugal this concubinage, often with slaves of African origin, resulted in cross-breeding, a fact not often appreciated, probably because of the absence of any social or even statistical study of urban societies in these two countries, but which the historian cannot ignore. In Italy, where all the female slaves were Oriental and white,[66] the effects are of course much less visible, but it is easy to judge, to imagine, the anthropological consequences of slavery, especially in the family groups of the noble and the rich.[67]

Obviously, these consequences could only be judged if we had some idea of the quantity of slaves. This is a question which has scarcely been discussed, and the information which we do have seems quite contradictory, as in any survey of medieval demography. Even the best writers have until recently been completely unaware of the presence of slaves in urban Italian societies of the Middle Ages. Literary texts are extremely reticent on this point: it seems that the slave, in Italy, was not a social type which attracted much attention from, for example, either moralists or satirists. More significantly, family records, chronicles, very rarely mention them; is this a refusal, an unwillingness to face facts, or at least a tacit agreement by contemporaries to conceal the problems, both moral and social, posed by the presence in their towns and villages of slaves? Should we imagine a sort of collective conscience, of responsibility, a feeling of guilt in the face of certain religious or social rules? In Italy there is a similar lack of statutes and legislative texts, of regulations – the reverse of the situation in Aragon, where they abound.

Again in Italy, censuses such as those which were transferred to the registers of the 1427 Florentine cadastre, and which were, however, very accurate, show only a very small number of slaves in Pisa[68] and in the other towns of the Florentine seignory.[69] This could give the impression that slavery had practically disappeared from the towns of Tuscany by the end of the Middle Ages. However, other documents tell a very different tale. Using both the accounts of the 'Catalonian slave keeper' and a series of notarial acts, C. Verlinden arrives at the figure of 4,375 for the fourteenth century; he raises this to 10,000 to take account of the incomplete nature of the sources.[70] This estimate seems to me to be very reasonable, modest even: certainly, statistics based on fiscal sources are always well below the real situation.[71] Señora Cortes has noted that in the last years of the fifteenth century merchants still sold an average of 300 slaves per year in the single town of Valencia;[72] these figures, which seem to indicate a much higher total number of slaves than that mentioned above, are also based on tax records, but these are of a different kind.

D. Gioffré's work on Genoa, based primarily on the records of the *Gabella sclavorum*, a tax raised from slave-owners,[73] clearly demonstrates the existence of slavery in the city throughout the Quattrocento. These fiscal accounts reveal about 2,000 slaves for the years 1400–1450, probably representing 2 per cent of the population. The figure drops noticeably throughout the following period, especially from 1457, with the increasing difficulty of the oriental slave trade. I believe that these last estimates, the only ones available to us which are scientifically established, are nevertheless still below the real figures; as always, and more especially so in Genoa, we must take account of privileges and exemptions, and of frauds.[74] Other signs point in this direction. According to the customs record of 1458 dealing with imports to Genoa, the only one which has come down to us, ships were still bringing thirty or forty slaves each year to the West;[75] and this after the fall of Constantinople and the Turkish seizure of the straits. A notarial act, more precise and less unreliable than this tax record, attributes 185 slaves to a single Genoese ship on its return from the East, in 1455.[76] Moreover, slavery impressed itself deeply into Genoese society, at different levels of wealth; slave-owners were not only very rich nobles and merchants, but also men of lesser fortunes, master craftsmen, shopkeepers, modest burgesses. The social level of masters, the social spread of slavery is, I believe, as significant an indication as a statistical evaluation.[77]

Venice seems still to have been an important market at this time; from Constantinople the Venetians sent many slaves to the western Mediterranean: in 1436 a single ship took 164 to Majorca;[78] in 1488 3,000 slaves from "the orient and Ethiopia" were apparently sold in Venice itself.[79]

It does not seem to me that the disappearance of slavery by the end of the Middle Ages can be accepted as an indisputable fact, even in towns of the interior, in Tuscany and Lombardy: quite the reverse. In 1252, in Bologna, Baruffaldino de' Geremei left his wealth in his will to his two brothers, and all his *servi*, numbering 152, to his grand-daughter Bolnisia;[80] in 1257 his brothers, Francesco and Giuliano, owned 29 and 24 *servi* respectively.[81] In the same city, a little later, between 1290 and 1300, two nobles named Loderinghi and Castellano, brothers perhaps, certainly relatives, apparently owned between them 105 *servi.*[82] I. Origo, for a much later period, notes different pieces of evidence indicating the presence of slaves in numerous Tuscan towns and villages.[83] The influence of these women in the society of the time was not inconsiderable. Petrarch called them "domestic enemies", and a treatise of domestic economy, more sincere than others, or more directly affected by the attitudes of the mistress of the house, also says: "We have as many enemies as we have slaves".[84]

In conclusion, it seems reasonable to accept that, though assessment of the number of slaves is difficult, they were far more numerous than fiscal sources indicate. In their duties and their way of life these slaves, primarily oriental women, were integrated into the family, where their influence was marked in a number of different ways; they formed part of the group, part of the clan, whose patronym they bore. Finally, slavery may have deeply penetrated these medieval Italian societies, but slaves were naturally much more numerous among the rich and the noble, who often owned several in a single house. The statistics adduced by D. Gioffré show clearly that noble *alberghi* were much more highly taxed, because of their slaves, than were the families of the *popolani*: two Grimaldi di Oliva brothers declared six slaves of their own.[85]

Without doubt, cohabitation of brothers and even cousins, whether married or single, the presence of domestics and all kinds of servants, and of the slaves themselves, explain the preservation of very many cohesive groups; and this, long after the supposed dissolution (according to administrative regulations) of great families. In Italy at least, even at the end of the Middle Ages, examples of such family groups are forcefully presented to those who read documents of all kinds. In Pisa, a study of the cadastre of 1428[86] shows that multifamily households formed from the association of two or three brothers, although only 6 per cent of the total number of households, included more than 10 per cent of the total population. Often they were groups of more than ten people living together, and their fertility too seems to have been very high; in the quarter of Fuori Porta, twenty-seven women from such groups had seventy-six children; that is an average of 2.8, against only 2.0 for households living alone.[87] These groups were in all circles: in the quarter of Fuori Porta again, a family of "workers of the land" numbered twenty individuals; the men, who here were three brothers, bore no patronym and were referred to only by their Christian names.[88] Alessandra Macinghi, a lady of Florence, speaks in one of her letters of an estate, with a house, let to a rich farmer who had seventeen people with him.[89] In all, Tamassia asserts that families of twenty and even forty souls were not of the rarest; he cites a chronicle of Forli in which the author gives an example of this kind: *E queste vide come con li occhie miei dare grano a uno di Valentino, che era più di 40 bocche in la famiglia.*[90] He also cites a Venetian regulation which states clearly that *agli effetti del porto d'arme, si considera una famiglia come composta di 24 personne*;[91] this, in the fourteenth century.

These scattered and diverse elements of evidence obviously prove nothing statistically. They only show the permanence of family customs, which in their attitudes favoured the continuation of very large groups. These groups, as we can see, were not rare in modest or poor circles. But, we repeat, the rich and 'noble' group, with its much greater numbers of children and dependants and, above all, in a much more general way, easily surpassed the others.

The family groups of the nobles not only remained more willingly united, they also formed more powerful, more artificial and more complex federations than those of the lower ranks of society. Some of these social structures are of very ancient origin; they go back beyond the feudal ages proper. R. Boutruche has stressed the importance of ties and even of personal bondservice in western societies in the early Middle Ages. Alongside each leader, or rather, each 'master' clan, lived a greater or lesser crowd of "domestic warriors"; their nomenclature varied according to region and time: *gasindus* in Germania and Lombardy, *criado* in Spain, and elsewhere, *puer, home, gwas* or *vassus*; this last name, given at first to "slaves in the private custody of great personages", spread subsequently to all free men who had served a master.[92] In England, pre-feudal vocabulary clearly emphasized gifts of food, the fact that the master kept his loyal followers around him, sheltering and feeding them; texts reveal the strong solidarity and the common way of life which united the "kept", the "bread eaters", and those called, in fact, the "loaf givers", the *hlafords* (from which word is later derived the word *lord*); the *gesith*, from the German *gisind*, was also a companion in action, a man-at-arms often kept in the master's house.[93]

"It is definitely in the sphere of the domestic warriors that feudalism was born";[94] but not without difficulty. The strength of 'family' or 'clan' links was evidently an obstacle to the setting up of loyal followers on individual fiefs far from the master. This explains the resistance of pre-Norman England, where guilds and dependencies occupied such a position in social life, to the development of true feudalism and to the placement of vassals, who for a long time remained loyal household servants. In Scandinavian countries, where kings surrounded themselves with a personal guard of warriors and administrators, the *hirdh*, and where the great "ploughed, with their companions, the occidental and Nordic seas", feudalism, opposed by these ties of lineage or dependence, and by the vigour of village communities, asserted itself and its fiefs only very late, in the fourteenth century, under German influence, in a "slight and superficial manner".[95]

Later, this time in the whole of the West, although the fief triumphed, there was opposition between the sometimes contradictory duties of the lineage and those of vassalage based on land-holding. In any case the masters always kept close to themselves many loyal followers who were not established but united by an absolutely personal dependence, by ties of a quasi family nature. According to R. Boutruche, in the years 1180–1200 these men, the "knights of the castle", still formed a "fluid crowd of domestic vassals, mingled with the servants of the *familia* who had no freedom". A courtly poem, *Raoul de Cambrai*, shows one of these loyal men, Bernier, a dependant of his master, brought up in the house of Raoul's father; although he was of good birth and dubbed knight, he remained kept, receiving "horses, clothes, harness" and all kinds of gifts; he served the head of the clan at table.[96]

Often those 'kept' in the castle were young men, younger sons, committed to their masters in order to preserve the inheritance of the eldest and to avoid the erosion of their patrimony; they led more or less cohesive, corporate lives there, and wrought their own special culture.[97]

These noble clans persisted for centuries. Right at the end of the Middle Ages they still deeply affected social structures in the countryside and in the towns of the West.

It seems that very often these noble lineages accepted amongst themselves, often on an equal footing, the masters' bastards, whether they were born of servants, peasants or noblewomen. From 1350 to 1500 the wills of the small nobles of Franche-Comté show clearly that they provided richly for their illegitimate sons (but not, apparently, daughters). On the death of their fathers, these bastards were by no means rejected by the families; quite the reverse, their half-brothers, uncles or cousins assumed responsibility for them. Texts refer to them, very significantly, as 'given', and above all as *alumpni* or as 'kept'. So they, like the other relatives, lived in the master's house.[98] This increased the size of the lineage, probably by an appreciable amount.

In Italy all these sons, whether legitimate or not, all these 'kept' young men, were the group's very strength; Dino Compagni speaks with admiration, or envy, of one of his fellow citizens, Menetto Scali, *potente d'amici e di seguito.*[99] When Florence conquered Arezzo the commune signed a pact with the counts Tarlati di Pietramala and their *consorti*, granting them citizenship of Florence, undertaking to defend their castles and authorizing them to have ninety men-at-arms for all the *consorti.*[100] Sometimes such dependencies included numbers of poor relatives, more especially young men who were in no position to raise enough money to establish themselves; thus they set up no homes, but continued to live in the master's house or on his land, always at his disposal. In his own *gente*, L.B. Alberti states that he could count *pochi di fa non meno che venti e due giovani Alberti vivere soli senza compagna, non avere moglie, niuno manco che sedici, niuno più che anni trenta e sei.*[101] This group of young bachelors living with the leaders of the clan remained at their service through thick and thin; this, in the Quattrocento, and inside a mercantile town.

Other, more numerous dependencies, extending to persons from other social ranks, developed more artificially through the multiplication of ties of personal dependence. In Orvieto nobles surrounded themselves with *fideles* and *familiares*; in 1348 a repressive edict of the commune extended all the penalties suffered by refractory or rebellious nobles to their dependencies at large; a *familiaris* was one who had lived close to a noble for one year before a crime, or continued to live with him. A noble leader must provide regular lists of names of all members of his *familia*; he must clothe them at his own expense with one or two pieces of cloth, of a single colour. Moreover, these nobles had as much success as before in recruiting armed mercenaries from among the peasants of the mountains.[102]

In Florence, during the 1370s, at the time of the serious civil disturbances and of the famous Ciompi revolution, the heads of the great noble families, such as Benedetto degli Alberti, Tommaso degli Strozzi, Giorgio degli Scali or Giovani degli Dini, had at their service vast dependencies of *seguiti*, artisans, shopkeepers, and even workmen.[103] More or less close personal ties kept around each of these heads a clique of associates and dependants, consisting of men of different trades and very varied social positions, especially wool journeymen and artisans. The chronicler Ser Nofri di Ser Pietro is correct in stating that the patrician leaders retained very close relations with groups of 'bandits' from extremely modest social classes.[104] The new men, later arrivals in the city, although less involved in competition or political conflict, quickly tried to create such links, more artificially, in order to compensate for a certain isolation, for the absence of such solid natural family structures, and thus in order to gain the reassurance of security. The father of this chronicler, Ser Pietro di Ser Grifo, commanded his own band of dependants and a whole network of alliances woven around his native canton, Figline, on the Arno: *Avea in quello paese grande seguito; perrochè quando era in Firenze ed in istato, era egli e' il padre quasi un signorello di tutta quella provincia.*[105] In 1381, Francesco del Bene, an official in the Valdinievole, received many letters from artisans requesting favours and benefices for their friends.[106]

This cohesion of the family clan stands out much better in some regions and cities of Italy than in others. M. Berengo notes that in the sixteenth century, the greatest families of the Venetian aristocracy had long been divided into several branches, whose only common factor was their name; yet in Lucca the greatest families never split up; essentially, this was a function of the permanence of solid ties between relatives and dependants: *Nella vita pubblica i Cenami, i Poggi, gli Arnolfini, i Burlamacchi, i Trenta si presentano come blocchi compatti, non incrinati ma resi più forti dalla moltitudine dei loro uomini e dal sviluppo interno delle parentele.*[107]

These dependencies of poor or indifferent allies also gave the noble lineages of northern countries, in town or country, considerable political and social weight. Joinville criticizes the bad administration of Paris at a time when the city's provostship was in the pay of the great merchant families; and, he says, "It invariably happened that those who bought this office condoned all offences committed by their children or their nephews, so that these young delinquents became accustomed to relying on those who occupied the provostship". The king, still in the words of the now eulogistic Joinville, acted so that "no wrong-doer, thief or murderer dared to remain in Paris, for all who did were soon hanged or put out of the way; neither parentage, nor noble descent, nor gold and silver availed to save them".[108]

G. Espinas, with reference to Douai and other towns of Walloon Flanders in the thirteenth century, has studied a considerable quantity of documents which give a clear indication of the importance of the 'family' group, in their constant use of the words *linagie*, *parents* and *amis*; the masters of the clan, the *mestres*, surrounded themselves with a *mesnie*, household servants but also dependants; moreover, the word *amis* refers in addition to those who contended or acted together in lawsuits.[109] In Douai, still in the thirteenth and fourteenth centuries, on the occasion of negotiations held to prepare and seal truces, the adversaries would arrive accompanied by the greatest possible number of their friends, their *amis.*[110]

However, these words are not always synonymous, and sometimes make it possible to ascertain the dependants' own relationships. The word *amis*, when used by the magistrates of Metz from the thirteenth century, described the relatives of a family clan, of a *paraige*; and J. Schneider believes that the use, a little later, of the words *aidants* or *coadjutores* indicates that the relationship in these cases went beyond the strict family, even multifamily, compass;[111] these were dependants.

In Bruges the words which refer to the relatives as a whole emphasize firstly the notion of common ancestry, the ties of blood, (*aeldinghers, hoyres, bloetvrinden*), but immediately afterwards, affective ties, neighbourhood links, dependencies (*naercommers, magen, maegschap, vrienden*).[112] In Strasbourg, the two principle lineages of the 'patriciate' gathered to themselves vast dependencies of relatives and friends; these extended right down to the common people, thanks not only to matrimonial alliances and neighbourhood links, but also to the fact that the masters of the lineage were often money-lenders.[113] In the Netherlands the memory of links uniting the dependant to the leader of the group was demonstrated until a late date by visible signs, marks of dependence: in 1307 the mayor of the village community of Herenthals near Antwerp complained that he had not, as in the past, received the vestimenta from his lord, the chapter of St Waudru.[114]

At this period and for a very long time afterwards, English landlords were abandoning the direct farming of their own estates; they also lost many tenant-farmers so that they were no longer, as before, masters of great manors and veritable heads of village communities. However, the farmers still dressed in the lord's colours, which proves their membership of the seignorial household. This dress, this *livery*, was in fact worn throughout the West by the members of a particular group, and especially by the relatives and dependants of a noble clan. This usage was particularly strong and tenacious in England, where texts of an economic and even specifically of a book-keeping nature show the existence of more or less widespread and, admittedly, more or less artificial dependencies, in the pay of great leaders. The English lords, as war-lords, gathered about themselves, in their houses, at all events under their command and at their disposal, troops of armed relatives and dependants, who wore their uniform, or at least their colours (their livery and badges). Moreover, these armed groups, formed of paid companies but tied also by personal loyalty and the feeling of really belonging to a clan, were called *liveries*. In 1390 the king strictly ordered:

> that no prelate or any other man of Holy Church, or any bachelor, or esquire, or any other of less estate, shall give any kind of such livery called livery of company: and that no duke, earl, baron or banneret shall give such livery of company unless he is retained with him for the term of his life in peace and war by indenture,[115] without fraud or malice, or unless he is a servant and family retainer dwelling in his household: and no such noble shall give such a livery to any 'vallet' called a yeoman archer nor to any other person of lower estate than esquire unless he is a family servant living in the household.[116]

In fact these armed companies of men wearing the master's colours disturbed public order and threatened the peace of the realm: therefore the king intervened repeatedly to forbid or restrict these practices. We should by no means fail to note, however, that although the king could not tolerate the establishment of veritable private armies, he recognized the existence of dependencies (*familiae*) of servants of modest status, living in their master's house; and he accepted that through alliances the master brought into his livery troops of friends who were loyal throughout their lives.

Other, newer and completely artificial social groups, such as the brotherhoods and, especially in England, craft guilds or companies, gradually introduced the wearing of livery, at least for their richer members. It is possible that they wished to show by this, in a single external sign, their own solidarity, as at least equal to that of the noble clans. This sign, which was obviously borrowed from the dependencies of the lords, became essential: eventually the word 'livery', here as in the case of the noble companies, came to signify the group itself. This happened in the case of the principal trade associations of London, such as that of the grocers, whose 'livery', in 1470, consisted of only seventy-five persons who wore the colours; these were the aristocrats of the trade, above the common members of the company.[117] Whereas in France the words used emphasize social solidarity (*frairies*, *fraternités*), the idea of mutual help (*hanses*) and charity (*charités*) or simply the specialized nature of a profession (*métiers*), the English terms emphasize equally precisely collective solidarity and the parallel with the noble clan. This clearly shows the decisive impact of noble family clans on the whole of the society of the time.

All these dependencies, in every country, increased the political and military power of family clans. They constituted a threat to peace, for they inflated private conflicts, giving them another dimension; and their social importance rapidly transformed a simple family vendetta into a civil war which mobilized the whole city.[118] Thus the state attempted by all possible means to suppress at least the excessively obvious signs of these dependencies, to make their existence and power less tangible, less obvious to the man in the street. Moreover, by restricting meetings and assemblies – opportunities for men to become aware of group solidarity – the state also attacked the prestige of the great families. Such, I believe, is the significance of certain provisions to be found in many sumptuary laws decreed by princes, and apparently more often by the communes of Italy. Limits set on family pomp in no way reflect any moral ethic, by which all magnificence would be banned; these restrictions aimed not only to reduce extravagance, to prevent excessive spending and enormous investment of unproductive money; they also sought to weaken nobles' clans by abolishing occasions on which their dependencies might be reaffirmed. In 1322, in Florence, a provision of this kind limited to ten the number of women permitted to accompany a fiancée to her husband.[119] Other regulations were more precisely concerned with marriages themselves, and others with funerals.

The prohibitions against appearing in great numbers show the care taken by the state to reduce a group's solidarity, and if possible to disperse dependants. Significantly, no clause of this kind appears in the sumptuary laws of Genoa, which are nevertheless numerous and strict: here family clans remained all-powerful and the commune could undertake no action of this type against them.

Similarly, the sumptuary regulations of French towns attacked not only sartorial luxury and every kind of excessive expenditure, but also a certain 'luxury of assembly'. They particularly attacked the great family ceremonies and, by all kinds of restrictions which seem quite petty, attempted to limit the scope and social repercussions of these solemn or unusual meetings, to reduce them to simple celebrations, restricted to close relatives, without any wider significance in the city. These family celebrations were in fact in themselves spectacles which provided powerful evidence of social prestige, and in many cases strengthened the links between friends, dependants, and the masters of the group. Marriages were celebrated in the open air, on the square before the church, and the ceremony was the occasion of a great gathering of people: in Ypres, in 1294, they were not permitted to attend the signing of a marriage contract.

These ordinances were aimed primarily at processions and banquets. Echevins and consuls wished to limit the number of these, and they insisted that only one meal might be given on the occasion of a marriage; in 1436 the magistrates of Limoges condemned parents who "have become accustomed to giving a dinner the next day, at which are served pastries and roasts and all they please; which dinner, little by little, has gained such importance that at present as many attend as on the day of the marriage". The same ordinances also state that "those men that are bidden to attend baptisms may neither eat nor drink at the house of the father of the infant, but some constrain the father of the infant to invite them to his mansion or else to give them a drink in another place". Then again, god-parents might accompany their god-children to church for the ceremony in the company of only a small number of persons, generally between eight and twelve; similar restrictions applied to the fiancé who visited the young lady in her parents' home, and to those female relatives who visited a woman in childbirth. The wish to restrict assemblies and processions, to reduce attendance to a few people, is constantly reaffirmed. Municipal edicts repeatedly refer to "a small number" of "close relatives and friends"; in Limoges this amounted nevertheless to twenty-four people, excluding the priest and the notary; but the frequent occurrence of prohibitions is a certain indication of much larger processions.

Finally echevins and consuls wished also, more precisely, to break the ties of dependence which might unite relatives, *amis* and clients with the masters of the family. They condemned gifts of all kinds: it was forbidden to give any present, "except to those of the same house"; it was even forbidden for any guest at a wedding feast, "be he man, woman, servant, jester" to eat at the marriage unless he pay his share "as the bread is put upon the table" (Ypres, 1294).[120]

In order to condemn this luxury of assembly the authorities invoked varying pretexts: excessive expenditure and immodesty, the resulting congestion in the city, the delay caused to church services, the excess of revellers going from one celebration to the next, eating and drinking. But one of the principle reasons for such rigour certainly seems to have been the wish to weaken the prestige and power of family groups. It is striking to observe that out of six royal ordinances studied, three condemn sartorial luxury, three attack various other manifestations of luxury, but not one attacks the luxury of assembly itself; in complete contrast, out of ten municipal regulations, seven treat of the luxury of assembly, devoting a total of thirty-one articles to it. Municipal magistrates were thus much keener than kings to combat family clans which threatened their authority, although they had become obedient to the prince. The seven regulations referred to, between 1264 and 1493, were decreed in Ypres and in five towns of the French Midi (Auterive and Montauban in 1291; Cahors, Castelnaudary, Carpentras, Limoges and Montauban in 1493); precisely where the clans remained more cohesive and more powerful.

Formation and disintegration of family groups

It is very difficult to make any detailed study of the formation of complex family clans. Normally they resulted from the closeness of neighbours, from accidental alliances, through a slow process of maturation; these very varied social groups escape all juridical or institutional definition. Rather, they were organized according to tacit agreements which are difficult to find or to reconstruct; their links, then, are not easily traced.

Only later did their leaders think to draw up a contract for signature. The elaboration of more or less detailed 'statutes' marks a second phase of the history of family clans, as probably of all artificial social groups – a less spontaneous, more institutional phase.

Be this as it may, these statutes, if they were drawn up, are nearly totally lost to us, for the majority have been destroyed. For example, it is impossible to study Tuscan family clans from statutes, although this may easily be done in the case of rural or urban communes in almost every region of Italy. Hence the importance of the astonishing statute of the *Casa dei Corbolani*, published by S. Bongi.[121] On 14 December 1287 nineteen heads of families met in the monastery of San Salvatore in Mostolio; they already belonged to three great and complex families of Lucca, bearing three different names: Corbolani, Del Veglio and Cerlotti; their property was in three areas, in the centre of the town. Here, then, was a numerous and imposing suprafamily clan, already highly developed, formed by the amalgamation of two consanguineous groups with another branch, probably stronger than they were; this last gave its name to the new *consorzio*. Ties of proximity most certainly played a preponderant role. The idea of the family remains clearly asserted in the very terms of the agreement: *Statuta, ordinamenta et capitula constitutionis domus filiorum Corbolani et consortum* ; but the initial group grew and embraced men of other families.

Given the lack of such documents as would allow us to date, not so much the origins as the expansion of family clans, and better to define their characteristics, we may only observe their existence and workings, be they open or covert, in many areas. Their real origins and the different phases of their increase in numbers are lost to us.

In Italy, the only obvious exception, at least regarding knowledge of the clan's growth, appears to me to be the city of Genoa.[122] Here the family clan, the *albergo*, an institution and a political framework which all the city's courts recognized, shows its influence quite openly in all texts, whatever their nature may be. To these might be added the permanence of notarial deeds, the use of which seems to have been more necessary and more widespread here, and seems to have lasted for much longer, than in many other towns.

In fact in Genoa, the formation and even more the consolidation and expansion of the *albergo* are the subjects of notarial deeds, drawn up in good and due form. This initial document naturally had to give a precise list of the heads of families coming into the alliance, to give the name and arms of the new clan, and to establish the rules of their common life. Some alliances were spontaneous, governed for a long time by tacit agreement; they came into the open only when they were already well developed; this was done through a highly formal treaty, concluded before a notary. When, in 1453, the Franchi family came together to admit a new member, they very clearly referred to the rules drawn up by the deed of foundation of their *albergo*, written by a notary sixty years previously, in 1393.[123] But in truth, none of these contracts forming *alberghi* seems to have survived. We have only much later documents called, in the jargon of the Genoese notaries, *aggregations*, which simply mark the stages of the expansion and strengthening of the *albergo*. These are very numerous and can be found by the dozen, at least for the years 1450–1480; they give valuable information on the size of the group and on its inner structure and government.

New members were admitted either by unanimous agreement or as the result of a vote held, as tradition demanded, by the use of white and black balls. Heads of families who were already party to the alliance heard the request of the person who wished to be admitted to the clan. This man, who would be recognized for his 'nobility', his ancestry or his merit, acted not as a single individual but as the head of a family, just as did his audience, "in his own name and in the name of all his family, of all his heirs and successors", or "in the name of his sons, of his grandsons, of his great-grandsons and of all his descendants, in perpetuity, to the end of time". The contract was collectively binding on the family, and indefectible.[124]

More spectacular are those *aggregations* which linked two already complex, well developed family groups, bringing them together artificially in a new clan; these mark another stage in the concentration of the Genoese 'nobility' into more and more powerful groups. Of all alliances, that between the Grimaldi and the Ceba families offers a perfect, and a highly significant example.[125] On 25 October 1448, sixty-four heads of Grimaldi families appointed two procurators, Luciano and Dorina, to receive the Ceba representative. Several of these Grimaldi declared that they acted equally in the name of their brothers and of their sons. The initial number, and these details, give a concrete idea of the clan's astonishing size. The Ceba family sent a single delegate, Nicolà Ceba, who declared that he committed himself on behalf of six other heads of families bearing the same name. This occurrence seems to have been of such great importance that the two parties had not called upon an ordinary notary, but upon Giacomo di Bracelli, chancellor of the commune of Genoa. This act of incorporation was not the first in the history of the clan – far from it; in 1448 the clan already appears to have been very complex: some of the Grimaldi had their seignories precisely detailed, some had none; two brothers who are cited right at the end of the document still styled themselves *Grimaldi olim de Castro*; it seems that they had been quite recently incorporated into the clan.

These amalgamations, of which there were many, constantly changed the list of *alberghi*, and with it the relationship of forces within the city. The very powerful clans all developed from an alliance of several families. Some, which are the easiest to isolate, evolved around an already strong noble line; this family would be the masters of castles and seignories in the mountains or on the Rivieras, and often of land in the town itself or in its immediate vicinity. This is true of the very great names of the Quattrocento: Doria, Spinola, Grimaldi, Lomellini. In previous centuries their leaders admitted either other, less rich and less influential nobles, or ruined nobles of decaying families who, having dwindled in numbers, were threatened with erosion or complete disappearance. They also received non-nobles, *popolani*, newly rich, *parvenu* merchants, who became valuable allies. Then, of course, the clan's name was borne by all; but for some, the fact that they owned a seignory and for others, some indication of their original, common name, might for a time point to the difference between them.

The most remarkable amalgamations called thoroughly into question the whole political balance in Genoa; here the seignorial clan, which was thus expanded and above all enriched, benefited; it had a greater influence on the destiny of the city and, through its new members, could intervene more directly in city affairs. Therefore this clan's opponents, or even the normally unworried commune, sometimes attempted to forbid such mergers. On 3 December 1448, the Elders observed that Federigo, Nicolà "and others of the Ceba family" had recently joined the Grimaldi;[126] at that time the Council of Elders included no Grimaldi, but one Fieschi and one Spinola; the magistrates, although their hostility is evident, had nevertheless to recognize that they found no trace of any law forbidding such a merger.

Throughout the fourteenth and fifteenth centuries other groups arose from completely artificial alliances of families of more or less ancient nobility, but whose power was about equal. In that case none could impose its name, and the new clan chose its own name and arms. The abandonment of old ancestral names clearly points to the interest taken in these completely artificial associations. New names and devices, totemic emblems almost, took on a symbolic aspect: *Gentile*, probably in a reminiscence of the past, and especially *Mari*, *Marinis* and *Usodimare*, to indicate the source of their wealth and the great importance of the sea. Other names seem inexplicable. Some of these quite artificial groups had fine fortunes: for example, the vast Cattaneo clan, which united the very ancient, but often decimated and enfeebled families of the old city, on the hill of Sarzano; the Gentile clan which around 1465 already numbered about fifty heads of families, and which shortly afterwards incorporated the Pallavicini, an illustrious line of Genoese nobles, established primarily in the East but defeated and uprooted by the Turkish conquest of Pera and Phocaea; this clan applied itself to the search, in Genoa, for solid new bases; and the Scipioni, the Pinelli and above all the Centurioni, formed from rich merchant families of rather obscure origin, who quickly lost their original names.[127] A last example of the characteristic expansion of a great, noble, suprafamily clan, is that of the Campioni, based in a quarter of the old city not far from San Lorenzo. They were already cited in 1447, but were not very numerous at that time; but in 1479 thirty-two heads of families among them paid the *avaria*; in the intervening period they had incorporated several noble names, not all negligible: Savignoni, Cibo, Maraboti, Guizulfo and Piccamiglio.[128]

Apparently this reorganization, in the second half of the Trecento, quite soon came to affect also the *popolani*, who similarly, from completely separate entities, and in the presence of notaries, developed into powerful family clans. We may see the full economic and human significance of these initiatives if we remember that the *alberghi* of the *popolani*, in distinction to those of the nobles, could not be frameworks for political life; their delegates to the city councils were always elected by districts or by trade associations, not by family grouping.

In Genoa these *alberghi* of the 'people' modelled themselves quite precisely on the noble *alberghi*: they had that group's imposing size, the same administration and inner structures. They were not numerous, but they all seem to have been very powerful.

The principal participants of the *Maona* of Chios, a sort of colonial company which in 1346 had mounted an expedition from Genoa to reconquer that island, and which from then on administered its main revenues, abandoned their different names in 1362 and took the name Giustiniani; this new name stemmed from the Venetian palace in which the meetings of the *Maona* were regularly held. Admittedly, a century later the Giustiniani still added their previous names, which they had borne before their amalgamation into a solid *albergo* (*Giustiniani olim de Banca, olim Longo, olim de Castro*, etc.); but they formed a large (fifty-four heads of families on a fiscal register of 1465)[129] and rich clan; in all, it was the richest of all Genoese clans. The *albergo popolare* of the Franchi, founded in 1393, grouped at that time thirty heads of families with nine different names; others joined them a little later; in 1453 they met in the great hall of one of their houses, situated on their own square; the twenty-four present belonged to fourteen different primary families.[130] The Promontorio, Sauli, Soprani and Fattinanti families, all *popolani*, were also chosen by good fortune.

Thus, in Genoa, the social structure of powerful family clans is not encountered exclusively among the nobles. It therefore seems evident that the formation of these confederations of suprafamily clans cannot be interpreted as a defence reaction of the nobles against the *popolani*. In complete contrast, it was the most powerful of the people who imitated the nobles' ways of life and their structures; these structures were very ancient, the legacy of feudal times. But this in no way implies the forced purchase of land or seignories, but merely the fusion of several primary families and of different names into very powerful groups where all bore the same name. In Pisa too, E. Cristiani notes that *consorterie*, which were very strong among the magnates, were also very often to be found among the 'people'; the families of the *popolo medio* and even of the *popolo minuto* owned, not single houses or pieces of land, but many different houses and nearby lands all at the same time, linked *in forma consortile*.[131]

There is no doubt about the existence of vast suprafamily groups in numerous towns of the western world. Under a common name these clans brought together several families who originally did not bear the same patronym, and could not therefore claim a common ancestor; they probably belonged to different circles. The developments which I have described in the case of Genoa could certainly be observed in many other cities, at least in Italy and the Empire. We may lack private documents with which to define the clan's nature and different ways of integration, but records of a political character enable us to pinpoint the main stages of formation and consolidation of great suprafamily groups: thus for example in Metz, where Jean Schneider noted three *paraiges* established by 1224 (Porte Moselle, Outre Seille and Port Sailly), then the appearance of other 'patrician' clans (Saint Martin and Jurue) just before 1250.[132] There were never more than these five clans of 'great burgesses', which were therefore veritable confederations of families, each group being divided into a certain number of branches (four in the case of the Jurue). Towards 1200 this situation was institutionalized by the division of each of these *paraiges* into four branches.[133] A charter drawn up at the request of Henry of Port Sailly "bears the names of several witnesses who seem to form the family grouping whose leaders the Port Sailly were at that time";[134] the sizes of clans are also confirmed by the fact that in each *paraige* the leading positions were held by twenty or thirty persons. Subsequently, about 1270–1320 new families which were at first strangers to the 'patriciate' became integrated into such and such a *paraige*,[135] but this renewal or expansion of the existing *paraiges* of Metz seems very limited. Hence the later formation of a sixth *paraige*, apparently around 1350–1367, which was known as the *paraige du commun*, and brought together all the rich men who were not yet members of a *paraige*. These men had become echevins or magistrates, but were outside the clans' solidarity; they quite naturally forged closer and closer family ties between themselves.[136] Thus, the official establishment of this *paraige*, born of the wish for mutual aid and solidarity, merely serves to confirm once more its slow maturation.

In all, although it is more difficult to grasp in detail, the social and political structure of the town of Metz does not seem substantially different from that of Genoa; its development appears parallel; a few 'patrician' or 'noble' clans, whose fortune was solidly based on the land, and who monopolized most of the public offices, moved in and settled; these clans strengthened themselves by integrating new families; and finally there came onto the political scene a more artificial clan, formed from the rich men of the 'people', of the *popolani*.

The formation of this, the sixth *paraige*, of the 'people' meant that all offices were from that time totally monopolized by the members of the six *paraiges*. This confirmation and recognition of the clans' power corresponds exactly to the reforms which, much later, in 1528, Andreà Doria carried out in Genoa.[137] The twenty-eight Genoese *alberghi* and the six *paraiges* of Metz were the results of the same social and political development.

The parallel between the two towns, geographically so apart, and so different in population and economic activity, seems to me to be striking. There is no doubt that a detailed study of many other urban areas would enable us usefully to extend these comparisons, and better to define a phenomenon which is not limited to Italy.

There is no doubt that, whether officially or in a less conventional way, family clans dominated cities' whole lives. Often, they were part of the essential framework of political action: whence important reorganizations, the progress of new alliances or their failure, divisions and internal conflicts. The outline of these alliances was constantly changing and generally speaking a group was attracted by two opposing forces. On the one hand it seems certain that the fact of belonging to a powerful group was a necessary condition of success, and even of survival, for these extended families. This would explain a very clear natural tendency, especially at quite a late period, for them to concentrate in clans whose power became greater and greater. But on the other hand the very wish to unite in a few more influential groups conflicted with the clan's in-built tendency to disintegrate, with its internal conflicts and with the activities of the commune. When the 'people' were kept apart from the 'noble' clans they were resolutely hostile to these federations of great families. The clans' real size and their development therefore depended, at least in Italy, on the balance of forces between the nobles and the commune.

In Genoa, certainly, the largest *alberghi*, the most populous and powerful, finally divided into two clans, which were not rivals, for they were based in two separate areas of the city; the two new branches also rejoiced in different *colours*, the one black, the other white. This allowed them to present their members more often before the councils and magistratures governing the city. Some alliances, on the other hand, could not stand the test of time. The popular Scipioni *albergo* was well established by the 1420s, although apparently of recent origins; between 1447 and 1458 it underwent a sudden upheaval; each branch revived its individual name and even its own way of life; they all played a distinct part in the city economy: Ardimenti, Conforti, Ceba, Dentuto, Embroni, Luciani, Pinelli; but only these last, the Pinelli, became leaders of a new *albergo*, attracting the heads of other families to their ambit.[138]

These, however, are exceptions or accidents in Genoa. The total number of clans declined at the end of the Middle Ages, and through the process of alliances each surviving group acquired greater strength. Here, the list of *alberghi* entered on tax registers provides decisive information. The *Mutuum* of 1379 shows sixty-four *alberghi.*[139] The *Gabella possessionum* of 1445 gives the names of fifty-nine noble *alberghi,* to which must be added those of two or three exempt families.[140] The number of noble households therefore remained more or less stable for these eighty years. The disappearance of weaker families or the often spectacular reinforcement of the more powerful *alberghi* were not evident until a little later. The least populous families gradually faded away, and the tax registers made only passing reference to them. In the 1460s some clans had only two or three members listed on tax records; this was the case of the Venti, the Malocelli, even the Zaccaria and the Embriaci. These old aristocratic families of noble Genoese merchants, who had been so enterprising at the time of the crusades or towards 1300, left the political limelight and abandoned public affairs; this resulted from isolation, and from the absence of large, cohesive social groups which might have bolstered up their fortunes. Many others emigrated and became established in the areas colonized by Genoa: Sicily, the Orient, southern Spain. For all these reasons, in 1465, the records of the *focagium*, a direct tax levied on personal chattels, showed only thirty-two *alberghi.*[141] Such concentration increased in the following years, and this quite officially: in the famous institutional reform of 1528, Andreà Doria reduced the number of *alberghi* to twenty-eight; they nearly all retained the names which were known in the 1460s, and now they included all the families of the aristocracy: *noblii* and *popolani.*

The amalgamation of several clans into larger federations is probably not an exclusively Genoese phenomenon. There are no studies however, which enable us to make comparisons, and we must be content with external signs or simple indications. P. Dollinger notes a distinct increase in the number of lineages, from about 1200 to 1400, in the case of the German Hanse towns; in Lübeck, twenty-four lineages were counted in 1150, forty-six in 1230 and 130 in 1408.[142] These figures may be explained by the city's growing wealth and population. Later, the number of family groups drops noticeably throughout the fifteenth century, and P. Dollinger attributes this to the weakening of the 'patriciate'; but it is possible that here too a general weakening, and the threats which affected the patriciate, caused families to regroup.

In the towns of central Italy, the general tendency, at this time, was clearly towards a more or less marked upheaval of clans. In Tuscany some *consorterie* became so powerful that they finally divided into minor groups, into two or three *ladi*: this for the Frescobaldi and the

Donati in Florence, from the 1300s, for the Cancellieri of Pistoia, *divisi in due rami par la discendenza da due donne diverse.*[143] In Orvieto in 1313 the large Guelph clan of the Monaldeschi, having conquered the Ghibelline Filippeschi clan, soon divided into four branches which more or less vied with one another.[144]

Writing in 1472, Benedetto Dei proudly affirmed that Florence had more than 250 noble households, against the fifty-nine (a figure which seems slightly excessive) of Genoa.[145] But this optimistic opinion took no account of the fact that in Florence the *consorteria* probably had not the same importance as the Genoese *albergo*; families divided more, or did not regroup into such powerful confederations. They suffered from the ever hostile actions of the commune, which used every possible means to break up excessively large groups. Measures against the rich and influential probably weakened only very few families but in the long run they perhaps caused desertions and upheavals within the *consorterie.* Throughout the fourteenth century, especially between 1380 and 1390, many families among the magnates wished to assume the status of *popolani*; they changed their names and, in fulfilment of a very significant and apparently necessary condition, abandoned the constitution of their *consorterie.* Thus, for example, the Ricasoli, who became the Bindacci, and the Della Toro (whose new name was Bilisardi), the Donati (Bellincioni) and the Bondelmonti (Montebuoni).[146] At the same time other family clans suffered from the attacks of the 'popular' commune and also from their expansion, from the excessive difficulty which they experienced in keeping a considerable number of primary families and individuals cohesive under the same name and a common authority. This was the case with the Tornaquinci, the only Florentine family clan whose fortunes we are able to follow, thanks to a recent and detailed study.[147] From 1000 the Tornaquinci were confirmed as one of the great households of Florence; they possessed at once, as did all the other influential *consorterie,* properties in the country, houses, shops and two towers in the city, near the Porta di San Pancrazio. This family devoted itself to commerce: in 1290 one Tornaquinchius de Tornaquinchis resided in Anjou, then in Aix-en-Provence, buying French wool and cloth.[148] But a century later the unity of this household of *grandi* was broken by the departure of several heads of lineages in succession; one, Niccolo di Ghino, joined the ranks of the *popolo* in 1364, and by his own choosing, in an act symbolic of their new situation, took for his family and heirs the name Popoleschi; others formed new groups, giving them their own names:

Giachinotti (from two brothers, sons of Giachinotto) and Marabottini (in 1386, from Marabottino, son of Marabottino). Simone di Tieri, the head of another group, being left all alone, assumed a new name, which was however very close to the original name: Tornabuoni. Here the increase in the number of clans certainly indicates a weakening of their cohesion and power.

Later, in Florence, it is possible that the action of the commune made it difficult, if not impossible, for these clans to regroup into vaster federations; this would explain why, in the Quattrocento, as Benedetto Dei emphasizes, the number of families bearing different names was much larger in Florence than in Genoa.

The size of family clans: their human and economic importance

How can we ascertain, precisely, the sizes of these groups, the numbers of their members? This aspect of medieval social structures has seldom engaged the attention of historians. Through the study of private documents such as notarial deeds, wills, contracts of sale or apportionment, and the examination of genealogies, we may, albeit very imperfectly, become aware of the number of individuals who bear the same name, in the same town, at a given moment. These scarce indications have no overall statistical value, but they are not without their interest.

Between 1362 and 1457, in three generations, Matteo, then Giovanni and Matteo de' Chorsini, in their *libri di ricordanze*, listed 103 people who bore the name of Chorsini; if we discount eighteen children who died very young there were still eighty-five people over the three generations.[149] Between 1379 and 1427, Lapo di Giovanni Niccolini alone listed thirty-three individuals with this name, excluding his ancestors – in a single generation, therefore.[150] Of course these two lists are not exhaustive, and in any case the compilers of the *libri* had little occasion to furnish the names of wives and daughters.[151] Additionally, simple transactions for the purchase of land caused this Niccolini to list ten men, obviously adult and emancipated, who bore the name Buondelmonti.

Another indication, possibly more conclusive and certainly more complete, is a peace treaty signed in 1316 after a great vendetta between two rival Florentine *consorterie*; for the Cavalcanti eighty-one people appeared before the magistrates of the commune (they were obviously all adults and freemen, and to them were added ten allies, referred to as *seguaci*), and for the Pazzi, thirty, plus two allies.[152]

Finally, again in Florence, tax records enable us to identify twenty-eight Strozzi among the heads of families who were taxed in 1351, and thirty-one in 1427; even at this late date this obviously implies more than a hundred individuals.[153] The activities and interests of these men are probably different, but I do not think that this implies any break-up of the group's cohesion; despite his very pessimistic viewpoint on the evolution of these great families, R.A. Goldthwaite is right to use the expression "the Strozzi clan".

So in the case of Florence these very brief and incomplete estimates still give the impression of very powerful clans uniting several primary families and a large number of individuals.

In Genoa all the records of land and chattel taxes class the nobles by *alberghi*, which in turn are classified according to their place of residence. In this way the register of the 1445 *Gabella possessionum*, which has come down to us intact, gives a complete picture of property inside the city;[154] only the regularly exempt families are absent, and there are very few of these, notably the families of the doges, Adorni

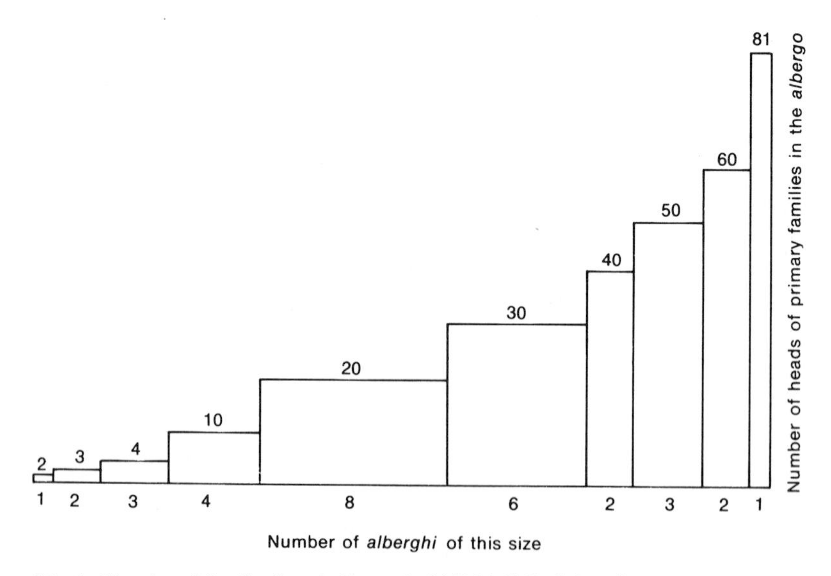

Fig. 1. The size of family clans in Genoa in 1465 (*A.S.G.*, Sala 42/66. Focagium 1465).

and Fregosi, then the Fieschi and the Spinola di Luccoli. The fifty-nine *alberghi* on the list account for 1,360 taxpayers, an average of twenty-three individuals taxed in each *albergo.* The much less complete register for 1455 lists 745 people as taxed in twenty-nine *alberghi*, an average of more than twenty-seven.[155] The records of the *focagium*, the chattel tax, of 1465, list thirty-two *alberghi* with an average of twenty-two individuals taxed.[156] Finally, the average for the twenty-nine *alberghi* in the *avaria* of 1479 is about twenty-four.[157] All these figures agree and appear conclusive. They show indisputably that the Genoese *albergo* was a suprafamily clan, a very large social group. In fact we see here only the adult and emancipated heads of families; when brothers kept their property indivisibly or ran their affairs communally they were sometimes counted together; children never appeared on the lists, and widows were only a tiny minority; often, at least for landed property, the census officers used the term *heredes*, implying cohabitation and thus more people. Then again, the members of a clan, even of a noble clan, did not necessarily all own a house, however modest; neither were they necessarily all wealthy enough to be taxed on their personal incomes; I have often, without success, searched the accounts of the *Gabella possessionum* or of the *avaria* for evidence of nobles whose existence is attested by lawyers' deeds, for example the Doria family and others; they are not mentioned there.

So, fiscal registers give only names of men, and then only of those who were already heads of primary families and rich enough to fall victim to the tax. It is impossible to know the numbers of exempt heads of families. We can only remember that we should definitely multiply the number of men taxed by a substantial figure in order to find the number of adult men, and by a still larger figure to obtain the number of people.

In any case the sizes of the *alberghi* seem very unequal and we should remember that the averages given are only simple indications. In 1465 the records of the *focagium* list thirty-two *alberghi* and 720 heads of families taxed (the others, being exempt, do not appear on this register). In fact the importance of each of these thirty-two *alberghi* is very varied.[158] So some noble family groups were represented only by a single family head; others by two or three. But in the *focagium* of 1465 fifty-nine Doria were taxed, and fifty-nine again in the *avarium* of 1479. In 1455 ninety-five Lomellini and 104 Spinola di San Luccà were taxed on their houses; to the latter we should add the Spinola di Luccoli, traditionally exempt, but who were listed in 1463 as being thirty strong for thirty-six houses.[159] The Spinola *albergo* therefore included at least 134 heads of families who were taxed on their houses, signifying certainly more than 600 individuals. Here then is the perfect example of a vast clan, or rather of a confederation of clans, a sort of tribe, powerful and populous, capable of exerting great influence on the town's every destiny.

This inequality of numbers is disconcerting. Only the most powerful clans, fifteen or twenty perhaps in Genoa, really succeeded in asserting their sway.

In the whole of the West, the strength and cohesion of these vast clans which asserted themselves to a greater or lesser degree, but which were almost always powerful, depended essentially, on the one hand on ties of blood and the fact that they looked to a common ancestor, on the other hand on close links of proximity, so imperative in the medieval city.

Notes

[1]For the exercise of political power by lineages and other family clans, see below, pp. 233ff. For the Hanse, see Dollinger, P., *The German Hansa*, London, 1970, Chapter 6. More generally, see also Dollinger, P., "Les villes allemandes au Moyen Age; les groupements sociaux", in *Recueils de la Société Jean Bodin*, vii: *La ville*, part 2, 371–401. Several towns have been the subject of very detailed individual studies. See Schneider, J., *La ville de Metz*, 114–142, for a lengthy and important discussion of the formation of lineages and of their political action. The author cites the two old studies of Klipffel, H., (*Les Paraiges messins. Étude sur la république messine du XIIIe au XIVe siècles*, Metz and Paris, 1863) and Prost, A., (*Le patriciat dans le cité de Metz*, Paris, 1873) and disputes their conclusions. See also Dollinger, P., "Patriciat noble et patriciat bourgeois à Strasbourg au XIVe siècle", in *Revue d'Alsace*, 1950–1951, 52–82; Martens, M., "Note sur l'époque de fixation du nom des sept lignages bruxellois", in *Cahiers bruxellois*, iv, 1959, 173–193; Joris, A., *La ville de Huy au Moyen Age des origines à la fin du XIVe siècle*, Paris, 1959.

[2]The study by Gerbet, M.C., (in progress), of the social structures of the nobility in Estremadura at the end of the Middle Ages emphasizes the role of the lineages and of their clans in the municipal life of the region.

[3]See below, pp. 234–235.

[4]Cristiani, E., *Nobiltà e popolo*, 48. The list is published by Cecchini, G., *Il Caleffo vecchio del comune di Siena*, 1931, 365–388.

[5]Herlihy, D., in *Essays in memory of Robert L. Reynolds*, 179–180. On indivision of property Herlihy asserts that town houses were too small at the end of the Middle Ages

to shelter a large family group; he gives the figure of 3.5 persons per house in Bologna (after Montanari, P., *Documenti sulla popolazione di Bologna alla fine del Trecento*, Bologna, 1966, 6) and 3.6 in Pistoia (from his own work, *Medieval and Renaissance Pistoia*, 75).

[6]Cristiani, E., in *Nobiltà e popolo*, asserts the permanence of the same aristocratic families at the head of the city, despite many institutional arrangements which were sometimes claimed as 'revolutions'. On this permanence, see also Dollinger, P., *Revue d'Alsace*, 1950–1951.

[7]Brattö, O., *Liber estimationum anno MCCLXIX*, Göteburg, 1956.

[8]See for example the documents published by Liagre, L., and de Sturler, *Les relations commerciales entre Gênes, la Belgique et l'outremont d'après les archives notariales génoises (1320–1400)*, Brussels and Rome, 1969.

[9]See Heers, J., in *Annales de démographie historique*, 1968.

[10]On all these points, see below, pp. 146ff.

[11]The Grimaldi adopted the Ceba on 25 October 1448; the Ceba promised *quos deinceps ipsi et eorum quilibet, filique, ac nepotes, prenepotes et universae ipsorum posteritates se se nominabant ex familia et cognomento Grimaldorum* (see Ascheri, *Notizie*, 74). In 1453, Cristoforo Tonso similarly promised the Franchi *pro se filiis descentibus et posteris suis* (*A.S.G.*, Notaio Cristofero de Rapallo, senior, filza for the year 1462, no. 376). As another example, Domenico Scotto requested and was granted incorporation into the Salvaighi *suo nomine et nomine heredes et successorum suorum* (*A.S.G.*, Notaio Oberto Foglietta, filza 6, no. 233, 25 April 1460).

[12]Specifically, for the Grimaldi–Ceba aggregation referred to above; it is difficult to see the reason for this exception: French influence is a possibility.

[13]Berengo, M., *Nobili e mercanti nella Lucca del Cinquecento*, Turin, 1965, 32.

[14]Anonymi Ticinensis, *Rerum Italicarum Scriptores*, xi, 1, 31.

[15]The only example, to my knowledge, concerns the Doria clan; in 1460 Batista, one of the members of this clan, abducted a young Doria girl who was promised to another member of the clan (see Salvi, D.G., "Il ratto di Bianchinetta Doria", in *Giornale storico e litterario della Liguria*, 1930).

[16]Aubenas, R., "Réflexions sur les 'fraternités artificielles' au Moyen Age", in *Études d'histoire à la mémoire de Noël Didier*, Paris, 1960; Dussourd, H., *Au même pot et au même feu*, Moulins, 1962.

[17]Lugli, V., *I trattatisti della famiglia nel Quattrocento*, Bologna and Modena, 1909; Bec, C., *Les marchands écrivains, affaires et humanisme à Florence (1375–1434)*, Paris and The Hague, 1967.

[18]Petrucci, A., *Il libro di ricordanze dei Corsini (1362–1457)*, Rome, 1965; Niccolini, G., "Libri di ricordanze dei Niccolini", in *Rivista delle bibliotecche e degli archivi*, ii, 2, 1924, 1–30, 88–91, 172–187, 243–252.

[19]Bec, C., *Il libro degli affari proprii di Casa de Lapo di Giovanni Niccolini de' Sirigatti*, Paris, 1969.

[20]There are unfortunately very few of these for France, or they are very ill-known; see however Guibert, L., *Nouveau recueil de registres domestiques limousins et marchois*, Limoges and Paris, 1895; Guigue, G., *Le livre de raison d'un bourgeois de Lyon au XIVe siècle*, Lyons, 1882; Gauthier, J., *Notes sur quelques livres de raison franc-comtois.*

[21]Macinghi-Strozzi, Alessandra, ed. Guasti, G., *Lettere di una gentildonna fiorentina del secolo XV ai figliuoli esuli*, Florence, 1887.

[22]Alberti, L.B., ed. Grayson, *Opere volgari*, 1960–1966, i, 34, quoted by Herlihy, D., "The Tuscan town in the Quattrocento. A demographic profile", in *Medievalia et humanistica*, new series, 1, 1970 (1–109), note 34.

[23]Klapisch, C., "Fiscalité et démographie en Toscane (1427–1430)", in *Annales E.S.C.*, 1969, 1313–1337.

[24]After Herlihy, D., in *Medievalia et humanistica*, 1970, table 2, p. 90. These figures are not directly comparable with those of Mrs Klapisch (in *Annales E.S.C.*, 1969), for the age-groups used are not the same (for example, 28–32 years in one case and 30–34 in the other).

[25]Bautier, R.H., in *Annales E.S.C.*, 1959.

[26]Herlihy, D., "Population plague in rural Pistoia", in *Economic History Review*, 1965, 225–244.

[27]Herlihy, D., in *Medievalia et humanistica*, 1970, 98.

[28]*San Bernardini di Siena, Opera omnia*, Florence, 1950, ii, 82, quoted by Herlihy in *Medievalia et humanistica*, 1970, note 30.

[29]Macinghi-Strozzi, Alessandra, *Lettere*; quoted by Gage, J., *Life in Italy at the time of the Medici*, London, 1968, 29.

[30]Quoted by Tamassia, N., in *La famiglia italiana nei secoli XV e XVI*, Milan, Palermo and Naples, 1910.

[31]*Opere volgari*, i, 108–109; quoted by Herlihy in *Medievalia et humanistica*, 1970, note 34.

[32]On this practice, which was so widespread that these *moltiplicati* for dowries represented an appreciable proportion of the shares on the register of San Giorgio, see Heers, *Gênes*, 148.

[33]See below, p. 230.

[34]D'Addario, A., "Un fiorentino del Tre Quattrocento", in *Vita privata a Firenze nei secoli XIV e XV*, Florence, 1966, 39–40 (the author gives no reference). One may also refer to Ammirato, S., *Dell'Istorie Fiorentine*, Florence, 1600, Lib. xx, and to Varchi, B., *Storie Fiorentine*, Trieste, 1858.

[35]Bib. Nat., Paris, Coll. Moreau ms. 1162, f. i, published by Tuetey, A., *Testaments enregistrés à Paris sous le règne de Charles VI*, Paris, 1880, 554–562.

[36]Gage, J., *Life in Italy*, 30.

[37]*Journal de voyage de Michel de Montaigne*, Paris, 1954, 163–164.

[38]Morelli, Giovanni di Paolo, *Ricordi*, ed. Branca, V., Florence, 1956, 207; quoted by Herlihy in *Medievalia et humanistica*, 1970, note 33.

[39]Morelli, Giovanni di Paolo, *Ricordi*, 96–97. Such practices seem to have been especially prominent among the Italians; in the sixteenth century Benvenuto Cellini, a Florentine, was accused, in Paris, of performing, "in the Italian fashion", practices reputed to be contrary to nature; see Morelli, 97.

[40]For all this, see Herlihy in *Medievalia et humanistica*, 1970.

[41]Women awaited their delivery with dread; it was the cause of the death of many young women. I have found in Genoa a large number of assurance policies on the lives of pregnant slaves; these policies were taken out for the benefit of the master, and the premiums were paid by the putative fathers, before the birth of the child. But the rate, in the sole case where it is mentioned, seems particularly low: only 2 per cent. See *A.S.G.*, Sala 57/57, no. 1865, 7 October 1485, p. 32. On these life assurance policies, see Heers, *Gênes*, 214–215.

[42]On this see Herlihy, *Medieval and Renaissance Pistoia.* The last wife thus remains a widow even though she is very young or rather young, and she retains a large fortune. Herlihy believes that in this way a considerable part of the wealth of a Tuscan town was in the hands of young widows; he thinks that this fact might explain some aspects of urban civilization in the Quattrocento, for example in the field of art.

[43]Cazelles, R., "La peste noire en langue d'oïl, épidémie prolétarienne et enfantile", in *B.P.H.*, 1962 (1965), 293ff.; Mollat, M., "Notes sur la mortalité au temps de la peste noire d'après les comptes de l'oeuvre de Saint-Germain-l'Auxerrois", in *Le Moyen Age*, 1963, 505–527.

[44]Heers, J., *Le livre de comptes de Giovanni Piccamiglio, homme d'affaires génois (1456–1460)*, Paris and Aix-en-Provence, 1958, 98, 132.

[45]Petrucci, A., *Il libro di ricordanze dei Corsini*, 89–93.

[46]Petrucci, *Il libro*, 137–139.

[47]Petrucci, *Il libro*, 144.

[48]See Pernot, A., *La noblesse*, 44–51.

[49]Alberti, L.B., *Opere volgari*, 214, 267.

[50]Alberti, *Opere volgari*, 285.

[51]See especially Verlinden, C., *L'esclavage dans l'Europe médiévale*, Bruges, 1955; Cortes, V., "La esclavitud en Valencia", in *Archivio*, Denia, iv, 1890.

[52]Origo, I., "The domestic enemy: the eastern slaves in Tuscany in the XIVth and XVth centuries", in *Speculum*, 1955.

[53]Bib. Bat., Paris, n.a. lat. Fonds Montreuil, vol. 1324 (L. Delisle's catalogue) entitled: *Captifs. Esclaves* (150 documents).

[54]Ladero Quesada, M. Angel, "La esclavitud por guerra a fines del siglo XV: el caso de Màlaga", in *Hispania*, Madrid, cv, 1967, 63–88.

[55]Callet, E., "La famille et la population pisanes d'après le catasto de 1428–1429", unpublished dissertation, University of Paris X, 1968; the clerks of the cadastre counted only a single black slave in Pisa (p. 70).

[56]Bénesse, D., "Les esclaves dans la société ibérique aux XIVe et XVe siècles", unpublished dissertation, University of Paris X, 1970, 140; statistics after studies by Verlinden, C. and Cortes, V.

[57]Callet, E., "La famille" 70. In 1428–1429 there were three male slaves and fifty-seven female slaves in Pisa.

[58]Bénesse, D., "Les esclaves", 23, 112.

[59]Heers, *Gênes*, 355.

[60]Bénesse, D., "Les esclaves", 115–116.

[61]Verlinden, C., *L'esclavage*, 431.

[62]Heers, J., "Un autre exemple de colonisation médiévale: Bonifacio au XIIIe siècle", in *Anuario de Estudios Medievales*, 1964, 561–571; texts published by Vitale, V., "Documenti sul castello di Bonifacio nel secolo XIII", in *Atti della Regia Deputazione di Storia Patria per la Liguria*, lxv, 1936, 144.

[63]Heers, *Gênes*, 554–555.

[64]Tamassia, N., *La famiglia italiana*, 230.

[65]The text is to be found in *Archivio storico italiano*, series 3, ii, 33; quoted by Tamassia, *La famiglia italiana.*

[66]The absence of black slaves in Italian households is indeed striking. Was this the result of some prohibition, of collective controls? Or was it linked to concubinage?

[67]Livi, R., "La schiavitù medioevale e la sua influenza sui caratteri antropologici degli italiani", in *Rivista italiana di sociologia*, xi, 1907, parts 4–5, 557–581.

[68]Casini, B., *Il catasto di Pisa del 1428–1429*, Pisa, 1964; Callet, E., "La famille", 67ff.

[69]This information was provided by Mrs Klapisch at the first congress of the *Société des Médiévistes de l'Enseignement supérieur public* in Nice, in 1969; see the transactions of this congress in *Annales de la Faculté des Lettres et Sciences Humaines de Nice*, Paris, no. 17, 1972, 65; but the reader should take account of frauds, for slaves were taxed as chattels; their masters attempted to pass them off as members of the *famiglia* in order to receive *detrazioni per bocche*.

[70]Verlinden, C., *L'esclavage*, 427f.

[71]Verlinden, *L'esclavage*, 432.

[72]Cortes, V., in *Archivio*, 1890, 50. All these figures are quoted by Bénesse, D., "Les esclaves", 23–24.

[73]Gioffré, D., *Il mercato degli schiavi a Genova nel secolo XV*, Genoa, 1871.

[74]Thus, to take an easily attested example, in 1456–1460 Giovanni Piccamiglio owned two slaves and his mother owned another: Heers, J., *Le livre*, 69, 92, 96, 138, 144, 148, 181, 185, 196, 248, 252, 270; but there is not a single mention of the Piccamiglio *albergo* in the list of slave-owners classed, as nobles, by *alberghi*, which is given in the *Liber slavorum* of 1458 (published by Gioffré, D., in *Il mercato*).

[75]*A.S.G.*, Sala 38/55, Caratorum Vetterum Anno 1458, no. 1553.

[76]*A.S.G.*, Notai Giudiziali, Pilosio Benedetto (Gazarie): several documents from the end of May and the beginning of June.

[77]It should however be noted that slavery is here essentially, perhaps exclusively, urban: Genoa and its suburbs, Savona and Albenga, imported slaves; but there were no slaves in Sestri Levante, a large township of at least 265 households. See Robin, F., "Sestri Levante", 126.

[78]Bertelè, T., and Dorini, U., *Il libro di conti di Giacomo Badoer*, Rome, 1956, 524.

[79]Quoted by Origo, I., in *Speculum*, 1955, 354.

[80]Gozzadini, G., *Delle torri gentilizie di Bologna e delle famiglie alle quali appartennero*, Bologna, 2nd ed., 1965, 286f.

[81]Gozzadini, G., *Delle torri*; this, according to the *Ruolo de' servi emancipati*, but the author does not give the exact reference. On this subject see also Simeoni, L., "La liberazione dei servi a Bologna nel 1256–1257", in *Archivio Storico Italiano*, 1952.

[82]Gutta, S., and Plessi, G., eds, *Liber paradisus*, Bologna, 1956, quoted by Gioffré, D., *Il mercato*, 76.

[83]Origo, in *Speculum*, 1955, 325.

[84]Origo, in *Speculum*, 1955, 330.

[85]Gioffré, D., *Il mercato*, 74–75.

[86]Casini, B., *Il catasto*.

[87]Callet, E., "La famille".

[88]Casini, *Il catasto*, no. 1345.

[89]Macinghi-Strozzi, Alessandra, *Lettere*, quoted by Tamassia, *La famiglia*, 112.

[90]Tamassia, *La famiglia*, 116, after Bernardi, *Cronache forlivesi. Monumenti storici pertinenti alle provincie di Romagne*, Bologna, 1895.

[91]Tamassia, *La famiglia*, 115, after Minotto, *Acta et tabulario veneto*, Venice, 1870, ii, year 1314.

[92]Boutruche, R., *Seigneurie et féodalité*, i: *Le premier âge des liens d'homme à homme*, 2nd edition, Paris, 1968, 169.

[93]Boutruche, *Seigneurie et féodalité*, i, 270.

[94]Boutruche, *Seigneurie et féodalité*, i. 170. On these domestic warriors, see Larson, L.M., "The household of the Norwegian kings in the XIIIth century", in Thrupp, S.L., (ed), *Change in medieval society*, New York, 1964, 133–151.

[95]Boutruche, *Seigneurie et féodalité*, i, 274.

[96]Boutruche, *Seigneurie et féodalité*, ii: *L'apogée (XIe–XIIIe siècles)*, Paris, 1970, 174.

[97]Duby, G., in *Annales E.S.C.*, 1964.

[98]Pernot, A., *La noblesse*, 8–11.

[99]Quoted by Alberti, L.B., *I primi tre libri*, 213.

[100]Tabarrini, M., "Le consorterie nella storia fiorentina del medio evo", in *La vita italiana nel Trecento*, Milan, 1904 (147–187), 173.

[101]Alberti, L.B., *Opere volgari*, quoted by Herlihy, D., in *Medievalia et humanistica*, 1970, 81, 109 and note 29.

[102]Carpentier, E., *Une ville*, 32–33. In Venice itself, 'medieval' chroniclers, writing of the early years of Venetian society, and especially of the great aristocratic families, often refer to the *domus de statio* where the leaders lived, and to the *domus a sergentibus* or house of the dependents. See Pavan, E., "Maisons, urbanisme et structures sociales à Venise à la fin du Moyen Age", unpublished dissertation, University of Paris-Sorbonne, 1975, 36.

[103]Brucker, G.A., "The Ciompi revolution", in Rubinstein, N. (ed.), *Florentine studies. Politics and society in Renaissance Florence*, London, 1968, 323–324.

[104]Brucker in Rubinstein, N. (ed.), *Florentine studies*, 332.

[105]Brucker in *Florentine Studies*, 332, note 3, after "Cronaca fiorentina di Marchione di Coppo Stefani", in *R.R.I.S.S.*, xxx, part 1, 1903–1905.

[106]Brucker in *Florentine studies*, 332, note 4, after the personal letters of the Del Bene family.

[107]Berengo, M., *Nobili e mercanti*, 32.

[108]*Quant il avenoit que aucun l'avoient achetée, si soustenoient lour enfans et lour neveus en lour outraiges; car li jouvencel avoient fiance en lour parens et en lour amis qui la prevostei tenoient; nus malfaiterres, ne liarres, ne murtriers n'osa demourer à Paris, qui tantost ne fust pendus ou destruiz; ne parentés, ne lignaiges, ne ors, ne argens ne le pot garantir*; Joinville, *Histoire de Saint Louis*, ed. de Wailly, N., 1868, 254–256. English translation by Shaw, M.R.B.: *Joinville and Villehardouin, Chronicles of the Crusades*, Penguin, 1963, 341–342.

[109]Espinas, G., *Une guerre sociale interurbaine dans la Flandre wallonne au XIIIe siècle*, Douai and Lille, 1930, 187, 219–220.

[110]Espinas, G., "Les guerres familiales à Douai aux XIIIe et XIVe siècles", in *R.H.D.F.E.*, 1899 (415–473), 435.

[111]Schneider, J., *La ville de Metz*, 121.

[112]Béthune, J. de, *Les Méreaux des familles brugeoises*, Bruges, 1890, p. xxvi.

[113]Weill, G., in *B.P.H.*, 1969, 288–289.

[114]Sivery, G., *Structures*, 314.

[115]This was the contract by which a man, often a knight, engaged in the service of a high-ranking noble for the rest of his life, in return for an annual salary. An example of an indenture between Richard Neville, earl of Warwick, and Sir John Trafford (1461) is published by Myers, A.R., in *English historical documents*, iv: *1327–1485*, London, 1969, 1126.

[116]Myers, *English historical documents*, iv, 1116.

[117]Unwin, G., *Gilds and Companies of London*, London, 1908, 103–104; Thrupp, S., "The grocers of London, a study of distributive trade", in *Studies in English trade in the XVth century*, London, 1933, 247–292.

[118]See below, pp. 108–109 for the size of vendettas and private wars, and pp. 111ff. for urban revolts.

[119]Quoted by Herlihy, D., in *Essays in memory of Robert L. Reynolds*, 182.

[120]For this see Mansuy, G., "Les ordonnances somptuaires dans les villes de France à la fin du Moyen Age", unpublished dissertation, University of Paris X, 1972.

[121]Bongi, S., "Statuto inedito della casa de' Corbolani", in *Atti della reale Accademia lucchese di scienze, lettere ed arti*, xxiv, 1886, 471–487.

[122]D.O. Hughes is preparing an important study of one Genoese *albergo* in the fourteenth century; for the present, see her article: "Toward historical ethnography: notarial records and family history in the Middle Ages", in *Historical methods newsletter*, University of Pittsburg, vii, no. 2, 1974.

[123]*A.S.G.*, Notaio Cristoforo di Rappalo senior, year 1452, no. 376, 14 September 1453; the decision was taken *juxta formam instrumenti primae institutionis dicti albergi scripti manu q. Dexerini de Pastino notarii 1393 die vigesima octava januarii.* This document of 1393 has not survived, and I have found no other document of this kind.

[124]There are very many examples: see *A.S.G.*, Notaio Oberto Foglietta, filza 6, no. 233.

[125]This document was published by Ascheri, A., in *Notizie*, 74.

[126]*A.S.G.*, Diversorum Registri, nos. 46–541, year 1448.

[127]For further detail on these alliances and on the numbers and conditions of the original families, see Heers, *Gênes*, 564–566.

[128]*A.S.G.*, Sala 41, Sg 103, B, Avariorum, 1479, no. 536.

[129]*A.S.G.*, Sala 42/66, Focagium, no. 612, anno 1465, Compagna Piazza Lunga conestagia Chiavicca.

[130]*A.S.G.*, Notaio Cristoforo di Rappalo senior.

[131]Cristiani, E., *Nobiltà e popolo*, 81.

[132]Schneider, J., *La ville de Metz*, 120–122.

[133]Schneider, *La ville de Metz*, 123, 146.

[134]Schneider, *La ville de Metz*, 117, 147.

[135]Schneider, *La ville de Metz*, 139–140.

[136]Schneider, *La ville de Metz*, 141.

[137]See below, p. 85.

[138]It is possible to study these amalgamations and disintegrations of *alberghi* in the fiscal registers on which the nobles were specifically classed by *alberghi.*

[139]*A.S.G.*, Mutuum of 6 per cent, 1379, Compere e mutui, no. 1866, f. 1, v°; this information was kindly supplied by J. Day.

[140]*A.S.G.*, Sala 42/65, B, Gabella possessionum, 1445.

[141]*A.S.G.*, Sala 42/66, Focagium, 1465, no. 612; one section of this register is missing, but study reveals that in any case there were only eight or ten alberghi which should appear on the missing pages; this gives a maximum figure of forty-two *alberghi* for that year.

[142]Dollinger, P., in *Recueils de la Société Jean Bodin*, vii.

[143]Quoted by Enriques, A.M., "La vendetta nella vita e nella legislazione fiorentina", in *Archivio storico italiano*, xci, 1, 1933, 117.

[144]Carpentier, E., *Une ville*, 67.

[145]*Archivio di Stato di Firenze*, MS. 119, f. 69 v°.

[146]Becker, M. B., "The Florentine territorial state", in Rubinstein, N., (ed.), *Florentine studies*, 114.

[147]Pamploni, G., "I Tornaquinci, poi Tornabuoni fino ai primi del Cinquecento", in *Archivio storico italiano*, 1968, 331–362.

[148]Pamploni, G., in *Archivio storico italiano*, 1968, 347. It is worth noting that family names still seemed uncertain and little used.

[149]Petrucci, A., *Il libro*.

[150]Bec, C., *Il libro*.

[151]Niccolini lists twenty-four males out of thirty-three people; some may not be listed if they had not attended some solemn occasion which would have brought them to the notice of the writer.

[152]*A.S.F.*, Provisioni XV, c. 24f., quoted by Enriques, A.M., in *A.S.I.*, 1933, 127.

[153]Goldthwaite, R.A., *Private wealth in Renaissance Florence*, Princeton U.P., 34.

[154]*A.S.G.*, Sala 42/65, B. Gabella possessionum, 1445.

[155]*A.S.G.*, Sala 42/63, no. 583, Gabella possessionum, anno 1455.

[156]*A.S.G.*, Sala 42/66, Focagium, 1465, no. 612.

[157]*A.S.G.*, Sala 41, Sg 103, B, Avariorum, anno 1479, no. 536.

[158]See above, p. 88, figure 1.

[159]*A.S.G.*, Sala 46/65, B, Gabella possessionum, Nobili. The 1479 *avaria* still counted 91 Spinola di San Luccà.

CHAPTER 3

Clan solidarity: blood, inheritance and the family name

External signs: names, blazons, banners and palaces

Family clans owed their varied destinies and their more or less strong solidarity to several highly complex factors.

Firstly, they claimed to descend from a single stock. Men felt themselves united by ties of blood and by their pride in belonging to an illustrious tribe. Bernardo, the obscure chronicler of Forlì, proudly affirms: *E forza, che il nostro sangue convegne sentire la passione del'altro suoi sangue, o segreto, o paleso.*[1] This unity of blood characterizes all the ceremonies which, in the feudal West, joined companions in arms. These ceremonies, probably inherited from those of the German and Scandinavian tribes, which were already to be found among the Greeks of the Iliad, created real consanguinity, and exerted a profound influence on noble attitudes and customs. It seems certain that they were not merely a literary theme. There is a long passage in the chronicle of Matthew Paris, who cannot be accused of invention or fancy, describing in great detail this ceremony of mixing the blood of two or more nobles at the time of the upheavals in Henry III's reign, in 1236 to be precise.[2] He describes how a number of nobles, wishing to put off the king's yoke, made alliances between themselves *secundum tamen antiquorum suorum abominabilem consuetudinem.* Each put some of his blood into a large vessel, mixing it with the others' as a sign of indissoluble and consanguine union: *Quod essent ex tunc in antea indissolubili et quasi consanguineo foedus colligati, et in prosperis et adversis usque ad capitum expositionem.* In other ceremonies the future brothers in arms also poured wine into their blood, or again dipped their arms into the blood.[3]

Many other chroniclers, nobles or just important burgesses, the authors of the *libri di ricordanze* themselves, such as Lapo di Giovanni Niccolini, speak very enthusiastically, respectfully and at length of their tribes' origins; here they mixed serious research and obscure legend. Anselmo Adorno, a Genoese who had moved to Bruges and become a stranger in his native city, stayed in Genoa on his way to the Holy Land and, musing on his family's past, was proud to think that he belonged to one of the four illustrious tribes from which the doges were chosen;[4] but he was mistaken: the brilliant success of the Adorni, originally *popolani*, was only recent; but the need to search for ancient antecedents shows the desire to be connected with a well-established tribe. Genealogical works had a definite vogue: a manuscript of 1360, the *Liber Ludi Fortunai*, devotes a whole section, called *De generatione aliquorum civium urbis Padue, tam nobilium, quam ignobilium*, to a scrupulous study of the origins and varying fortunes of a hundred Paduan families.[5]

Every noble wished to ensure his own immortality by preserving the clan's name. It was reassuring to belong to a large, strong tribe. The name was the symbol of the clan: a totemic sort of word with reputedly magic properties. These names were chosen in the 1320s, in Orvieto, for the four clans which evolved out of the great Monaldeschi confederation; they remind us of totemic animals: the stag, the viper, the dog, the eagle.[6] These names were invoked at every opportunity.[7]

This presents no problems, of course, when it concerns an ancient lineage, all of whose branches remained cohesive through the centuries. In the case of very great families, noble families which were the masters of strong seignories, the different branches might occasionally be distinguished only by reference to a fief. But the clan's name was also very often pressed on groups formed through the amalgamation of several different families or lineages. In this case, the first, and principal duty of the new members was to bear the same name as the others. We have already noted that in Genoa the ancient names were more or less quickly abandoned; the fact that the expression *olim de*... was kept shows us clearly enough that they were not abandoned without regret.[8] However, in this case the name was a sign of a very close alliance, as strong as that of blood. Documents of admission to the Genoese *alberghi*, whose form differed very little from notary to notary, show that the new members had to "act and comport themselves in all things as if they were born of the said name" (*de dicto cognomine*)[9] or, more clearly, that the original members received them as if they really were *de ipso albergo et cognomine ac de eius stirpe propria.*[10] Thus the name and the tribe were closely linked.

The coat of arms, the blazon, is another triumphant sign of the preservation or new formation of alliances. Such a tribe was obviously proud of its men, of its martial virtues, of its virility. Lapo di Giovanni Niccolini speaks very highly of the first of his ancestors, one Ruzza (Ruzza d'Arigho di Luchese di Bonavia de' Sirighatti), *chi è l'origine di noi e del nostro llato,* whom he describes as *Uno huomo grande del chorpo, e bello, e pro delle personna, e vivette circha a ciento trenta ani.*[11] Once the early years of the communal period were over, these family clans of the Italian towns confirmed their entrenched agnation. The *Morgengabe,* the portion of the husband's wealth settled upon his bride at their marriage, a survival of Lombard law which here was called the *quarta* or *tertia,* was still respected in Genoa and Milan in the 1130s, but had disappeared by the end of the century; the same development took place a little later in the other towns of northern and central Italy.[12] In Florence, in 1174, an agreement made for the sale of a portion of a tower forbade its passing, by inheritance, into the hands of any woman.[13]

This respect for martial ancestors and martial virtues is revealed in coats of arms. The fact that nobles bore the same blazon or the same arms, or even just a common colour, a known distinguishing sign, seems to the noble mind to have been the affirmation of a loyal alliance, as strong as that of blood. In medieval tradition companions-in-arms, who were often more or less distant relatives, assumed dress and arms of the same colour;[14] whence, later, the various colours, arms or insignia borne by all the companions of chivalric orders. The ancient war banner was flown not only by direct descendants, those who really were of the name and tribe, but also by all the relatives who followed and served the fortunes of the house. The blazon evidently indicated common origins or an alliance. The anonymous chronicler of Pavia speaks at one time of those very great families who *sub uno insigne, vel signo, diversa vocabula secundum diversas lineas habent.*[15] The new members of an *albergo* promised and swore *defferre insigna et arma dicti albergi et non alia,*[16] or *defere et uti armorum et insignibus ubicumque dicti albergi et de colore ipsius albergi*;[17] this, under pain of a fine of 1,000 ducats, a very large sum; the refusal to bear arms was the only offence punished in this way. The Grimaldi, when they received the Ceba into their clan, allowed them

Quod in suis ædibus, et aliis celebrioribus locis sacris, ac profanis ubi erant vel ut vulgo dicitur arma Cebarum celari aut pingi curabunt signa GR. familiæ, et si nova signa ab se post hac erunt alicui sculpenda, vel pigenda relictis Cebarum signis Grimalda ibi signa fingentur.[18]

Even in peacetime and in different countries the blazon was a rallying sign for the different branches of the same clan: thus in Poland, and in Scotland where clans wore their colours in their clothes, each having one or more tartans distinguishing them from the others. In Italy too, when Benvenuto Cellini saw that the Cellini family in Ravenna had fixed above their houses the same arms as the Florentine Cellini, he deduced with certainty that the two *casati*, from Florence and Ravenna, belonged to the same *gente.*[19] In the Tuscan mind, then, the clan was by no means restricted by city boundaries.

The blazon characterizes the noble house, the palace, in the city. N. Tamassia, whose work is very valuable on this topic, says that each house bore the family's name and arms, its *stemma*. Occasionally this was clearly required by the regulations of prince or commune: *Domus in qua debeant essent picta arma . . . testatoris, intaliata in quidam lapide, ita quod bene et clare videatur.*[20] This large stone, on which the blazon was cut, was placed above the main door; we see the arms again at the top of the tower, either cut once more into the stone or sometimes on a banner. Around their Piazza, in Croce di Canetto, along the main street of Canetto, all the large Genoese houses of the Giustiniani, rich *popolani* grouped in a vast family confederation, were adorned above the entrance gates by massive stones or blocks of white marble on which were carved their common arms. Nobles or important burgesses would have their arms depicted on tapestries or frescoes covering the walls of ceremonial rooms and chapels; on 24 July 1387 Matteo Chorsini and his wife Lorenza degli Strozzi gave to the church of the Holy Spirit, to embellish their chapel of St Jacob, a *baldachino* of silk cloth with hares, birds and dragons on a white ground, a central motif representing Christ's Passion and the arms of the Chorsini and those of the Strozzi; three silken *chamici* also depicted birds and the Chorsini arms, as did the two great candlesticks of the altar.[21] Arms also graced books, jewels, certain garments and, obviously, armour; these insignia, or at least their colours, were also to be found on servants' livery. Great merchant families used their trade mark (the Medici's famous heart surmounted by a cross) only for bales of merchandise and for the addresses of business letters; for every other aspect of social life these families used their blazons and colours.

In Genoa, naturally, arms were flown from every merchant ship, even in peacetime; the Franchi, although they were only *popolani*, insisted that Cristoforo Tonso, whom they had just admitted to their *albergo*, undertook to bear *arma et seu signo Albergo in vexilis paventibus, guarminentis Dominorum, aliisque omnibus in quibus uti solitum est armis et signis.*[22] This armorial pride, this wish to use the blazon to signify, often ostentatiously, their membership of a noble tribe, is clearly confirmed in pictures of the houses, and especially of the ships. Here, the famous painting by Cristoforo Grasso which is kept in the naval museum in Pegli, near Genoa, provides decisive iconographic evidence. It is in fact the only important picture of Genoese buildings in the Middle Ages. L. Volpicella has shown[23] that this is a copy made in 1597 of an earlier picture which portrayed the armed fleet leaving the port of Genoa in good order, in 1481, against the Turks: twenty-three warships and seven large vessels. The city is clearly represented in the background, with its churches, palaces and towers. From the iconographic point of view this work is extraordinarily rich. For our purpose we may observe that each ship flies at least six banners, flowing well out; we cannot identify them all; some, especially at the prow, seem to be trophies. The banners of Pope Sixtus IV and of the admiral, Paolo Fregoso, fly over each warship. Then, the vessels fly the flag of the commune, the famous red cross on a white ground. But in addition the warships have the arms of their owner and those of their master, of their commander; these banners are those of powerful and very ancient families, of true 'nobility': Doria (three warships), Lomellini (three more), Fieschi (three more) and Cattaneo; there are also the arms of less prominent families (Biassa, Carmadino, Interiano, Davagna and Giudice) and finally those of *alberghi* of *popolani*, such as the Giustiniani and the Franchi. Thus, every Genoese *albergo*, whatever its origins or power, claimed by its blazon membership of a tribe and of the nobility.

Throughout Italy, the blazon showed the pride of the tribe, and its power and independence in the face of the state, or of the commune's political emergence. In 1266 Venice forbade dependants to bear the arms of their patrons:

> Quod nullus homo in Veneciis parvus vel magnus possit nec debeat habere in scutis, lameriis, capellinis, çuppis, banderiis, vel alii arnesiis, aut in aliquibus aliis armis, nec a modo faciat fieri, et illi, qui habent, faciant destruere infra dies XV.[24]

After the family name and arms, the remaining symbol of a family clan's unity was the house. The city palace, often fortified, and surrounded by the other palaces of the clansmen or by the houses in which their dependants lived, retained the prestige of the feudal castle, proudly rising from its *rocca*. In Italy the house symbolized the clan's power; in the event of treason, condemnation or exile, the victorious enemy would attack buildings as much as people. The house was confiscated, or more often was demolished, razed or burned, in a spectacular and symbolic manifestation of the defeat of the guilty traitor, the enemy. This was not only a military precaution, but also a sort of magical operation upon the public mind.

Between 1260 and 1266, when the Guelphs were exiled from Florence, they lost many houses and towers which were completely destroyed, not only in the city itself but also in all the townships and villages of the *contado*; on their return they had to be compensated and this required a special census, or *estimo*.[25] A naive but very interesting drawing in a margin of the manuscript of the *Annales genuenses* of Caffaro shows the *podestà* of Genoa, mounted upon his horse and heavily armed, ordering the destruction, with picks, of a rebel noble's house.[26] Such judicial destruction, by fire or steel, became so common that in Orvieto in 1348 the city council, believing that too many houses were in ruins *ex quo cives bene appetentes vivere et alii forenses mercatores aborrent* forbade, thenceforth, any magistrate or officer to destroy any house, for whatever reason, whether condemnation, or banishment, or misdemeanour, or any other.[27] But in Florence, as late as 1380, Matteo di Chorsini bought a house on the Piazza and Via Maggio; this house had belonged to Bartolomeo Ridolfi and was sold to Matteo by *gli ufficiali de' beni de' rebelli chiamati per lo Chomune di Firenze*.[28] In 1382, again in Florence, the commune even had the Giraldi houses partly destroyed and the ruins burned; this was to punish the murder of Francesco di Giandonato, who was killed by a young Giraldi.[29] In Venice too, the Quirini and Tiepolo families, who were found guilty of leading a serious conspiracy against the Seignory in 1310, had to submit, albeit thirteen years later, by a decision of the Council of Ten, to the obligation to change their *arme gentilice*; and one of the conspirators also suffered the dishonour of having to keep his door open day and night as a sign of disgrace.[30]

In many towns of northern France and Flanders, municipal magistrates also punished exiles and murderers with harsh sanctions against their houses; their rights of *arsin* (fire) and *abattis* (demolition) were kept for centuries. Sometimes, in order to avoid too much destruction and the resultant disfigurement of cities, they permitted guilty men to pay heavy fines, equal to the value of their houses; in 1395, in Abbeville, they decided to burn only the doors and windows.[31]

The symbolic value attaching to the house probably explains the wish to keep one's ancestors' house always in the family, at a time when the fragmentation or excessive expansion of clans was leading to the dispersal of patrimonies. The house, which reaffirmed the prestige of a clan's name, had to remain the property of the descendants – and that, as far as possible, indivisibly. On his death bed, Francesco Sassetti was ruined by debts, but he wished to save the Montughi Palace which "has given our family great renown" and which was "highly praised in Italy and elsewhere, for it is beautiful and cost a great sum of money"; further, "it is superb, and brings small return . . . it is a dwelling for rich men".[32] In Lucca too, by tradition or by a sort of superstition which strongly characterized collective attitudes, the *domus magna* had to remain in the family; in 1536 still, Stefano di Antonio Bernardi writes in his will: *Ipsa domus magna semper postea teneatur, habitetur et usufructetur per maiores natu de domo et familia illorum de Bernardis de Luca in perpetuum.*[33]

Concords and vendettas

The continuance or reinforcement of family clans ensured above all internal peace and close alliances against neighbours, rivals and enemies. The members of a group remained cohesive and united, and had to live on good terms with one another. In Douai and in every other town of northern France, each great family, each lineage, constituted a union "in law and in peace"; the word *Sippe*, still frequently used to denote large family groups, also meant peace and friendship.[34]

The first duty of clansmen was to settle their disputes rapidly, or to submit them to arbitration within the group itself. Very often we find here the same orders not to bear arms against one another or to insult, wound or even speak ill of one another, as we find in all the oaths or regulations of brotherhoods, guilds or hanses. All these societies for mutual aid and defence were originally organizations to keep the peace, internally. Here, the idea of common descent and the members' horror of spilling their common blood made the duty to keep the peace still more compelling.

The Corbolani clan were nobles from around Lucca; their statutes, drawn up in 1287, emphasize above all things and at great length their absolute obligation to maintain peace between the menfolk and, apparently as difficult, given the wording of the text, between the womenfolk of the *Casa*; there is no doubt that this was the main reason for the enactment of these statutes. All the men had to swear never to *alium alterum manumictere in persona, irato animo, nec ferire vel percutere, nec amenare ferro vel baculo*. Sons and daughters of more than sixteen years also took this oath. The principal duty of the consul, the governor of the *Casa*, was to prevent all discord and restore peace: anyone who offered insults was fined from five to ten sous by him; he had to *ad concordiam facere devenire* those who had fought. This internal peace, this protection of persons, honour and wealth, extended also to guests and clients: none of the members of the clan, none of their wives, might speak insulting words *aliqui inquilino, vel eius uxori, qui starent in domibus vel apothecis suprascriptorum consortum*.[35] Indeed, the statutes were merely the formalization, in writing, before a notary and by oath, of the more or less tacit rules by which the family group's concord, the protection of relatives and allies, and therefore respect for hospitality were assured.

Almost two centuries later, in Genoa, the clan's internal peace still seemed to be the goal to which all the rules of the *alberghi* led. On 17 September 1459 sixteen heads of families of the De Pinu *albergo* who lived in Castagnola, a hamlet on the mountain overlooking Levanto on the eastern Riviera, affirmed before their notary, in a fine and especially significant preamble that they considered that: "to preserve the unity of a line born of common ancestors it appears politic especially to ensure harmony between all its members, regarding their persons and their wealth; that they may, by common action, calm conflicts which may arise and avoid the suits and the expense occasioned very often, and for all, by enmity and affrays".[36] They wished "everyone to keep his *parentela* and house united by fraternal love, by every means and in every way". So they agreed to elect each year two governors "who may have, without restriction, power and authority to regulate and terminate disputes and controversies which might arise between those of the said house and name". These governors would give their judgements and would fine those who refused to respect them. The last provision was very important: it was absolutely forbidden, under pain of similar fines, to have recourse to any other magistrate.

In effect, the maintenance of internal peace was the responsibility of the clan itself, which declined any intervention from the state and more especially, in Italian towns, from the commune. Tradition had long demanded that family affairs be handled by the group's members. From the judicial and political point of view membership of a clan precluded membership of any other organized group, and especially of any group bound by oath. In 1287 the Corbolani forbade all their members *facere aliquam sectam, iuramentum, vel compagniam aut sacramentum aliquid cum aliqua persona vel loco.*[37] This was a very real prohibition: the *compagna*, in Italy, was often the first form of political organization, preceding the commune. Thus, originally, the members of a family clan refused to become part of another community.

For a very long time in the Italian towns, and even in Tuscany, which was more highly urbanized and apparently policed earlier than other regions, the commune could not assert its authority, its police system or its courts over these powerful social groups. In 1330, still, the *consorteria* of Ripafratta dispensed justice in its fiefs to its members through a *consul nobilium de Ripafratta eorumque fidelium*, established in the very city of Pisa.[38] Much later, in Genoa, the magistrates showed themselves unable to act against the kidnapping of Filippo Doria's two daughters, the heiresses to the fief of Sassello, by their two cousins Ceva and Batista Doria; these rejected the intervention of the commissioners entrusted with the enquiry and affirmed loudly, with harsh words, that the family affairs of the Doria concerned only the Doria.[39]

In Florence, in the fourteenth century, the authorities administered the law rigorously, and the nobles had to recognize the authority of the commune; but it was accepted that some slight offences were not punishable if they were committed inside the family; conversely, if strangers were involved, these acts were condemned.[40]

Family solidarity is encountered especially in the private wars which constantly troubled the peace of the cities. In those towns of the West which escaped the harsh oversight of a princely state, the struggles of the great noble families encouraged intestine quarrels and, very often, endless violence, veritable armed conflict. All the bourgeois chroniclers deplore this unending discord and upheaval. Giovanni Villani clearly accuses the *maledette parti* of the nobles of provoking in Florence a *si diversa e aspra guerra, che quasi ogni di, o di due di l'uno, si combatteano i cittadini insieme in più parti della città da vicinanza a vicinanza, com' erano le parti.*[41] Dino Compagni also holds the *nobili e grandi cittadini* responsible and Marchionne di Coppo Stefani blames *la discordia e l'ambizione . . . e la superbia de' grandi.*[42] In fact, the quarrels of the great drew all their clients and lesser relations into armed conflict, often with more fury than the masters themselves.

These conflicts might arise from all kinds of disputes: neighbours' disagreements over rights or property, attacks on one's honour, for example when marriages broke up. A treatise of domestic economy written in Sicily asserts that a good father must reserve a quarter of the revenues of his patrimony in order to deal with the conflicts and disputes which will not fail to assail his household.[43]

The most violent struggles obviously arose from the wish to avenge the dead or injured. Violent death always demanded compensation. Even accidents sometimes set two families against each other for many years. The Scholari killed a nephew of the leader of the Niccolini of Florence in a dispute about their hunting grounds, after their respective packs had clashed at a joint hunting party.[44]

The whole of medieval life was affected by the vendetta, especially in the cities up to at least the fifteenth century. It took root as a literary theme – an extraordinarily fertile source of inspiration which all authors exploited. First among these, with his strange vigour and his astonishing persistence, was Dante, and the theme was continued with the same richness, well beyond the 'medieval' period. Apart from this, the vendetta gave birth to special institutions, to a specific law, all linked to the practice or regulation of vengeance.

It was an act of deference and respect to the memory of a comrade to avenge his death; failing this, his memory and all his line remained sullied. Therefore it was an overriding duty for his descendants and friends. In Florence, tradition demanded that a man killed by the sword be buried with his wounds unwashed, so that his bloodstained corpse would inevitably attract the vengeance of his close relatives.[45] Death demanded vengeance even if there were no premeditated crime, but simply imprudence or ill-luck.

Normally the injured family sought to apply the law of retaliation, to attack in precisely the same way: the same wound, or mutilation of the same limb, in the same place and at the same time of day. This of course was aimed at complete erasure of the insult. Yet vengeance often went much further than the original offence: relatives killed in return for a simple wound. Vengeance could also be taken in strange ways; all opportunities seem to have been regarded as propitious, especially those which presented the least risk and made anonymity possible. Nothing here points to even the most rudimentary code of honour. Sometimes an avenger would wait for many years, so that his enemy would be more easily taken by surprise, less on his guard; in Florence, a Mamelli was killed by the Velluti twenty-eight years after his crime. The laws of the Seignory had to attempt to combat unworthy acts of vengeance; a regulation of 1321 dealt with those who attacked men sentenced and imprisoned by the commune; it forbade those *maleficia que committi consueverunt in carceribus Communis Florentie maxime contra bannitos*; another regulation prohibited the use of disguise in order to attack a man with impunity.[46] At other times those seeking 'justice' entrusted the deed to a paid mercenary. In his *Memorie* Luca di Dato da Prato notes the day on which he went to Pirato to kill one of his enemies; he details his expenses on that occasion: *Pagai al sicario per lo fatto che fece a Prato di che fu preso e smozzicato . . . per le spese fatte in camparlo delle forche . . . perfarlo guarire . . . Ebbe mozza la mano, cavato l'occhio, scopato e bollato.*[47]

Inevitably, vendettas caused private wars, for here the solidarity of family clans was fully involved on each side. When the wronged man was only wounded the right of vengeance belonged rather to him or to his heirs, but clan solidarity necessarily applied in the case of the protection of the wrongdoer, who could therefore count on the assistance of all the members of the *consorzio*. The statutes of the *Casa de' Corbolani* state unambiguously that if an affray broke out between one of the *consortes* and any person who was not a member of the clan, the clan must immediately inform the consul, who then called together the *consortes*.[48] Vengeance could be taken, not only on the guilty party, but also on another member of his family; this led to an extension of quarrels, involving progressively more friends and allies. The inevitable responses prolonged these conflicts and often, with the help of alliances, finally divided the city into two opposing factions.

This solidarity of lineage never faltered. It actively and dramatically involved many members of the clan, and it seems that it was more strongly and lastingly applied in the towns which governed themselves and were further from any prince's law. In Florence, in the 1290s, still, the members of the *consorti guelfi* all promised one another total assistance:

Che tutti noi comme che per adietro siamo stati parenti, vicini e amici d'uno medesimo animo . . . vogliamo che da quinci inanzi, per fortificare i sopradetti animi, promettere e giurare d'aiutare l'uno l'altro e favoregiare con cià che bisogno facesse comme fanno e debano fare i veri consorti d'un sangue.[49]

A century later Baldo, a doctor of law who taught in Perugia, Pisa and Florence, detailed the obligations of the members of a family, a family clan: *Omnes de casato offensoria sumunt arma – nam iniuria facta uni totam domum decolorat.*[50]

The group's total unity necessarily led to collective responsibility in the face of sanctions and reprisals. In all cases Florentine law held the whole family to be jointly guilty. After political prosecutions for treason or grave offence to the commune, or for corruption, magistrates did not fail to punish the guilty individuals severely, but they also banished their children and relatives. Punishments decreed against 'magnates', in the fourteenth century, were nearly always extended to all the members of their families. In 1380 after the murder, in Arezzo, of a Florentine ambassador by Tommasino de Panzano, all the murderer's *consorti* were immediately warned that if after one year he was still alive, they would be considered to be in rebellion against the commune.[51]

It is evident that the state attempted to break the cohesion of the clan and to prohibit relatives and allies from offering help or even refuge to a guilty fugitive;[52] but their solidarity was still very evident in Milan in 1451; through Francesco dela Capra, his commissioner, Francesco Sforza, at that time ruler of Genoa, addressed all the *gentiluomini* (the text is in Italian, not in Latin like those originating from specifically Genoese courts) of the Spinola di Luccoli *albergo*, and their *subditi* or *feudetarii* of the Valle Scrivia or the Valle Borbera; his message forbade them to help or to shelter Filippo Spinola di Luccoli or any other bandit allied to him; as an encouragement to traitors within the clan he offered a reward of 1,000 golden ducats.[53]

In Flanders too the *faide*, or private war, involved any lineage as a whole; in Douai, adversaries negotiating a truce would enlist the assistance of the greatest possible number of relatives and friends, who would all have taken part in the fighting.[54] The situation in Normandy was the same.[55]

The customs and documents of the Paris *Parlement* clearly show the cohesion of the lineage in all cases of private conflict or vengeance. It was the 'kindred friends' who instituted prosecutions in cases of misdemeanour or crime; in the fourteenth century, in Rheims, when a suspect was arrested, the officers of justice requested all the friends of the victim to bring an action against the prisoner; if none did, then the suspect was often acquitted; the family would be present at every stage of the procedure, and when the sentence had been carried out the injured family had to consent to the prisoner's release.

The towns of Flanders also accepted and applied the notion of collective responsibility; friends of a guilty fugitive could be arrested in his place. In 1364, in Tournai, forty-seven people came as guarantors of a friend, upon which they were imprisoned for seven weeks within the city gates. In the following year a rich burgess, Jacques Mouton, refused to appear in court and took refuge in a monastery: eighteen of his friends were incarcerated.[56] Letters of pardon were sought, not by the guilty party, the fugitive, but by a large number of 'kindred friends'; the king granted this pardon only if, for their part, the friends and relatives of the victim declared themselves to be content that "satisfaction was received by the plaintiffs".[57]

J.M. Turlan, after C. Petit-Dutaillis, gives a very significant example of the cohesion of the clan or alliance even among the common people: in the fifteenth century, in order to defend themselves against the armed bands which ravaged the countryside and threatened the towns, commoners enlisted the help of many armed relatives and friends.[58] In the 1250s, in Metz, 'letters of peace' drew a very nice distinction between those who were members of a *paraige* and could carry out their own private vengeance with the help of their friends, and those who were alone and did not have such help.[59]

In some regions of course, this cohesion did not necessarily involve the whole of a clan; nor did it drive all of a man's friends to avenge him. In French towns vendettas seem to have been more limited than in Italy. From the 1250s the obligation to give help applied only to relatives up to four times removed; this, at least, is the evidence of Beaumanoir and even of the law of Tournai;[60] but there is no indication of whether this limit was observed, or whether private vengeance did not drag more armed men into interminable conflicts. These two provisions show rather the wish of the state, be it kingdom, principality or municipality, to limit and subsequently to quell these private wars. In fact, even in northern France, the solidarity of the lineage remained very strong in the matter of quarrels and private conflict; the king's justice even took account of it.

Private quarrels and urban revolt

Private conflicts involved many dependants, relatives and allies of all kinds, of all ranks and of every level of wealth, in addition to their leaders; the importance of these conflicts may in large part explain the origins, if not the expansion and the persistence of great urban uprisings throughout the Middle Ages.

These revolts have primarily been studied only from a strictly economic point of view. Historians still generally provide only stereotyped analyses of them, which are absolutely sterile in terms of historical research. Up to very recently all authors invoked, and some still invoke, a materialist explanation, ordered according to a schema more or less directly inspired by pseudo- or neo-Marxism.[61] On this basis the reasons for revolts remained relatively simple: on the one hand misery, on the other hand the inevitable class struggle.

Whether they were angry outbursts of misery, rural *Jacqueries* or urban uprisings, 'medieval' revolts could obviously be explained by a very low standard of living among the less fortunate, the humble or poor, the exploited. Hence the temptation to link these revolts with economic 'crises' and to attempt to place them exactly, and to explain them with as precise a study as possible, even with graphs showing the economic situation. Here, social and political analysis relies on increasingly detailed statistics; this is also dangerous, or at least uncertain and weak in the conclusions drawn. In any case, a number of studies have well shown, especially in the case of the peasant uprisings of 1340–1390, that the insurgents were not at all miserable wretches reduced to famine and impelled by despair, but rather relatively well-off freemen, certainly with some property, who farmed their own lands, sometimes even with the help of paid employees.[62] The idea of surges of despair, in town or country, must be greatly modified.

Further, to link the idea of famine to that of revolt often leads us to ignore the true reaction of hungry people, which was not necessarily rage, but rather a great migration of souls, peaceful or aggressive, such as the extraordinary shepherds' crusades, or the processions of more or less heretical wanderers, at the end of the Middle Ages. These large movements of men, characterized at once by hunger and an exasperation with religion which bordered on collective hysteria, were more diffuse and are more difficult to define than revolts; chroniclers refer to them only intermittently, here and there; knowledge is very scanty. In any case, historians have not been greatly tempted by this subject, but have surrendered themselves more willingly to the idea of a revolt of the 'oppressed'; this, more than flight, more than refuge in another faith, corresponds to an ordinary, ready-made schema of social analysis. The hypothesis of hunger riots merely follows the path of conformity.

Another aspect of the 'Marxist' schema which still tempts most present-day writers is, to keep a very crude image, the struggle of the poor against the rich, the struggle between two socio-economic classes for the conquest or defence of political power and the means of production. This second analysis is scarcely more subtle than the first; its extreme artificiality and its desire to reduce all to a simple level are surprising. We now know that 'medieval' urban society was very mobile, very open, and also very ill-defined; it seems impossible to be exactly certain of the true political, judicial and economic situation, and even of individuals' actions; to assert that this society could be reduced to a fixed picture of the owners and the exploited, rich and poor, masters and workers, the great and the 'people', demonstrates an extraordinary lack of analysis and historical imagination. On the part of a researcher, this would be to limit himself voluntarily to an *a priori* idea which has only the merit of simplicity; it would be to surrender to an academic idleness – which is very cosy, but has serious consequences – before the problems of proper research, which alone might unravel the tangled and complex skein of men's conditions and fortunes. This totally simplistic viewpoint, wilfully or unconsciously inspired by those who look to a vague kind of Marxism, was and still is widely held with reference to at least two periods of urban history.

First of all, we must re-examine the famous 'communal movement' which occupies so much space in our school books and so captures our children's imagination (an obvious example is the bishop of Laon in his barrel). Communal emancipation is still thought to have been the result of violence; to have brought new men to power, merchants who formed a 'burgess class', divorced from the sway of the feudal lords. But we know that such an analysis, which it is not possible to discuss at length here, by no means corresponds to reality in any of the cities of the south: in Italy, Provence, Languedoc, Catalonia, where the commune was confirmed without clashes, where the noble aristocracy held at once landed property in towns, fiefs in the countryside, the means of commerce and political power. In northern and central Italy urban riots did not bring a new 'social class' to power; these riots arose, not from 'class' conflict, but rather from internal opposition to the aristocracy on the part of the merchant-nobles who had the same interests in common; they were sometimes worsened by religious conflicts, especially after the Investiture Contest. In fact these religious quarrels often concealed simple age-old opposition between family factions. In all these conflicts the allies, relatives and *amis* of the most powerful clans confronted each other; these were the mainstays of all political life in Italian towns in the so-called 'communal' period, up to the creation of the *podestà*, a stranger, judge and peace-maker.[63]

Even in the north, especially in France, real communal revolts were not very common. In any case, a number of recent studies have cast doubt on the originality of the 'burgess class'; the men who established the communes were by no means newcomers who lacked roots in the soil, landed property and fiefs. On the contrary, in several cities, as for example in Metz, the first aristocrats were important landowners in the country and in the town, where "the development of urban land was one of the sources of burgesses' wealth".[64]

The earliest aristocrats in these cities of north-western Europe, rich and influential men, built their fortunes through lay or ecclesiastical office. They were the *ministeriales.* F. Vercauteren showed this clearly in the case of another imperial city – Liège.[65] The situation was the same in Rouen in the eleventh century, when, according to L. Musset's very detailed study, the real moneyed aristocracy was born, not in the merchant world but "in the ducal entourage and in the shadow of the Church"; these men who amassed money and possessions, assembled large landed patrimonies and lived in stone houses, were originally book-keepers, ducal almoners, episcopal treasurers.[66] This was also the case in Rheims, where the origins of the urban aristocracy were decidedly ministerial.[67]

In his study of the origins of the Metz aristocracy J. Schneider shows firstly that these 'burgesses', these 'patricians', came from very varied social circles; but his very detailed analysis demonstrates clearly that the richest and most powerful of the *majores urbi,* for example the mayors of all three quarters and the senior echevin, almost always belonged to the episcopal *familia*;[68] the same author also describes, in the same era, the twelfth century, a certain number of knightly families solidly established in the city.[69]

It is therefore difficult to conclude that there were two different aristocracies, the 'feudal' and that of money and commerce; it would certainly be illusory to see in the opposition between them the origins of the communal movement. It would be more rewarding to seek deep-seated enmity between factions and families as the root of many urban disturbances, riots and acts of violence. The famous commune of Le Mans, which is normally presented as typical of a 'burgess' uprising, asserted itself with the help of a strongly-fought struggle between two dynastic factions which contested the succession of the county in 1070. In Rouen, from the 1090s, peace was particularly disturbed by the harsh conflict between two parties of townsmen: the *Pilatenses* and the *Calloenses*;[70] there is nothing to indicate any sort of social opposition between these parties – quite the contrary; these were struggles of political factions, each side bearing the name of its leader. And in Metz, the whole political rise of the 'patriciate', the 'burgesses', is summed up in the entrenchment of office holders who gradually freed themselves from episcopal oversight. These men were already aristocrats, members of the bishop's *familia*; they freed themselves, as in many other western cities, without violence. Later, as in Italy, conflicts arose at the time of the Investiture Contest, which gave some men the opportunity to assert themselves. The political rise of the Metz 'patriciate' was also achieved through alliances and the formation of factions. At first the burgesses had the support of the cathedral chapter against the bishop and the priests of the outer parts of the city in setting up fairs;[71] later, the document of 1214 which contained the first official mention of the existence of family clans, of the *paraiges*, was in fact only a pact of alliance between Duke Thiébaut I of Lorraine and two of these groups (those from Porte Moselle and Outre Seille) against a third group from Port Sailly, who were defeated and, for the most part, exiled.[72]

The schema of the class struggle is more often applied to the study, or rather to the description, of other urban revolts at the end of the Middle Ages, especially between 1360 and 1440. These revolts are habitually known as 'popular'; this epithet, for which we are indebted to nineteenth-century historians, contains a serious ambiguity, which since that time has been more or less consciously preserved. In fact the word 'popular' obviously implies for us the idea of a struggle of the oppressed, or at least of the 'people', in the modern sense of the word; but in fact the risings and governments of the 'people' in the medieval sense, especially in the Italian cities, concerned only the *popolo*, that is, the masters of guilds, and therefore to some extent an already well-established aristocratic body.

The classic picture which we are generally offered of urban revolt in Flanders, Paris and Rouen, and in all the Italian towns, is basically that of conflict between, on the one hand unimportant men, especially journeymen of guilds, weavers, fullers, dyers, and on the other hand the masters, important merchants and captains of industry, who controlled the municipal offices. This analysis should be examined critically.

It is true that in the 'troubles', and in riots of all kinds which disturbed or sometimes (although rarely) blooded the city, men of modest or wretched condition took to the streets and fought; these, in fact, were workmen, clerks, recent immigrants, outcasts, who were not well integrated into the urban community, all kinds of men who had often been relegated to the outlying parts of the city, outside the gates. It therefore seems certain that the rich were well aware of the social danger which these masses presented, whether they were hard-working or idle parasites, because they were always on the border of poverty or misery, or even of starvation. These people all seem to have been easily swayed by the kind of sermon which preached a messianic or egalitarian message.

There is also no doubt that these poor people, more than others, felt the harsh effects of bad harvests and the expense of food, of industrial unemployment and of what some have rather vaguely termed economic 'crises'. There is no question of denying either the extreme inequality of conditions and wealth, or economic misery, or the consequences of fluctuations in harvests and employment.

So in large cities at least, there was a mass of workers and unemployed who were easily mobilized; when trouble broke out they often threw themselves into the attack on public and private wealth. But this by no means implies that this mass was responsible for riots, or provoked them. Nor is it at all certain that they were impelled by class feeling or that they followed leaders who were conscious of this; it is by no means certain, indeed, that the true origins of these conflicts are to be found in any kind of class confrontation.

There is a serious lack of detailed and scholarly studies on this subject; with rare exceptions, these urban revolts are known solely through the accounts of chroniclers, who were interested in the exterior, dramatic aspect of any incident. We have no information on the identity, and therefore on the condition, of the rebels and their supporters and it seems difficult to trace this, even by extensive research; but we might at least reflect on the personalities of the leaders. It is curious that writers have not given greater attention to the fact that the leaders very often belonged to the urban aristocracy of commerce or the guilds; for example, Étienne Marcel in Paris, the van Arteveldes in Ghent, the Paris butchers in the Cabochien revolt, Salvestro de' Medici in Florence in the Ciompi revolution. How can we reconcile this simple observation with the simplistic schema of class conflict?

The explanation is to be found elsewhere, largely in the struggles of different factions. As far as the Ciompi are concerned, this has, I believe, been decisively demonstrated.[73] G.A. Brucker totally rejects Rodolico's views[74] as well as those of Rutenburg,[75] which E. Werner has more recently adopted,[76] which speak of the class struggle provoked by the hypothetical development of the small *botega* into a large capitalist enterprise. In his careful study of the situation of the Ciompi, which was based on individual records such as notaries' acts, which had not previously been examined from this point of view, G.A. Brucker has shown that the insurgents were by no means ordinary workmen, but were themselves small employers, dyers, carders, washers of wool and cloth, who had their own small wealth; some had invested more than 1,000 florins in the public debt, the *Monte.* These men, who had come to power at the time of the *Balia* government, were politically very conservative and devoted their energies to the suppression of disorders; they claimed no programme of economic, social or political revolution.

Apart from these points which he has developed in a masterly fashion, G.A. Brucker indicates above all that the real leaders and instigators of the riots were aristocrats: Salvestro de' Medici is the best known, but there were also Benedetto Alberti, Tommaso Strozzi, Giorgio Scali and Giovanni Dini, who probably had most followers, and were most effective and eager in their struggle for power. These men were hostile to the movement for peace which reigned in Florence; they attempted to impose their own politics by force. They had at their disposal the help of all their relatives, who followed varying professions, sometimes very modest ones: in the Santa Croce quarter several dyers bore the great family name of Busini; one Giovanni di Neri Pitti plied the very modest trade of cloth stretcher; in 1378 four Busini, three Antellesi and three Cafferelli were registered among the members of the *popolo minuto*, which benefited for a time from political reorganization. Moreover, they had hatched all kinds of plots and had gathered a dependency of shopkeepers, artisans and workmen, in the town and in the country.

The Ciompi 'revolution' was born of a struggle between different factions of aristocrats, of the desire to pursue a vendetta and to avenge exiles. These aims, this approach, were strongly maintained throughout the affair: Benedetto Alberti and Tommaso Strozzi dominated the Ciompi *balia*; later, at the end of August 1378, hundreds of workers marched behind Lucà da Panzano, an adventurer from a great family, then accepted as their leaders three other very powerful magnates, among them Anibaldo Strozzi; finally, in August 1379, after their defeat, the exiled Ciompi joined aristocratic magnates and rich merchants such as Benedetto Peruzzi, Antonio da Uzzano and Piero Canigiani. Petitions presented at the end of July and in August 1379 reveal no ideological aspiration; they were requests for benefices on behalf of named persons, and for sanctions against other persons; briefly, compensation, vengeance, and the settlement of scores.

All this precise information allows G.A. Brucker to aver strongly in conclusion that this revolt was "a characteristic Florentine imbroglio", marked as much by personal hate and fidelity as by any hypothetical class consciousness. From this point of view the development of industry could only introduce new elements, especially through the presence of more and more workers who had recently moved to the city; it thus gave events a further dimension. But in Florence the deep-seated nature of the revolts did not change; these conflicts certainly still related to the traditional struggles between factions, each supported by its dependency of lesser men.

It is unfortunate that serious research of this type, that is, research undertaken without prejudice, using authentic source material, has not been undertaken with reference to other cities.[77] Without any doubt, it would enable us to replace the very simplistic attitude which, let us not forget, is still almost universally accepted; such research would enable us finally to sketch a history of urban disturbances in the Middle Ages which has never really been written.

It should however be noted that some writers, free of the shackles of others' hypotheses, have felt, despite the lack of very detailed studies, the true complexity of these urban disturbances. P. Dollinger, referring to the Hanse towns, says distinctly that "we cannot speak of revolts by the poor against the rich, or even of clear-cut opposition between the patriciate and the guilds". In 1391, in Stralsund, part of the 'patriciate' had caused the guilds, which were themselves led by Karsten Sarnow, a very rich merchant, to overthrow the tyranny of the Wulflam, the all-powerful lineage of the city.[78] Here, so far from Florence, we find a real struggle between rival factions.

Peace movements, state intervention and the clans

City authorities were long unable to forbid these conflicts of factions, despite their harsh attitudes and, sometimes, prohibitive ordinances; they simply attempted to re-establish peace between opposing sides. In Tuscany they appointed special magistrates, *pacieri*, who sought to make the belligerents accept arbitration. The public interest was so threatened by great family quarrels that in 1290 Florence devoted a large sum to cover the expense of establishing peace between the Lamberti and the Della Tosa.[79] In Flanders the echevins were initially involved in regulations of this kind, but private wars became so common that it became necessary to establish a special jurisdiction, that of the *Paiseurs* or *Paismakers*, who were installed in numerous towns in Flanders, Brabant and Hainault, for example in Ypres, Douai, Brussels and Valenciennes.[80]

Truces took on their full reality with the consent of all relatives and *amis*. In fact peace was often established between two lineages, at least in Italy, only after much haggling and bargaining, with a precise contract, signed and sealed before a notary. In such cases the affair took on the appearance of the settlement of a commercial dispute. Firstly the two sides appointed procurators,[81] who could seek the opinions of independent arbitrators and draw up the foundations of an agreement. This was then duly registered and ratified by all the members of the lineage, or by the greatest possible number of members. These official contracts are still often found, sometimes several per year, in the records of Florentine notaries.[82]

If a man guilty of murder were to ask a pardon of the injured family, all his relatives would accompany him. In Saint-Omer, when the Zoene family obtained peace from their opponents over the blood which had been spilt by one of their number, they all had to go up the nave of the church under the eyes of the assembled throng, in a greater or lesser state of undress depending on their degree of relationship; it was indeed a collective humiliation, their surrender to the mercy of their enemies: the guilty man gave up his naked sword to the head of the other family, who awaited him in the chancel.[83]

In these cases, where the forgiveness of offences was so loudly proclaimed, peace was quantified in substantial financial settlements.[84] These transactions depended primarily on the amount of compensation claimed by the victim's clan; a vendetta might be turned to excellent account if the clan were sufficiently populous and powerful. This again shows the importance of keeping the lineage's solidarity very strong, and of embracing many other allies and dependents. On the other side the same cohesion was obvious in the collection of money for compensation. J.M. Turlan has shown the extent to which the financial help of relatives and *amis* was necessary in northern regions; on this subject he cites two very significant texts. On the one hand there was a chancery document of the fourteenth century entitled *De la finance des amis*, which thus bears witness to a practice which was very normal at that time and shows clearly that to this finance the 'kindred friends' *contribuere teneantur, quilibet pro rata sua.*[85] On the other hand there was the *Livre Roisin* which showed the exact portion owed, in Lille, by each relative up to the third remove.[86]

Such financial considerations are of course no strangers to the search for peace. Often, too, clans found these reconciliations to be opportunities for new alliances, thanks to marriages which forged mutual links and brought obvious advantages to all. Speaking of the origins of his family, Lapo di Giovanni Niccolini recalls that the serious conflict between them and the Scholari ended in "peace through marriage". Ruzza Niccolini had first provoked *da sùa parte e de' suoi consorti* the members of the opposing *casa*; then, with all his relatives, he met them in the field, the clans drawn up on respective sides of a small river. *E tanto si fè che si tratto la pacie, e Nicoholino . . . gharzonetto, il Ruzza suo padre, gli diè per moglie la serochia . . . degli Scholari che fu morto, e faciesi la pacie cho' loro.* Lapo obviously considers that this marriage *per pacie* had contributed to his house's fortunes.[87] The anonymous writer of Pavia says, for his part, that fathers married their daughters to members of other noble families, and sometimes to enemies, to make peace.[88] Marriage also made it possible to reinforce or renew links between two branches from the same stock which had become strangers or even enemies; in 1303, in Siena, Ciampoli Gallerani married his daughter Buida to Bonsignore, the son of Orlando Bonsinori, *pro concordia inter consanguineos stabilianda.*[89]

There is no doubt that peace between lineages was encouraged or even caused, especially from the 1300s, by a powerful religious movement which demanded the end of all conflict in the name of Christian charity, of the forgiveness of offences and of the common good. Bonaccorso Pitti congratulates himself on the great religious reawakening of Italy in 1309, saying that discord is more easily calmed: *. . . è termino bene, pero che molte paci se ne feciono.*[90]

Originally at one with the established Church and under its authority, this religious revival often led to the formation of assemblies for peace, probably initiated, in the case of France, by the Council of Charroux in 989. This movement, encouraged by the Council of Bourges in 1038, involved spectacular meetings around holy graves and relics, first in Aquitaine, then, according to Raoul Glaber who describes this magnificently, in the whole of France.[91] Later, sometimes outside the Church, more or less stable assemblies were formed which united men wishing to observe and to impose a very precise, very severe, oath of peace.

These social and religious groups unified all those who were exasperated by the insecurity of those troubled times, by the extortions of the robber-barons and especially by the struggles of factions in the cities. Little is known about these groups, which were often spontaneously formed, except in the case of the Languedoc peace movements, the model for which seems to have been the very famous Brotherhood of Peace which arose in Le Puy in 1183 after the miraculous apparition of the Virgin to a poor carpenter.[92] These brotherhoods or assemblies appointed guardians of the peace, *paciarii*, and then levied regular taxes to administer them; they remained in existence for centuries, organizing themselves increasingly, and finally took in hand all the interests of the city, so as to become the first consuls of the commune, or consulates.[93] There were Brotherhoods of Peace in Nîmes in 1207 and in Avignon in 1215. In Marseilles the Brotherhood of Peace of the Holy Spirit, which began in 1189 as an association of charity and devotion, became dominated by the merchants, and in 1216 took in hand the administration of the city.[94]

At the local level these brotherhoods were also the first representative assemblies; at first they were councils of priests, provosts and archdeacons of the diocese, then of lay barons and even, in the Gévaudan region, of burgesses and villagers; they were convened by the bishops of Mende, Le Puy and Viviers, and they administered finances and the hearth tax; up to about 1260 they still retained important judicial powers.[95] This was especially the case in mountainous regions where urban development took place later and was less universal than in the large traditional centres of town life and in the mainstreams of trade: in upper Languedoc and even, although less certainly, in Rouergue and Quercy, and around Albi and Agen. Elsewhere, in the plains and valleys, in lower Languedoc and in Provence, the aristocratic consulate-communes, led by the very great families, also suffered the onslaughts or the influence of these peace movements, which bore significant names and had serious effects upon the political destinies of various cities.

In the south of France, then, Brotherhoods of Peace were either the beginnings of the original forms of urban administration and even of some forms of regional representative assemblies, especially within the framework of the diocese, or else asserted themselves at certain times in the political evolution of large cities. This emphasizes sufficiently the role of the myth of harmony and peace, linked to the idea of order and the common good, in opposition to the disturbances and private wars for which the great noble lineages are normally held responsible. To a certain extent the commune, which developed from a movement for peace, seems by its very nature to have been opposed to the clans, which through their vendettas and armed conflicts between different factions maintained disturbances and private wars. One of the commune's principal tasks was to avoid or to quell these conflicts.

The same wish for harmony asserted itself as strongly in other countries of the West; in cities other than in Italy it was the veritable leaven of many institutions thought of as communal or pre-communal. The first article of the charter of the Brotherhood of the Halle Basse in Valenciennes, the first urban movement, gives decisive proof of this:

Au nom de la sainte et individue Trinité, de sainte Marie, saint Nicolai et de tous les sains, Nous, très-amet Frère, avons voet a nostre Seigneur ensemble awarden le loyen de dilecion, pour coi besoing soroit que . . ., entre nous au mains ire ne estinchelle se discorde nullement aièche vigueur; car, dit li Psalmiste . . ..[96]

In any event, alongside these social and political groups, to which destiny often promised good fortune, the Christian ideal of peace was also asserted – later, at the time when the great popular religious movements so struck men's imagination with some of their more spectacular aspects: sermons, processions and chastisement, even flagellation. The famous Bianchi pilgrimages of the summer and autumn of 1399 thronged the roads of all north and central Italy with long processions of barefooted penitents, dressed simply in white – thousands of people who stopped to pray in chapels and oratories, preaching harmony to all. In Prato, the town was still counting the victims of the plague:

Una parte della città ando di fuori, vicitando le chastella d'intorno insino di lunge 40 milia e faceiano molte pacie . . ..
In verità, ch'è tuoi pratesi tornarono a chasa col magiore onore che brighata che ci sia

uscita. Eglino aveano une divoto crocifisso innanzi. Ragionata che feciono tanto pacie, che l'arme che fue loro conata – chi ispada, chi chotello et chi pianella – no' ll' arebe portate 2 muli.[97]

To discard arms and establish peace, that and penitence was the way to expiate the sins which had brought down the wrath of God in the plague.

We should also not forget the equally spectacular activities of those inspired tribunes, the great preachers. The idea of peace was ever in the forefront of sermons, being intimately connected with the ideal of Christian purity, whereas discord was harried as a vice. Examples are St Bernardino of Siena and later, although rather differently, Savonarola himself. Thus these more or less spontaneous revolts against vendettas and private wars almost always took on a Christian and 'popular' aspect. In fact it was commonplace in all these sermons and the popular movements to accuse nobles, magnates and the powerful of fostering wars which harmed the whole city; this "in their simple family quarrels, through their pride in their line". Any member of a clan could provoke a vendetta; often, as in Shakespeare's *Romeo and Juliet*, conflicts arose and grew from servants' quarrels, and the *popolani* families caused as many wars as the others, the families of more ancient origins; so what is really our concern is not the real or imagined 'nobility' of families, or their wealth, but the social structure itself, the very existence of family clans which the state – prince or municipality – could not overthrow. It was the main source of conflicts between factions.

In Italy the state forbade vendettas, in which the princes or magistrates of a city clearly saw a striking manifestation of the cohesion and power of family clans. The struggle against private wars was one of the most spectacular aspects of the attack on the clans. Shakespeare represented this policy admirably when he showed the ruler of Verona furiously trying to preserve the peace and prevent any armed conflict, but at the cost of terrible regulations. The communes of Italy increased their prohibitions and sanctions; sometimes they even took harsh action. In Florence between 1330 and 1340 seventy-two families were said to belong to the magnates; forty-six of these were convicted of gravely infringing the communal laws; they were said to have committed an average of four crimes each, ranging from murder to 'treason'.[98]

Yet despite all these efforts it is remarkable that in those very towns which provided themselves with powerful political institutions whose bases were 'popular' and professional, private wars still continued for a long time, often up to the last years of the Quattrocento and sometimes beyond. This was the case in Florence, where private wars continued their ravages despite the activities of the Seignory; Graziani gives an account of a particularly horrible vendetta in 1437, and refers to another in 1449.[99] In his *Domestic chronicle* G. Bianchi also mentions several bloody battles between *casati*; one in 1446 and another, very late, in 1497.[100]

In northern France, Flanders, Hainault and the county of Namur, the private wars which were common in the thirteenth century were still spilling blood in every city two centuries later.[101] So the permanence of private war and vendetta provides ample evidence of the existence of the family clan, whatever its name might be, and of its cohesion, whatever the cities' political institutions might be.

Notes

[1]Bernardo, *Chronache forliesi*, ii, 150, quoted by Tamassia, N., in *La famiglia*, 118.

[2]*Matthaei Parisiensis monachi Sancti Albani, Chronica Majora*, ed. Luard, H. R., in *Rerum Britannicarum Medii Aevi Scriptores* (Rolls Series), 57, iii, 1876, a. 1236, quoted by Tamassia, N., *L'affratellamento*, Rome, Turin, Florence, 1886, 13.

[3]Quoted by Tamassia, N., *L'affratellamento*, 14–15.

[4]*Itinéraire d'Anselme Adorno en Terre Sainte*, Lille, Bibliothèque Municipale, MS. 330, p. 5 a.

[5]Quoted by Hyde, J.K., in "Italian social chronicles in the Middle Ages", in *Bulletin of the John Rylands Library*, xliv(1), 1966–1967, 107–132. The manuscript is in Padua, Biblioteca Civica, San Daniele dei Friuli, MS. 204; another copy is in the Seminario Vescovile, Padua, cof. 11.

[6]Carpentier, E., *Une ville*, 67.

[7]Émigré families evidently retained their original names as a sign of their descent from that stock: see Hughes, D.O., "Antonio Pessagno, merchant of Genoa", unpublished Ph.D. thesis, Yale University, 1967. Villani asserts in *Cronica*, iii, appendix, that three brothers of the noble Tuscan family of Gherardini, who emigrated around 1300 to England, were the originators of three great families which retained the name Fitz-Gerald; in 1413 an English priest of this *casato* who passed through Florence was, according to Villani, treated as a relative by the Gherardini.

[8]It was also a matter of convenience: in a vast clan of recent formation there were many men who bore the same Christian name; their fathers' Christian names did not always provide sufficient distinction, so it was better to indicate the family of origin.

[9]*A.S.G.*, Notaio Oberto Foflietta, filza 6, no. 233, 25 April 1460. The Salvatici, with nineteen named heads of families, admitted Domenico Scotto.

[10]*A.S.G.*, Notaio Oberto Foflietta, filza 6, no. 61, 3 April 1460. The De Nigro, with twenty named heads of families, admitted Lucà Saliceto.

[11]Bec, C., *Il libro*, f. 1 v° (p. 56).

[12]Bellomo, M., *Ricerche sui rapporti patrimoniali tra coniugi. Contributo alla storia della famiglia medievale*, Milan, 1961, 2–8.

[13]Bellomo, M., *Ricerche*, 7–8: *ea lege ut de hac donatione non pervenia* (sic) *uxori tue neque uxoribus tuorum descendentium et ita adimpleas et observes omnia pacta et conventiones inita inter socios huius turris*; there are similar examples for 1180 and 1181.

[14]Compare *Lancelot of the lake*, iii, 244: "The Black Knight put on the same arms as his new companion"; this and other examples quoted by Tamassia, N., in *L'affratellamento*, 14.

[15]Anonymi Ticinensis, *R.R.I.S.S*, xi, 1, p. 31.

[16]*A.S.G.*, Notaio Oberto Foflietta, filza 6, no. 233, 25 April 1460.

[17]*A.S.G.*, Notaio Oberto Foflietta, filza 6, no. 61, 3 April 1460.

[18]Published by Ascheri, A., in *Notizie*, 74.

[19]Cellini, B., *La vita scritta da lui medesimo*, Florence, 1891, i, 50; quoted by Tamassia, N., in *La famiglia*, 115.

[20]Tamassia, N., *La famiglia*, 119.

[21]Petrucci, A., *Il libro*, 73.

[22]*A.S.G.*, Notaio Cristoforo de Rapallo, senior, filza for 1452, no. 376.

[23]Volpicella, L., *Genova nel secolo XV; note d'iconografia panoramica. Atti della società ligure di storia patria*, 1924.

[24]Cessi, R., *Deliberazioni*, ii, 212; quoted by Cracco, G., in *Società e stato nel medioevo veneziano*, Florence, 1967, 232, note 1.

[25]Brattö, O., *Liber estimationum*, 28.

[26]Paris, Bibliothèque Nationale, MS. Latin 10136, f. 109 v°.

[27]Taken from the records of *Riformagioni*, no. 135, f. 48–48 v°, Archivio di Stato, Orvieto, published by Glénisson, J., Day, J. and Grandmottet, O., in *Textes et documents d'histoire du Moyen Age*, Paris, 1970, i, pp. xviii–xx.

[28]Petrucci, A., *Il libro*, 63.

[29]Enriques, A. M., in *A.S.I*, 1933, 128.

[30]Lazzarini, V., "Aneddoti della congiura Quirini-Tiepolo", in *Nuovo archivio veneto*, ix, 1895, 81–91.

[31]Ledieu, A., "Abattis de maisons à Abbeville au XIVe siècle", in *B.P.H.*, 1901, 467–472; Delcour, A., "La vengeance de la commune", in *L'arsin et l'abattis de maison en Flandre*, Lille, 1930; quoted by Glénisson, Day and Grandmottet, *Textes*, xxviii.

[32]Warburg, A., "Francescos Sassettis letztwillige Verfügung", in *Gesammelte Schriften*, Leipzig, 1932, i (127–150, 353–365), 140–141.

[33]Berengo, M., *Nobili e mercanti*, 33.

[34]Espinas, G., in *R.H.D.F.E.*, 1899, 416.

[35]Bongi, S., in *A.R.A.L.S.L.A.*, 1886, 477f.

[36]*A.S.G.*, Notaio Oberto Foglietta, junior, filza 5 (2), no. 199.

[37]Bongi, S., in *A.R.A.L.S.L.A.*, 1886, 478; unless, of course, four-fifths of the *consortes* agreed.

[38]Cristiani, E., *Nobiltà e popolo*, 127, note 171.

[39]Salvi, G., "Il ratto di Bianchinetta Doria", in *Giornale storico e letterario della Liguria*, 1930: *Bene! vogliammo vedere se delle cose nostre faremo a capriccio vostro ...; ora vedremo chi se intremetterei nelle cose nostre ...; vi ha una turba di stolti che vogliano parlare, ora vedremo se chiuderemo loro la bocca e se delle cose nostre disparemo a nostro talento.*

[40]Quoted by Enriques, A.M., in *A.S.I.*, 1933, 127.

[41]Villani, Giovanni, *Cronica*, Florence, 1823, v, 9; quoted by Stahl, B., in *Adel und Volk im florentiner Dugento*, Cologne, Graz, 1965, 76–77. In *Cronica* ii, 5ff., Villani gives a long list of families who opposed each other in 1292, *in tanto brighe e discordie*: Adimari and Tosinghi, Rossi and Tornaquinci, etc.

[42]Dino Compagni, "Cronica delle cose occorenti ne'tempi suoi a cura di Isidoro del Lungo", in *R.R.I.S.S.*, 1913, iv, 11; Marchionne di Coppo Stefani, "Istoria Fiorentina", ed. I. di San Luigi, in *R.R.I.S.S.*, 1903, ii, 196, quoted by Stahl, B., in *Adel und Volk*, 76.

[43]Giuffredi, *Avvertimenti cristiani, Documenti per servire alla storia di Sicilia*, Series IV, V, Palermo, 1896, quoted by Tamassia, N., in *La famiglia*, 18.

[44]Bec, C., *Il libro*, 56.

[45]Bargellini, P., "La vita notturna", in *Vita privata a Firenze nei secoli XIV e XV*, Florence, 1965 (75–90), 84; Throughout this article, which is often very interesting, the writer gives neither notes nor precise bibliographical references.

[46]Enriques, A.M., in *A.S.I.*, 1933, 91f.

[47]Luca di Dato da Prato, "Memorie", in *Giornale degli studi archivi toscani*, v, 62, quoted by Tamassia, N., in *La famiglia*, 62, 67.

[48]Bongi, S., in *A.R.A.L.S.L.A.*, 1886, 480.

[49]Del Lungo, I., "Una vendetta in Firenze il giorno di San Giovanni 1295", in *A.S.I.*, Series IV, xviii, 367f.; quoted by Tamassia, N., in *La famiglia*, 107.

[50]Quoted by Tamassia, N., in *La famiglia*, 61.

[51]Enriques, A.M., in *A.S.I.*, 1933, 132.

[52]Cecchetti, B., "La vita veneziana nel 1300", in *Archivio veneto*, 1884, refers to those who, in Venice itself, were accused of crimes and lived in the palaces of the noble.

[53]*A.S.G.*, Politicorum filse, no. 2 (no. gener. 1648), no. 6, 11 December 1451.

[54]Espinas, G., in *R.H.D.F.E.*, 1899, 435.

[55]Yver, J., "La solidarité familiale en matière criminelle dans l'ancien droit normand", in *Normannia*, 1934, 195–215.

[56]Turlan, J.M., in *R.H.D.F.E.*, 1969, 686–687.

[57]On all this, see Turlan, J.M., in *R.H.D.F.E.*, 1969, 687, 690, 691, 692.

[58]Petit-Dutaillis, C., *Documents nouveaux sur le droit de vengeance dans les Pays-Bas au XVe siècle*, 1908, quoted by Turlan, J.M., in *R.H.D.F.E.*, 1969, 682.

[59]Schneider, J., *La ville de Metz*, 117–118.

[60]Turlan, J.M., in *R.H.D.F.E.*, 1969, 682.

[61]Among synthesizing studies the only exception is the recent book by G. Fourquin, who breaks firmly with this facile tradition and shows clearly that every uprising is not necessarily 'revolutionary'; that, on the contrary, individuals were questioned much more than institutions; that the origins of popular uprisings must be sought in greatly varying areas and that 'vertical' solidarity often played as important, if not more important a role than 'horizontal' solidarity. Fourquin, G., *Les soulèvements populaires au Moyen Age*, Paris, 1972, and Martines, L., *Violence and civil disorder in Italian cities, 1200–1500*, Berkeley, Los Angeles and London, 1972, provide interesting analyses of several urban uprisings.

[62]For the *Jacquerie* of the Paris region see Fourquin, G., *Les campagnes de la région parisienne à la fin du Moyen Age*, Paris, 1964, 229ff.

[63]Moresco, M., "Parentele e guerre civili in Genova nel secolo XII", in *Scritti giuridici in onore di Santi Romani*, Padua, 1940.

[64]Schneider, J., *La ville de Metz*, 91–93.

[65]Vercauteren, F., *Les luttes sociales à Liège*, Brussels, 1943.

[66]Musset, L., "A-t-il existé en Normandie au XIe siècle une aristocratie de l'argent?", in *Annales de Normandie*, 1959, 285–299.

[67]This information was kindly provided by P. Desportes, who is completing an important study of the town of Rheims in the Middle Ages.

[68]Schneider, J., *La ville de Metz*, 88–93.

[69]Schneider, *Metz*, 342–343. See also the conclusions of E. Bournazel (unpublished thesis in Law, Paris, 1974), who shows that in Paris in the eleventh century the counsellors of the king, small nobles, were allied in business to money-lenders and lived close to the bridge.

[70]Deck, S., "Les marchands de Rouen sous les ducs", in *Annales de Normandie*, 1956, 245–254.

[71]Schneider, J., *La ville de Metz*, 71–76.

[72]Schneider, *Metz*, 120.

[73]Brucker, G. A., in Rubinstein, N., *Florentine studies.*

[74]Rodolico, N., "Il popolo minuto e il tumulto dei Ciompi", in *Saggi di storia medievale e moderna*, Florence, 1963, 102–121.

[75]Rutenburg, V., "La vie et la mort des Ciompi de Sienne", in *Annales E.S.C.*, 1965, 95–109; "Ciompi and zealots" (in Russian), in *Visantijskij Vremennik*, xxx, 1969, 3–37.

[76]Werner, E., *Städtische Volksbewegungen im 14. Jahrhundert*, Berlin, 1960.

[77]But see Bowsky, W.M., "The anatomy of rebellion in XIVth century Siena: from Commune to Signory", in Martines, L. (ed.), *Violence and civil disorder in Italian cities 1200–1500*, University of California Press, 1972, 229–272, and Fédou, R., "Le cycle médiéval des révoltes lyonnaises", in *Cahiers d'histoire*, 1973, 233–247.

[78]Dollinger, P., *The German Hansa*, 138–139.

[79]Enriques, A.M., in *A.S.I.*, 1933, 124. See also Bowsky, W.M., "The medieval commune and internal violence: police, power and public safety in Siena, 1287–1355", in *American Historical Review*, 1967, 1–17.

[80]Espinas, G., in *R.H.D.F.E.*, 1899, 422–423; there are many bibliographical references.

[81]In Genoa the *alberghi* also appointed procurators in conflicts over property as well as individuals; for example, in 1464, between the Di Nigro and Di Mari *alberghi* (*A.S.G.*, Notaio Tommaso Duracino filza 7 (2), no. 15, 11 January 1464). In 1449 the four *alberghi* of Di Marinis, Lomellini, Di Mari and Pansani appointed two procurators to settle a quarrel between them and the Grimaldi, *olim Ceba*, over a chapel in the church of San Pietro in Banchi (*A.S.G.*, Notaio Risso Baromeo, filza 1 (2), no. 63).

[82]Enriques, A.M., in *A.S.I.*, 1933, 95; among others the author quotes *A.S.F.*, Notarile, A. 981, Attaviano di Chiaro, i, c. 25; iii, c. 25; C. 102, Johannes Berghi de Cartapecchis, cc. 64, 76, 82. For a detailed study see also Cecchini, G., "La pacificazione fra Tolomei e Salimbeni", in *Quaderni dell'Accademia Chigiana*, ii, Siena, 1942.

[83]Van Kempen, *De la composition pécuniaire pour homicide d'après la loi salique, son maintien dans les coutumiers de Saint-Omer jusqu'à la fin du XVIe siècle*, Dijon, 1902, 112.

[84]Van Kempen, *De la composition*, 115–120 and *passim*.

[85]Paris, Bib. Nat., MS. Latin 4763, f. 47, quoted by Turlan, J.M., in *R.H.D.F.E.*, 1969, 684.

[86]*Livre Roisin*, 106–107, quoted by Petit-Dutaillis, C., in *Documents nouveaux* and by Turlan, J.M., in *R.H.D.F.E.*, 1969, 578.

[87]Bec, C., *Il libro*, 57; on the origins of this conflict, see above, p. 108.

[88]Anonymi Ticinensis, *R.R.I.S.S.*, xi (1), 31.

[89]Bigwood, G., and Grunzweig, A., *Les livres des comptes des Gallerani*, Brussels, 1962, i, 44.

[90]Quoted by Enriques, A.M., in *A.S.I.*, 1933, 101.

[91]*Raoul Glaber, Les cinq livres de ses histoires (900–1044)*, ed. Prou, M., in *Collection de textes pour servir à l'étude et à l'enseignement de l'histoire*, Paris, 1886, i, a. 1041.

[92]Bonneaud-Delamare, R., "Les institutions de paix en Aquitaine au XIe siècle", in *Recueil de la Société Jean Bodin*, xiv: *La paix*, Brussels, 1962, 415–488.

[93]Grand, R., *Les paix d'Aurillac. Étude et documents sur l'histoire des institutions municipales d'une ville à consulat (XIIe–XVe siècles)*, Paris, 1945.

[94]Mundy, J.H., *Liberty and political power in Toulouse, 1050–1230*, New York, 1954; Kiener, F., *Verfassungsgeschichte der Provence (510–1200)*, Leipzig, 1900, 216, 235–236; Lesage, G., *Marseille angevine (1264–1348)*, 1950, 37.

[95]Bisson, T., "An early provincial assembly: the general court of Agenais in the XIIIth century", in *Speculum*, 1961, 254–281.

[96]Caffiaux, H., "La charte de la frairie de la Halle Basse de Valenciennes", in *Mémoires de la Société des antiquaires de France*, 4th series, viii, 1877, 1–47.

[97]Published by Mèlis, F., in *Aspetti della vita economica medievale*, Siena, 1962, i, 55–56.

[98]Becker, M.B., in Rubinstein, N., *Florentine studies*, 130.

[99]Graziani, "Chronica", in *A.S.I.*, 1st series, i, 415 (year 1437), 620 (year 1449).

[100]Bianchi, "Chronica", in *A.S.I.*, 1st series, ii, 162, 167 (years 1496–1497).

[101]Dubois, P., *Les asseurements au XIIIe siècle dans les villes du nord. Recherches sur le droit de vengeance*, Paris, 1900; Cattier, R., "La guerre privée dans le comté de Hainaut aux XIIIe et XIVe siècles", in *Annales de la Faculté de Philosophie et de Lettres de l'Université libre de Bruxelles*, i (2), 1890; Wodon, J., *Le droit de vengeance dans le comté de Namur* (*XIVe–XVe siècles*); Petit-Dutaillis, C., *Documents nouveaux*.

CHAPTER 4

Clan solidarity in neighbourhood ties

Family clans which claimed common descent, although the links were sometimes tenuous and even artificial, also owed their tight cohesion to a close, and in some respects communal, social life. Links forged, daily or at times of crisis, through neighbourhood, were the strength of the social group in town and country. This is another legacy of the family.

The family and the house

The family, even in its widest sense, even when it had become very large, had to remain united. For all the Italian chroniclers and moralists family life brought together all the relatives, their children and if possible their collaterals. It is one of the favourite themes of Alberti's *Libri della famiglia*; the author emphasizes this most frequently, and forcefully. One of his characters wishes that *sotto un tetto si riducano le famiglieri, e se cresciuta la famiglia, una stanza non puo receverla, assentissinsi almeno sotte una ombra tutti d'uno volere*; and later the author clearly expresses this decisive choice: *Pero a me mai piacque dividere la famiglia, uscire et intrare per più d'un uscio: nè mai mi pati l'animo che Antonio mio fratello abitasse senza me sotto altro tetto....*[1] Alberti's dreams even lead him to imagine a much wider communal life which would embrace not only all the brothers but also the members of the Alberti *gente*, who would live under the same roof: *Et a uno medesimo fuoco si scladassino et a una mesima mense si sedessero.*[2] Thus he imagines a community in fact of several dozen individuals living in a very lofty and vast house, sharing board and hearth.

In the period which concerns us, however, these family communities survived only in those country areas where property remained indivisible, where large family groups lived together, around a common hall.[3] In the cities the undoubted existence of these clans generally did not imply such a communal life; in only a few respects, in a few activities of social life, was there any community. The different branches of a single line each had their own houses. Journeys and long sojourns in foreign commercial branches, and sometimes rivalry, caused close relatives, brothers even, to separate. Alberti well knows that the time of which he speaks is gone; he thinks with nostalgia of bygone ways, or he imagines.

What was the position in the West, and especially in Italy, towards the end of the Middle Ages? Obviously, the family community may be measured by the size of a town house, when it was inhabited by only one family or by households bearing the same name, belonging to the same clan. Unfortunately such medieval houses are very little known. Often, we must be satisfied with vague assertions or old illustrations. Some authors have wrongly believed or implied that town houses were similar in all the cites of the West,[4] and they have generally underestimated the use of stone for private buildings and the size of these houses. The idea of a small, wretched cob house, with dovecots, built on poor foundations, another idea which goes back to a very old tradition, whose origins are more or less romantic, still appeals to us, despite ourselves. This view is well in keeping with the generally accepted idea of medieval technical mediocrity; it is still solidly rooted, and evokes dark, dirty tortuous streets and fragile, irregular, comfortless buildings; this tradition is linked to uncritically accepted ideas of the insecurity and harshness of the age.

In reality medieval houses, like the townscapes of western Europe as a whole, seem to have been extremely varied from one country to another and from one kind of civilization to another. From this point of view each city deserves to be individually studied. We should at least try to define a number of particular types of environment and ways of life.

Such a study could be made in several different ways; but it is obvious that to define the size of a house and the conditions of the environment from fiscal records is the least certain method of all, giving only very abstract results. It is preferable in every way to seek to establish the real aspect, a concrete picture of the house. This may be done either from texts: chronicles, often containing a wealth of references, treatises of morality or of domestic life, contracts of hire, rent documents, individuals' accounts, contracts or accounts for construction or repair, and finally, inventories made after a death, which sometimes give detailed lists of furniture; or, and especially, by scientific, archeological examination of the buildings themselves; admittedly their state of preservation may vary, but a critical study which takes account of previous modifications would give more concrete and definite information than any other approach.

What we already know of these town houses enables us to assert that they were not all small: quite the contrary. The great number of large or even very large houses must strike any attentive observer. These vast dwellings, with which we are more concerned for the present, were apparently very unequally distributed in towns. Some of these variations are significant, others are perhaps only apparent, because of the lack of sufficient information.

Differences in height are particularly astonishing: in some towns there were insignificant little houses of only two low storeys; in others, on the contrary, there were large buildings of up to three and four storeys above a vaulted ground floor. This latter type of dwelling, which of course absolutely contradicts our traditional preconceptions, was by no means unusual. Large, tall houses existed in many north European cities, especially in the fifteenth century; it may be possible to claim that they characterized Germanic civilization and the townscape of the cities of Bavaria, or the Rhineland, or sometimes of the Hanse. The few pictures which have come down to us very often give this impression. The admittedly old, but still very useful work of Otto Stiehl, on domestic architecture and the environment in the 'Gothic' period, contains interesting and detailed analyses, as well as pictures, of these imposing, lofty, German houses; from Cologne, Lüneberg, Ulm, Bamberg and Bern different types of house are shown of varying aspect, but all very tall. There was also, above all, that very fine house of a Nürnberg merchant, built in two parts which faced each other across a courtyard, each part consisting of four lofty storeys.[5] In Metz too, aristocrats lived in fine tall houses whose regular façades were several storeys high; in this same city the building plots, which were allotted by ecclesiastical 'courts', were apparently of greatly varying lengths, but the façades which lined the street were narrow: generally they were twenty-five feet wide, never more than thirty feet.[6]

We could easily find houses of this type in many other northern cities, as far as western France, Rouen[7] and even Brittany.[8] Most of Jean Fouquet's imaginary landscapes were situated in the Loire region; we may believe that the city of Tours was often his pattern, suggesting one street scene or another, as for example in 'Saint Martin sharing his cloak with a beggar',[9] and in 'The entry of Ptolemy into Jerusalem',[10] inspired by royal arrivals in France, and especially in the admirable 'Capture of Jericho'[11] in which, near the river opposite a fortified castle and a peasant village, the town has a long street lined with houses, behind the flattened city walls. All these houses – Touraine, or at least French – of Jean Fouquet are built of stone; many of them have narrow, very tall façades of three or four storeys, capped by pointed tiled or slate roofs; these too are lofty, valuable houses. Yet these facts, which prove decisively that there were tall houses in many western medieval towns, do not necessarily imply that the whole townscape was characterized by dwellings of this type. They could be merely exceptions, or rather indications of great wealth, of definite social status.

In Italy, on the contrary, several towns seem, at different times in the Middle Ages, to have possessed only tall or very tall houses. Such unusual townscapes surprised and delighted travellers, and not only men from the north. Pero Tafur, although a good Castilian and accustomed to the towns of Iberia, exclaims that in Genoa *all* the houses rise like castle keeps: "All the houses are like towers of four or five storeys or more".[12] When Anselmo Adorno, the Genoese who had moved to Bruges, stayed in his native town in 1470 before going to the Holy Land, he also marvelled at the height of private houses: the town "is adorned with very many houses, high, of marble, with iron gates"; and "three or four miles from the city there are also citizens' houses, very high, very vast, admirable to see.[13]

Indeed, lofty architecture established itself very early in Genoa and has not, to our day, been dislodged; from about 1150, the time when along the streets the rich inhabitants were replacing the old wooden porticos by heavy stone arcades, they built houses of four or five storeys, in stone up to the third floor, in brick above; moreover the use of these two materials was for several centuries one of the striking characteristics of Genoese domestic architecture. Subsequently, these lofty buildings became the rule, without exception. All the evidence agrees on this point: descriptions given in inventories, pictures such as the famous painting which represents the city in 1481, rising from its hills,[14] and even more the very many buildings dating from the fifteenth century which are still in good condition and even, as in the case of the very fine house of Lamba Doria, date back much earlier, in this case to 1260–1280. In the Via Luccoli, the address of the powerful noble *albergo* of the Spinola di Luccoli, two very modest looking houses, not at all palace-like, which date from the fifteenth century, prove that lesser men also lived, several families together, in very lofty dwellings. There were also many of these houses in essentially 'popular' and modest quarters such as Santa Maddalena. In fact Giustiniani well says, around 1530, that the houses of the *plebe minuta* were even more densely inhabited than the others.[15] Thus in the Middle Ages the whole city of Genoa, in every quarter, be it noble or popular, at every level of wealth, consisted mainly of very tall dwellings.

The houses of Pisa are equally well known to us thanks to a good, very detailed if now dated study by C. Lupi.[16] Normally the medieval house, in Pisa, was very narrow. It rested on two, or more rarely on four, stone pillars, joined by arches. It was ten or twenty metres high. This very narrow and very tall house, consisting always of more than two storeys above street level, is inevitably reminiscent of a kind of tower; contemporary documents often say *domus seu turris*, and in the fourteenth and fifteenth centuries Pisans themselves referred to their houses as *torri gergate*, short towers. Benjamin of Tudela really believes them to be towers, and in a characteristic exaggeration he counts at least 10,000 of these 'towers' in the city.[17]

The enthusiastic description of Milan which Bonvicinus de Rippa wrote about 1280 includes several articles devoted to the city environment; the author asserts that "there are 12,500 houses with doors opening directly onto the street, and in a great number of these several families live together with crowds of dependants"; he concludes: "this shows the astonishing density of the population of citizens".[18]

Those authors who have observed these contrasts, more often geographers and town-planners than historians, have attempted to explain them. Some point to the use of solid materials, of stone, in large houses; and they link this townscape to the Roman legacy, or to the proximity of large quarries, or to the wealth of the commercial towns of southern Europe. But in Italy, even in the small region of Tuscany, commercial towns do not all contain such tall or such vast houses. Other analyses have tried to point to different forms of geographical necessity: the wish for protection against the wind; shortage of space in towns built on foot-hills, or locked in narrow valleys. It has become a commonplace to show Genoa clinging to the last, still steep, slopes of the Apennines, overlooking a well-protected port, its houses rising very high through shortage of space. This very classical and rather simplistic explanation seems in no way adequate; firstly, there was nothing to prevent the Genoese from spreading their buildings right out into the two coastal plains of Polceverra and Bisagno, which surround the steep promontories, and there were still many empty spaces inside the walls themselves. We should certainly not ignore physical factors but they alone cannot explain the Genoese townscape, which was due much more to the political weakness of Genoa against the lords of the Apennines, which prevented it from protecting itself by the formation of a vast territorial state. The city could defend itself better on high ground against the direct threats of incursions by highlanders and of rapid intervention by the armies of Milan, so the lack of a protective surrounding territory led to the choice of an essentially defensive site. Moreover, and this is probably a more important factor, the tall house of Genoa represents the family group's stronger cohesion, its more marked adherence to the ancient forms of community life. In the Quattrocento the large houses of Genoa contained vast noble families whose cohesion was still strong; the same residential arrangements were found in the quarters of the rich *popolani* (for example, the Giustiniani). There, without doubt, is another sign of the clan's strength. In the poorer quarters a large house was sometimes inhabited by several households, each in a different apartment; but the plan of the house indicated a different past.

The Genoese retained this type of townscape with lofty houses in all the countries which they conquered, dominated or colonized. We find that there were in the Middle Ages, and still are, these very characteristic, tall houses, rising from the port itself, along an arcaded street (the *Ripa*), in almost all the townships of the Rivieras: in Camogli, in Portofino especially, in Rapallo and up to Porto Vènere, that forward bastion against Tuscany. In Sestri Levante between 1470 and 1500 there were an appreciable number of houses of this type: a narrow façade, about five or six metres wide, with one or two storeys above the vaulted ground floor; this was so both in the township itself and in the various hamlets of the locality. These houses were built of stone or brick. The ground floor was fronted by an arcade and often served as store or shop; each storey was an individual apartment for one family, reached by a stair at the side; sometimes two families shared a storey; very often those sharing would be brothers.[19]

These tall houses were found at that period, and are still found to the present day in the towns and villages of eastern Provence: for example in Grasse and its vicinity. One is tempted to see in this unusual townscape an especially Ligurian influence, that of the village perched on its promontory or spur, a village on an *oppidum*. But this hypothesis is not easily supported. Some places, such as Camogli, Rapallo and Portofino, are not perched high up at all, but are *marine*, by the water's edge. In Sestri the tall houses are in the 'township' of the plain, by the sea, as well as on the promontory of the 'isle'. Further, it is clear that these tall, narrow houses on the exact Genoese pattern occur in areas which underwent Genoese colonization and not elsewhere; such was precisely the case on the Riviera di Levante and in the Grasse region, which from 1460 was subject to intense Genoese settlement.[20] These houses are the same in some towns of Var, for example in Saint-Tropez and in Pontevès, where in 1471 and 1477 Louis II of Anjou introduced many Genoese families in order to repopulate the area.

In Corsica, under reasonably similar geographic conditions, the contrast between the towns subject to Genoese colonization and influence and the others appears even more clearly. Tall houses rose out of all the strictly Genoese villages, whatever their locations, fates and wealth might be: in Bastia, where the townscape of the port is very closely reminiscent of all those in the eastern Ligurian Riviera; in Bonifacio, roost of privateers and military bastion, hugging the cliff; and in all the ports of the Corsican cape, which are rather *marine* in the fashion of Portofino in Liguria.[21] Elsewhere the houses, although often perched high up, are more squat. As early as 1933 P. Arbos showed very pertinently that these differences in no way depended on special physical conditions, although some had tried to explain them thus, but rather that they resulted from different social structures and ways of life: from the different degrees of cohesion in the family, or in the family clan.[22] This certainly appears to be a direct effect of Ligurian colonization: many settlers, at least in Bonifacio, came from Genoa itself or from the Riviera di Levante.[23] Finally, it appears that in the Genoese outposts of the Black Sea, especially in Caffa, the many-storeyed houses created a townscape closely resembling that of Genoa itself.[24]

Elsewhere, and in Italy itself, the situation evolved, and the original townscape was more or less rapidly transformed. Pisa and Lucca kept their very tall palaces until quite late, but Florence lost hers in the Quattrocento. In 1334 the three sons of Jacopo degli Alberti, sharing between them their father's legacy, still owned the family palace in common; but their children left it.[25] The fragmentation of clans worsened and gathered speed; in Florence each head of a family established his own house; R.A. Goldthwaite believes that the great 'Renaissance' palace of Florence, a low-built palace, was a solution to the problem of the simple conjugal family's isolation, of its separation from the other relatives of the same name.[26]

The links between the family clan's cohesion and the construction of tall houses might be verified in many other towns of the West at the end of the Middle Ages. In Metz the tall houses are those of noble *paraiges*. It should also be noted that in other towns large dwellings, but this time low-built, could contain a vast number of people, numerous dependants scattered around a courtyard or in rooms bordering a patio. Thus the tall house is not the only type to indicate the permanence of the cohesive family clan; but it is the most notable. Originally it was also possible to add a storey on the marriage of a son, and to receive the new household beneath the same roof.[27] In every case, however, the type of house and thus of townscape reflects in large measure the social structures of the city.

Neighbourhood links and city 'quarters'

There is no doubt that a knowledge of social structures can bring much which is new and important to our knowledge, not only of the urban environment, but also of town planning itself.

The medieval town arose spontaneously; it often seems anarchic. In contrast to the cities of Roman and Greek antiquity, or to the capitals of monarchies in the so-called modern era, no overall plan was normally worked out or realized. In the West a town was nearly always rebuilt slowly upon the remains of an ancient city or near new focal points such as a count's or a bishop's castle, an abbey, a port or crossing-point. Such reconstruction, lacking firm direction and character, would occur without apparent order, depending on very different factors: market locations, the use of river banks or sea shores, access to bridges, the search for security, or the protection of the powerful. Among these factors a concern for family, ethnic, or professional solidarity most definitely occupied a very important place. Men could not remain isolated or strangers to one another in their own districts; by choice they joined together into strong, cohesive groups. In areas where land was intensively brought into cultivation or even where political colonization took place there seem to have been very few cities which were built from nothing, showing a deliberate will, an overall plan and true 'urban' civilization. Only the south-west of France, the Spanish Levant and the east of Germany present examples of this sort of town planning. But at first the *Reconquista* towns of Old and New Castile were merely disordered heterogeneous collections of tiny urban centres, separated by land devoid of all building, each bringing together men from different places around its small church; in this way, for example, the *fuero* of 1190 lists thirty-five quite separate parishes in the town of Soria; similarly in Salamanca; similarly too in Calatayud, where fourteen parishes shared the 1,063 families counted in 1253.[28] In short these cities, although they were built from nothing or completely rebuilt after devastation, were only collections of very small, individual urban centres with linguistic, ethnic or even family bases.

The disintegration of a town into more or less autonomous social units is one of the essential characteristics of medieval urban development. These structures were maintained and sometimes strengthened over the centuries.

In northern France, even, links between neighbours certainly played a very important part in social life. In Mantes, in the centre of the royal estates, family groups, which were of a tacit nature and made little impression on ordinary political life, but which are better revealed in judicial or private documents, brought together men who were regularly described as "kindred friends and neighbours (*voisins*)"; this expression emphasizes without any doubt the coincidence of ties of relationship and of neighbourhood. These friends and *voisins* did not bear the same surname; they were especially to be found among the well-off, although not among the very rich. Finally, and very significantly, a common profession sometimes further strengthened this double tie of neighbourhood and relationship: the kindred friends and *voisins* of Gervaisot Maillart's children included eight members of the tanners' guild; between 1279 and 1287 five of these were elected peers of the commune.[29]

Neighbourhood ties maintained political communities, and groups of neighbours, at first spontaneous then more artificial, held sway over the whole of a city's political life when there was no central power to break their hold. This was especially true in southern Europe. In Spain, certainly, the burgess, the citizen, was well named the *vecino*. In numerous Italian towns the political basis, for example for elections to the councils, and the fiscal basis which appeared in tax registers, was always the territorial district: *quartiere, sestiere, terziere, contrada, conestagia*, or very often, *popolo*, or as often, parish. Only those cities where the power of guilds was more strongly entrenched was a professional basis (in Florence, the *arti*) substituted for any of these; in Tuscany it was often a method of taking from the nobles all influence over the *popolani*, or even over their dependants.

To belong to one of these districts was not merely an administrative matter. It created and preserved solid ties. Before 1175, in Florence, where these topographic divisions remained very effective up to the end of the Duecento, six *sestieri* had replaced the four very ancient quarters which corresponded to the four gates of the city. From that date these *sestieri* contained varying numbers of *populi* (between four and fourteen). The *populi* bore the name of their church; they formed a social unit of probably very ancient origin which, in politics and religion, remained very cohesive. In a very original analysis, which would however lead us far from our present concern, B. Stahl has shown the deep unity of each of these districts, and the particularly close unity of the *populi*.[30]

These districts, these neighbourhood associations, spread their hold into the countryside. One of the origins of Italian political and social life was thus this extension of the topographical divisions of the city into rural areas or even into overseas colonies. Any *contado* conquered by Florence was divided into six parts, each assigned to one of the city's *sestieri*; Siena had a similar link between the three *terzieri* of the city and the parts of the *contado*. Similarly, when Venice colonized Crete the island was divided into six parts, which bore the names of the six *sestieri* of the metropolis; every settler had to establish himself in the *sestiere* corresponding to his original residence;[31] this was probably in order to maintain close links between the inhabitants of projected colonies. The same seems to have been true for the Genoese who settled in Caffa;[32] in any case the Genoese settlers in Caffa and Bonifacio, although they were so far from Genoa, never failed, if they came from the city, to indicate in all their public and private documents, their native district, their *compagna*, and even, more precisely, their *conestagia*.[33] Those men of Piacenza who settled abroad, and especially in Genoa, in the thirteenth century, also indicated to which *vicinia* they had belonged before departing.[34]

Among the members of the *popolo* such neighbourhood ties maintained or brought about solid political and social groups which were well organized and durable, and which primarily ensured the defence of the city; these people formed militias of foot soldiers – the *fanti portes* of Italian cities in the thirteenth and fourteenth centuries; they obeyed the orders of a captain or gonfalonier and gathered under their own banners in the local church; each year they faced each other in great games or sporting jousts, with the same lively enthusiasm which they had brought or still brought to bear in street fighting. In 1195 in Lucca: *Fu discorda in Lucca tra Porta San Frediani, Porta di Borgo e Porta San Donati dall'una parte, e dall'altra parte Porta san Cervagi e Porta san Pieri. E feceno stormo e combattéono* . . ..[35] In times of difficulty the defence of the city, or at least of the *popolo*, depended on these neighbourhood societies. In 1250 *i buoni uomini di Firenze* roused the *popolo* against the Ghibellines and presented twenty banners *a certi caporali partiti per compagnie d'arme e per vicinanze.*[36] This is why, even in peace time, these very powerful 'popular' neighbourhood groups were primarily found at the most exposed points, especially near the gates in the city walls where they formed 'Societies of the Gates', and were committed to the defence of the fortifications. In the sixteenth century and even later thirty-three towers of the outside wall of Metz bore the names of guilds: the barbers' tower, the butchers' tower, the bakers' . . ..[37] This emphasizes in a very significant way the interest which all the 'popular' groups took in the defence of the ramparts.

In the thirteenth century these popular Societies of the Gates which were powerful and, in many towns, well organized, opposed the great noble families which very often guarded one of the towers of the outer walls. Later, admittedly, they lost their peculiar military and political character, but sometimes continued under the guise of associations of neighbours, although of greatly varying kinds. In Pisa the ancient *vicinie*, the first organizations of citizens, evolved and at the beginning of the communal era gave way to those territorial districts on which the political structures were based: first the *quartieri* and the *sestieri*, and with greater stability the *popoli* and *contrade.* However these very ancient popular associations, the Societies of the Gates, never lost all their rights. In 1346 the *Maggior Officiale delle Vie e de' Pubblici* was flanked by a small council of five delegates of citizens, one for each of the city gates. This, of course, was a legacy of the past, but showed that the popular Societies of the Gates still played an important role, if not in political or military life, then at least in the administration of the city.

In Genoa, in the Quattrocento, these spontaneous *vicinie* lived outside the traditional institutional framework of the *conestagie*, which alone were recognized by the commune; the *vicinie* took no part in political life; they never sent delegates to the different councils. They were essentially human and social groups, groups of neighbours of good will, on the fringes of the normal patterns. For that very reason the *vicinia* is very little known and very rarely revealed in documents. I have found only a single example, but it is a valuable and significant one, certain proof of the permanence, among the *popolani* themselves, of social groups which arose from proximity. A booklet entitled *Ordines vicinie Sancti Donati* contains copies of several notarial acts drawn up in the first three years of the existence of this association of neighbours, dating from the day of its foundation, 21 February 1447.[38] The association's constant recourse to a notary well shows its private, spontaneous and uninstitutional character. It was a group of considerable size; on the first day 102 heads of families met in order to define the aims and statutes of the *vicinia*; they were all *popolani*, of very varied professions and social positions; some richer families such as the Albaro, De Oliva, Delfino and Leone, emerged from very modest circles; there was here none of the great names of commerce or finance. This *vicinia* certainly lived up to its name, for all its members lived near the church of San Donato, in a very old, popular quarter on the Sarzano promontory, where the first Ligurian *oppidum* seized a foothold, and which was the city's first focal point. Indeed the *vicinia* guarded the approaches to the Porta Soprana, the main gate in the walls in the thirteenth century.

Only neighbours had the right of admission to this social grouping. If a member left the quarter he was immediately expelled from the *vicinia*, and any new neighbour might be admitted if this were agreed by three-quarters of the members. Meetings were held either in the cloister of San Donato, following a tradition well rooted in Genoa and in many Italian cities, or, from December 1447, in the *loggia nova* on the square, another symbol of the group's social life which, we may imagine, was built at its joint expense. The rules which were made on the first day clearly asserted the wish to live in peace and maintain harmony together. All solemnly proclaimed their rejection of any distinction between parties (black or white): *nullo colore infringere volumus*.[39] Every six months at least forty members had to elect four *principales* to administer the *vicinia*, and more especially *curare omni affectu conservationem et preservationem bene dilectionis inter omnem societatem et viciniam*; every member owed respect and obedience to these *principales.* There was also harmony among the women: the *vicinia* appointed a body of first three, then four, *matrones* to oversee good manners and calm discord. Admittedly these elections became annual, then biennial, but the members still met regularly, according to these documents, at least up to the end of December 1470.

The *vicinia,* knowledge of which we owe to a scattering of documents, and of which we should like to study other examples, here in Genoa or in other cities, seems to have been a perfect example of a social unit – very cohesive, the probable result of political and military links, but exclusively maintained by the wish for peace and by neighbourhood ties.

Neighbourhood links among the clans: the seignorial court

The same neighbourhood links were also very strong within family or suprafamily groups. Proximity, after the blood and the name, cemented the clans, which sought at any price to maintain close residential cohesion. This was a fundamental characteristic of medieval towns, where the social structure reflected the power of great families. This, to give only one very characteristic example, was the case in Moslem towns, especially Mecca; tribes and even clans each occupied a very circumscribed area of the town (a 'gully').[40] In the East this arrangement seemed to represent the transposition to the city of a nomadic custom whereby all the members of great families gathered in a circle of tents; in any case, in the Middle Ages, such an arrangement characterized all the towns of the Mediterranean world, in Islam as in Christendom.

This separation was also to be found in many western cities in the Middle Ages, even in northerly regions; family clans would occupy several houses together or a whole quarter. In the country as in the towns, these same neighbourhood links appear to have been a legacy of feudal times, the result of the transference of rural customs to the town. Throughout the Middle Ages, 'noble' family clans tried to dominate their villages by maintaining close cohesion between their members, who led a kind of communal life in their castle, or at least built their residences very close together.

This tradition was still alive at a very late date, in country areas, where clan structures were maintained, whether nobles or simple peasants were involved. In 1470 the locality of Sestri Levante, on the Ligurian Riviera, numbered twenty *ville*, hamlets scattered on the mountain slopes or around the main town; at a census, out of eighty-seven great families, each of more than five heads of family, who were also land-owners, thirty-four had *all* their members in the same *villa*; thus, the sixteen Bernarselo leaders all lived in Cassagna, high up in the mountains; the thirteen Nausola were all in the hamlet of Bargone. But the other clans were not widely scattered: twenty-one of the twenty-three Bergante leaders were in Bargone; other groups divided into only two parts, based in two villages; only one case shows any real dispersal. Such great concentration of the family group meant that from a social point of view each *villa*, with one exception, was dominated by a single clan which was much larger than the other families, or by two or three at the most. To give a single example: the *villa* of Verici contained sixteen members of the Gallo *albergo*, eight families having only two or three heads, and two single individuals. Thus neighbourhood cohesion remained very strong, although this was at a very late period and in a locality inhabited specifically by freemen, without either fiefs or nobles. These links "increase a harmony which was not based simply on a common blood, but also on everyday relationships, which were all the closer for being in the restricted framework of one or two *ville* which never contained very many inhabitants".[41]

Further, in certain regions, ties were often strengthened by the protection afforded by the seignorial castle. Family friends and servants, or peasants, built huts, then makeshift houses, inside the grounds of castles or fortified abbeys, which were thus gradually transformed into first temporary, then permanent, groups of dwellings.

The high villages of eastern Provence were no strangers to this 'feudal' tradition. In the tenth century a lord would build a simple square tower on the summit of a hill which was reached only with difficulty. This tower, entered only through a door placed several metres above ground level, would offer only uncertain prospects of accommodation; so, at the base of the rock on which the tower stood, the lord would build outer walls which formed a kind of enceinte; inside, he would build houses for his men-at-arms. Later, the peasants would gradually abandon their ancient villages and establish themselves in these precincts:[42] whence those high, fortified villages, where houses jostled close together at different levels, according to the capricious plan necessitated by the irregularities of contour.

In these villages the castle precinct was a refuge, the centre of political and social life. In 1334 the men of the village of Cipières[43] who were men of the lady of Caussol, were "assembled in public parley by a crier in the precinct of the court of the said lady"; the officer who summoned them was referred to as "public crier and member of the said court".[44]

These very characteristic arrangements might equally be found in Liguria and Corsica, in Catalonia and in southern Italy, especially Calabria. The famous fresco called the 'Good Government' executed by A. Lorenzetti in the Palazzo Pubblico of Siena depicts several fortified townships or *castelli* in the mountains where the city had not imposed peace and respect for the law. One of these places gives a striking picture of these seignorial courts: rectangular in shape, bounded by an outer wall and protected by a tall square tower; inside were crowded the lord's mansion, several less lofty dwellings and the church.[45]

The fortified court, which was a centre of rural settlement, was probably one of the most characteristic elements of our medieval civilization. We could find many examples of it in all countries, and more especially at difficult times, in war and during outbreaks of banditry. Nor is it invariably found on precipitous heights, so that the plan of the village often presents a more regular pattern.

This process, with reference to the fortifications and settlements of lower Auvergne in the Hundred Years War, has been the subject of a remarkable analysis by G. Fournier.[46] In their poultry-yards several lay or ecclesiastical lords had small buildings erected – these were called *loges* or *chambres*; in them the peasants of the locality took refuge from the threats of misdeeds by armed men and brigands; these *loges* stood close to the external walls of the manor court, in concentric circles: whence the characteristic appearance of villages which grew up around such refuges: for example in Ambert,[47] where the position of the castle walls is still clear, or in the abbeys of La Chaise-Dieu and Saint-Alyre.[48]

The seignorial court was equally well established, although less easy to detect, in cities; this explains many aspects of our townscapes, for dependants always sought the protection of their masters, thus increasing the power and cohesion of the clan. In Germanic countries, in the very places where between 1180 and 1200 the burgesses struggled to destroy fortified houses and forbade the construction of any new fortress, fine stone houses still rose from the centres of noble and patrician courts, in reminiscence of the ancient seignorial courts. These houses had wide windows on the ground floor, without any protection, looking onto gardens or courtyards. In Strasbourg the *Römerhof*, which was surrounded by an exterior wall and had no windows on the street side, contained in a space measuring 25 metres by 14 metres a large stone house and, in contrast, a much smaller house; they were joined to each other by a wooden arcade.[49]

In the cities of Italy tradition and the memory of the more or less fortified seignorial court were still very strong in the years 1260 to 1266, when the destroyed property of the exiled Guelphs of Florence was described and valued in the *Liber estimationum*. This document, which is valuable in so many ways, shows clearly that the Tuscan towns and Florence itself contained these courts. In Empoli, in the *popolo* of Santa Maria Vecchia, at the place called Ripa, Rogerio Rosso possessed *unam domum magnam cum curia et duas alias domos in dicta curia*, and a further house in the same place, standing in a courtyard; true, this court was crossed by a street which considerably lowered its defensive value; even so, the influence of the ancient feudal court appears to be very clear here. In Florence, in the *popolo* of Santa Maria in Campo (*sestiere* of Porta San Piero), Bentivegno and Rinovanti Cambi owned a block of buildings, called a *residium*, with a tower and an adjoining house, built of stone; close by they also owned another stone-built house *ex tribus partibus*; all this *cum curia et lapidibus Bentivengne Rinovantis Cambii*; this court formed a whole, totally isolated from the rest of the city, bounded by streets on all sides. Finally, the same document informs us that these two brothers also owned: *Unam curiam muratam circumcirca cum scalis lapideis iuxta dictum resedium* – this, divided by a street.[50] If it appears difficult to reconstruct the townscape completely from such inventories, their terms are sufficiently precise and examples of this kind are numerous enough for us to imagine, throughout the city, these courts of seignorial origins, still more or less walled, protected by some kind of fortification, with tower and houses close together.

In Rome, on the Quirinal, stood, isolated and colossal, the tower known as *delle Milizie*; it was in the centre of a vast fortified area (*Militiae palatium*) which included a whole quarter formed from several buildings arranged around a *cortile*, crossed by two streets on an incline; all these houses, with several others in the vicinity, had originally belonged to the Arcioni clan; later the Annibaldi, then the Caetani, built right next to them a solid fortified castle of three storeys. The Colonna, for their part, owned a large fortress on the Monte

Accettorio; it had thick walls surmounted by several towers, enclosing a triangular court.[51]

This feudal court was also thoroughly established in Genoa, and long characterized many quarters of the city. Texts, especially notarial acts, of the twelfth and thirteenth centuries, commonly use the term *curia* when referring to the open space in the heart of a family clan's buildings, the interior courtyard of a kind of private fortress, or the equally private square on which stood the largest palace and its tower. According to a document of 1269, if any sharing of property took place this *curia* remained the property of the eldest son, as did the tower and the *domus magna* (*domus et turris cum iure curiae*). Later, however, there was a change of usage; notaries referred to the *platea sive carrebeus*, without signifying its origins.[52] The fact is that in Genoa, in contrast to several other cities such as Lucca, the seignorial courtyard did not remain hemmed in between the houses, away from the main thoroughfares; the court became a street, or a very elongated piazza.

When peace returned, the family clan's court lost its defensive characteristics; its general appearance changed. Yet it remained bounded by several houses: the clan leader's, those of the dependants and attendants who were sometimes very deeply subservient to the family or often were simply protégés or tenants. In Florence in the fourteenth century, the priests of the Congregation of Gesù Pellegrino owned many houses on the Via San Gallo; one, which they rented to a weaver, was called Palagetto; the *camerlengo* records mention three other tenants: one of a *palco*, another of a *bottega*, the third of a *palcho con una chucinetta*; all these buildings were said to be *nella corte del Palagetto*.[53]

Such arrangements were not peculiar to Tuscan or even Italian towns. In numerous cities nobles, great merchants and religious establishments leased to strangers small houses within their courtyards, which had previously been reserved for the clan's dependants. Behind the main house, beyond the court or the garden, were the shops, *dominiculae*, small houses, lodges or huts of the dependants. Thus the 'houses' enumerated in tax registers often, in fact, included a number of separate buildings, whose size varied.[54] They were light, very precarious, hurriedly built structures which were abandoned when populations decreased, and into which were probably crowded large numbers of insignificant people who were ill-assured of their future. These pent-houses and hovels bear witness to an astonishing press of humanity in those periods when urban populations were growing. The often excessive use and subsequent neglect of these courtyards around great houses can only be accounted for by large movements of population; movements which cannot be verified by studying variations in built-up areas or in enceintes, nor by studying variations in the numbers of houses found on the registers of property taxes.

The noble clan as masters of an urban quarter

Even outside their courtyards, great families kept their main houses and those of their protégés all close together in the same quarter. This is true, at least, of all the Mediterranean countries, on both shores, right up to Constantinople where, in the Middle Ages, the 'quarter' was in fact only a single, very large house, surrounded by the dependants' houses. The city had a considerable number of these 'quarters', each of which quite simply bore the name of the head or ancestor of its great family: "By quarter, we should normally understand large private houses which gave their name to the immediate vicinity."[55]

In the West, this tradition certainly goes back to the first period of urban development, to a time when the nobles owned fiefs and lands inside the town itself or, even more often, in the immediate vicinity of the walls. There, at the gates of the town, they built powerfully fortified, autonomous residences to guard roads and crossroads, bridges and the passage between hills; the Germans called them *Eigenbefestigungen.* The main part was a strong keep, inhabited when there was any dangér, which could often be reached or left by a tunnel. The tower known as the *Bischofshof* in Naumberg still offers a fine example of these keeps, which had no windows below the upper floor.[56] These nobles' strongholds very quickly became focal points, and others came to live in houses which were built first in the court, then right around the keep. In this way were formed hamlets or small villages which were loyal to the seignorial clans and subservient to their leaders. When the city walls extended to embrace these nobles' lands the clusters of buildings formed tight, cohesive units in the very midst of the city.

From that moment the family clan, as owners of the land, dominated a whole quarter and kept it under its authority and protection. For centuries this domination was maintained, sometimes with great vigilance. One of the group's essential goals was to keep for itself its own domain within the city, and to preserve it from outside influence. The results of this often unspoken policy were that strangers were forbidden, in all kinds of ways, to settle in the neighbourhood of great family houses, and that these families strengthened their roots and kept them intact for as long as was possible. Sometimes this desire even stands out clearly in oaths or contracts. When the three great families of Corbolani, Del Veglio and Cerlotti met in Lucca, in 1287, to form the *Casa dei Corbolani*, each was already well established in a *contrada* or *cappella* in the centre of the city. These three adjacent *cappelle* then became the protected domain of the new clan. The statutes drawn up on that day state that each *consorte* had to report to the consul of the clan any house, tower or property situated in any of the three *cappelle*, which was for sale; then the consul would at once convoke the members of the group and would have to *proponere coram eis quid placet eis facere de tali domo, casa seu possessione, et executioni mandare qui quid tunc fuerit.*[57]

The development of the medieval town long bore the marks of these origins and this legacy. All the texts, chronicles and tax records enable us to assert that despite the state's efforts, and in certain cases despite the political or military weakening of these great families, such neighbourhood cohesion was still unbroken in the fifteenth century. Each powerful clan kept a very firm grip on a quarter, on a group of houses.

In Italy, and especially in Tuscany, linguistic usage still reflected this very original aspect of the medieval town well after the final extinction of the large family federations. All the Tuscan authors wrote of *consorterie* or *federazioni di case e torri.* In Florence the Strozzi palace was certainly built *fra gli Strozzi.*[58] In Pisa, around the palace or *domus magna*, were crowded several houses for the poor people, known as *domunculae*; one part was occupied by the close attendants of the rich, either members of their clan or strangers; behind this very tightly crowded group of houses spread an extensive area of land, gardens or even a field, belonging to a single large family, a *casata* or a *consorteria*. Again in Pisa, an author writes not of one house but *di più case di abitazione della stessa famiglia.*[59] Throughout the 1200s, and still in the fiscal records of 1277 and 1287, several quarters (*contrade*) of Siena took their names from great families (in 1287, eight of the sixty-three *contrade*). For some, the name of the *contrada* was strictly that of the family, with the formula *Filii* (for example, *Filii*

Jacobi Meli); in other cases the clerks certainly entered the names of the churches, but the domination of the family clans and also some holding of goods in common, are clearly shown in the formulae: *ex parte* or *ex latere* (for example *San Donatus ex latere filiorum Rustichetti* or *San Desiderius ex parte Codenacii*).[60]

In Lucca, houses adjoining or near each other clearly show the existence of a family clan whose members often referred to themselves as *consorti di patrimonio* or more simply *vicini.*[61] In Tuscany, when a *consorteria* divided, several new groups of houses were often built very close to the old houses; each new branch of a *consorteria*: *fabbricava una casa nuova . . . ma quasi sempre dentro al perimetro del terreno gia posseduto in comune.*[62] All the Tuscan account books and *libri di ricordazione* also show that the newly wealthy merchants who invested their money in landed property were seeking primarily, either to regain ancient family houses which had passed from their possession, or to spread the extent of their property, while excluding strangers from their midst. From this point of view Francesco Datini adopted a precise and firmly followed policy in his acquisitions. A valuation of his property, dated 26 June 1407, shows that he owned twenty-five houses in Prato itself: six (three *chase* and three *chasette*) formed a single unit around his *chasa grande*, his palace in the Porta Fuia quarter; another *chasa grande*, in the same Porta Fuia quarter, was flanked by three houses, all bought in 1407. These two large houses, which of course were close to each other, had their own gardens and warehouses (*fondachi*).[63]

In Florence, in 1427, when the 'popular' commune had been trying for more than a century to break the clans' power, the cadastral registers still gave the names of thirty-one heads of Strozzi families, all living in the quarter of Leone Rosso, in the parish of San Pancrazio. R. A. Goldthwaite rightly emphasizes that in Florence it was the custom, when a family owned properties in one quarter of the city, for their descendants, however numerous they might be, to continue to reside there for centuries.[64]

We could find numerous examples of this cohesion of great or small families in other Italian cities outside Tuscany. In the case of Forlì, Bernardo's chronicle states clearly that all the members of each family elected for each quarter a *capo de parentà*, generally called a *centurione.*[65]

In Genoa the frequent concentration of each *albergo*'s residences inside a small quarter is seen indisputably in all the tax registers of the

Quattrocento. In these the nobles were clearly classified separately from the *popolani,* and were listed by *alberghi*;[66] but these *alberghi* were nevertheless presented in an immutable order, corresponding to their geographical situation. Each *albergo* gave its name to a *contrada.* These *contrade* were the ultimate homes of the tribes; for the oldest among them they were ancient fiefs; for the more recent clans they were their first establishments. No division changed this characteristic or weakened neighbourhood ties; no more, indeed, did the purchase of property: in the city a family acquired only houses situated in its *contrada,* on its own land near to its original centre, in order to strengthen the clan's power and cohesion. From this point of view, indisputable and totally conclusive information may be obtained from a study of the 1463 register:[67] of 888 houses belonging to fifty-eight *alberghi,* 846 were situated precisely in their own quarter, along their own street, around their own square. Clans with as much power as the Doria, Lomellini and Grimaldi had all their houses very close to one another, with very few exceptions (in the case of the Lomellini three, out of sixty-two houses; still fewer for the other clans). True, the Spinola formed two distinct groups, but the members of each owned residences in exactly the same place: thirty-one out of thirty-six of the Spinola di Luccoli in Soziglia, and the Spinola di San Luca owned sixty-two of their sixty-seven houses around the square of that name. The single, striking exception is the Fieschi clan; of fifty-three houses, twenty were near San Lorenzo, sixteen in Maccagnana and the remaining seventeen were scattered over five different quarters. But the fact is that the Fieschi were nobles of the Apennines rather than of the city and we know that they were not well-established in the city. The San Lorenzo branch, the only one to show the normal cohesion of the Genoese clans, was a specifically town-based branch, minor, marginal rather, and the result of an alliance; the clan drew its real strength from its fiefs and its highlanders, not from its fortified houses in the city; they did not dominate the city, but threatened it from without.

The neighbourhood ties of the Genoese nobles were maintained just as firmly in the case of their residences outside the city. These burgesses had no rural estates or lands far from the town; they owned only summer residences, spacious country seats, surrounded by vineyards and orchards, where they spent the hot months. The houses of each clan were compactly grouped, in two or three places at the very most.[68] All the summer residences of the Grimaldi were in Sampierdarena, those of the Lomellini in Fassolo and Pegli. Thus these large country houses, so close to the city and near a church or monastery, formed other groups, other social units, which were as cohesive as those of the city itself. In 1447 the Spinola di San Luca had eighteen fine residences in Quarto and twelve in Cornigliano.[69]

All the accounts of Tuscan merchants show clearly that they were happy to spread their investments in land across several districts of the *contado*, in different villages, guided by the desire for a good bargain; in this way they acquired isolated fields, vineyards or olive groves, even *métairies*, often at a distance from one another; but these same businessmen, who had often been townsmen for several generations, kept their personal country houses, or acquired new ones, in their families' places of origin. The master's house, with its tower and dovecot, recalling seignorial power and still bearing the marks of nobility, had to be in the *pieve* and *popolo* of a man's ancestors, close to relatives and dependants. Even a rapid perusal of the *Liber estimationum* of 1260–1266 would reveal, in the case of the wealth of those Florentines who were situated in the fortified villages or small towns of the *contado*, a considerable number of groups of family buildings, tightly clustered around a main house, a palace or even a tower. In the fortified village *castrum* of Castangnai(?), counts Guidoni Guerre and Guidoni Salvatici possessed *unam turrim* and *tres mangnas domos terrenas* adjoining; in Empoli, a much larger town, Rogerio Rosso was the owner of *unam turrim cum quattuor domibus parvis.*[70] Using this document alone, it would be easy to give a number of examples for each town and village of the *contado*.

Italians who had settled far from their homes, where business had led them, apparently retained the same customs, and in these foreign cities pursued policies of investment in property which followed the same traditions. This was not always, as for example in the Hanse towns, the result of insecurity and the wish to protect one another, to place themselves under the protection of a sovereign in a hostile country. It was not a matter of closed ghettoes, but, in towns where these men lived in peace and where they appeared perfectly well integrated into the rest of the population, there was still a powerful desire to recreate living conditions peculiar to their traditional social and family structures. A perfect illustration of this attitude is to be found in a specific example, that of Renier Acorre, a money lender and banker at the fairs of Champagne, who became the count's chamberlain. This man had acquired a large country estate of feudal origin, and with astonishing patience had become the owner of 350 pieces of land, through successive purchases, around his castle; about 1260, in Provins, he owned a group of five adjoining houses in the Rue de Froidmantel; in the same street he bought several other houses, two of which were adjacent; eventually, by purchase or exchange, he acquired other neighbouring houses on a second street;[71] these, together with the original properties formed a veritable block, a complete quarter of the town.

Obviously, such urban structures and such traditions were not peculiar to the Mediterranean world. The cities of Germany, and even of northern France, would probably provide more or less typical examples of this concentration of buildings in the ownership of a single family, of the constant desire to keep the members of a group or of a clan united by very close neighbourhood links. For example, in Paris, in the thirteenth and fourteenth centuries, streets often bore family names, indicating the domination of a group of relatives in a more or less well defined and limited quarter.

In Metz the five *paraiges* of the 'patricians' all bore the name of a quarter; it is easy to define the area of their settlement inside the city. Thus these suprafamily clans dominated a whole network of streets and houses; their neighbourhood links were one of their main strengths and the dispersal of residences, which in any case was always very limited, is noticeable only much later, at a time when conflicts had long since lost their virulence.[72]

Neighbourhood asserted itself as one of the essential elements of the family clan's cohesion. Velluti's *Cronica di Firenze* emphasizes the three bases of this cohesion: *A noi congiunto d'amore, parentado e vicinanze.*[73]

Very frequently these links were the beginnings of a suprafamily clan, of a confederation of groups. In Florence neighbouring *casate* joined into *consorterie.*[74] In Genoa powerful, large families admitted other, less prestigious and smaller families who lived in the same quarter, in their immediate neighbourhood. In this way most of the Genoese *alberghi* were formed. Others, originating more artificially from the merging of several households, which then assumed new names, brought together the nobles of one square, or of several neighbouring streets. The Giustiniani, a clan of extraordinary power and great extent, are the best Genoese example of these mergers, caused solely by neighbourhood links. It is known that this *albergo popolare* included most of the families of the Chios *Maona*, a sort of financial and colonial company which had administered the island since the famous expedition organized by Simone Vignosi, and which was financed by these families themselves; in 1362 they chose Giustiniani as their common name. Thus, originally, the households of merchants were apparently linked solely by a financial enterprise. All these families, about a dozen, lived in the same quarter, near the *Platea Longa*, the famous long street – a sort of *souk* – between Piazza San Lorenzo and the old port. We must therefore believe that when the commune floated the loan to mount the 1346 expedition the families of the *Platea Longa* were already sufficiently unified to make a massive and cohesive response, and thus to take the matter practically into their own hands. These neighbourhood links established in their town of origin were subsequently strengthened by common economic interests, the exploitation of the Chios monopoly of mastic and of the traffic in Turkish alum, by military and fiscal solidarity (the defence of the island and the refusal to pay taxes in Genoa itself); this all caused the creation of an *albergo*, as an institution, which had originated in neighbourhood links. In the Quattrocento the sale of shares in the *Maona* brought new names into the company: Castro, Rocca, Moneglia, Garibaldi. However, all these groups which thus joined the *albergo* also lived in this same quarter; so the original occupants did not pass their shares on to anyone, but rather, apparently exclusively, to neighbours. Neighbourhood links were therefore effective throughout the life of an *albergo*: initially in its foundation, and at all times in its expansion.

In the 1470s, more than a century after the first expedition to Chios, the Giustiniani, who of course had no common ancestry, were still united by neighbourhood and by business. Their houses, which were in general more opulent than those of any authentic noble *albergo*, formed a solid block right round the *Platea Longa* and the square which thenceforth was known as the Piazza dei Giustiniani. Just like nobles, they bought country houses which were also close together, without exception, in Carignano and Albaro.[75]

An equally detailed study of the other Genoese *alberghi popolari*, although they arose from more artificial unions than was the case with the *nobili*, would produce conclusions of the same order: in the absence of true blood ties an artificial community, whether caused by merger or by adoption, depended primarily on neighbourhood links. This was the case with the Franchi and the Fornari.

Even in 1528, at the time of the famous reforms of Andreà Doria, the twenty-eight *alberghi* which united all the families of the Genoese aristocracy, *nobili* and *popolani*, for the most part comprised mutual neighbours.[76]

These neighbourhood unions, which may have been spontaneous, but were also inevitable, obviously influenced the whole of the city's political and social life for centuries. Daily encounters on the square or in the *loggia*, the administration and maintenance of order in the area, the financial support given to the Church and to the poor, all created customs which gradually brought about more solid and stable links. The original families or *alberghi* whose houses bordered the same square often eventually united to form a single powerful clan. In 1449, twenty-five heads of families of the four noble *alberghi* of the parish of San Pietro in Banchi met in their *loggia* on the square by the church in order to appoint two procurators; they wished to defend their patronage of one of the chapels of this recently built church against another family group, the Grimaldi-de Oliva.[77] On this occasion the four groups were very unequally represented: fourteen Marini, six Lomellini, three Mari, two Pansani; as procurators they elected two Marini. This union, which was probably occasioned by the new and powerful threat of the de Oliva, recently admitted to the Grimaldi *albergo*,[78] affected as yet only one particular aspect of social life; but it shows the desire to strengthen links between neighbouring families which already shared a *loggia*: it heralded a more complete amalgamation.

Another, equally significant example: among the thousands of entries in the records of the *Colonne di San Giorgio* indicating the names and ranks of shareholders, in 1456,[79] may be noticed the mention: *Nobiles platee San Pancraciis videlicet Palavicini, Calvi, Riciis et Falaminice: Lb. 177.12.4.* So these four families, who were still independent at that date, and whose houses, probably very few in number, bounded the tiny square of San Pancrazio, set in the heart of the city, had already forged close enough links to own communally a small sum which was invested in the *Casa di San Giorgio*; this was probably for their alms and poor reliefs.[80] A little later, but before 1465, three of these *alberghi*, the Pallavicini, Ricii and Falamonica, together joined the Gentile,[81] in which *albergo* they still figured after the reforms of Andreà Doria in 1528.[82]

Unfortunately there is as yet no study which would enable us to verify with any accuracy the manner in which these neighbourhood links were established in other towns of Italy and the West. It seems however that in Languedoc and the extreme south of France the very great families each came to dominate a whole quarter. Such was the case in Bordeaux. In Toulouse, from the 1230s, the 'honour' of the Barravi extended over a whole street which bore the name of the clan: *Et tota illa carreria ex utraque parte faciebat sibi censum obliarum*; the quarter and gate known as those of Arnaud Bernard probably owed their name to the head of a family clan, Arnaldus Bernardus of Capiti Burgi.[83]

All indications show that these families and family clans, *casate, consorterie* and *lignages*, sought to retain their close neighbourhood links: politically, they wished to dominate a complete section of the city and to appoint from among themselves that district's representatives in the city's different councils; militarily, they wished to ensure a better defence against rivals and even against the commune. In any case, against the encroachments of the state, the clan retained this essential form of social life much longer than its real privileges, longer than its political and military power. The townscapes of our western world still often bear the very visible traces of these clans or federations of families.

Urban life and social structures

Various aspects of the medieval town which at first sight seem quite disordered are more easily explained when we take account of the existence and strength of family clans.

Firstly, we shall consider the city's very discontinuous aspect. The city did not fill the whole space contained within the walls: sometimes far from it. The low density of buildings, the extent of open spaces such as gardens, meadows or vineyards, vast areas which were still uninhabited and were left as waste lands or farmed as fields, all these have long attracted the attention of historians. Many have tried to perceive in these breaks in the continuity of the townscape a country tradition, the legacy of a still unforgotten rural past, proof in short that urban civilization did not really exist. This was one of the main arguments of W. Sombart, who tried to demonstrate the archaic and incomplete nature of commercial civilization in the medieval western world. It seems quite likely that the wish to keep the fields close to oneself, to drink the wine from one's own vines, planted close to one's residence, and to ensure, in time of war and siege, a safe source of supplies, did contribute to the continuance of these open green spaces right in the heart of the towns; but such breaks in the continuity of the townscape also depend on other, very varied reasons.

This tradition departs from that of Rome, but rejoins that of medieval Byzantium; Bertrandon de la Broquière, a Westerner and a Burgundian, visited Constantinople in 1432 and was astonished: "This city is constructed in villages and there is more land vacant than occupied".[84] Certainly, many Mediterranean cities, in Christian or Moslem countries, although rich and populous, were as discontinuous in construction. In the West such a townscape is explained essentially by the town's very past, in the different phases of its construction. For the medieval city seems to have been a collection of townships, a coming together of many units. The count's castle, religious establishments, and the fortresses of the nobles each put up a central group of buildings. But powerful families as well as religious houses were anxious to protect the cohesion and autonomy of their strongholds; and so for a very long time, sometimes to a very late date, right up to the end of the Middle Ages, they kept, behind or right round their houses, undeveloped land, gardens, vineyards and even woods, in order to isolate and protect themselves.

Temporal lords often encroached on the properties of abbots or bishops; by usurpation, by inheritance, by purchase too, they laid hands on ecclesiastical courtyards which they developed, establishing protégés or dependants there. Thus in the areas of the old courts the townscape took on a new aspect: straighter, better laid out streets, part of an overall plan; better ordered houses; regular, sometimes even geometric, plots. In Metz, from the early thirteenth century, settlement took place through the development of these ecclesiastical courtyards, in the city or in its immediate environs.[85] These quarters, whose style and structure were very new, can easily be seen in the plan of the city.[86] At the same time, or a little later, powerful families used the outbuildings of their large houses and built new, modest dwellings, which were used by dependants or protégés.[87] Woods, enclosures and vineyards were normally developed only later, at a time when armed conflicts had ceased, and the isolation of the different 'feudal' and family units was thus less necessary.

The commune also tried to construct public buildings in these open spaces, for example the communal palace or the doge's palace, and they also became large municipal squares, which were impossible to create elsewhere, for the noble clans obviously resisted the expropriation and demolition necessary for such public works. This is probably why the cities best endowed with rich edifices and communal palaces were those where the commune, through its own authority or following banishments or condemnations and the resulting destruction, was able to compel the demolition of houses belonging to certain great family clans. It is most significant that a city such as Genoa, where the *alberghi* remained so powerful, was precisely the city which had no large public square as late as 1460, and where the doge's palace was of such small size. The only public building with any imposing aspect was the famous Palazzo di San Giorgio, but this was built on the Rippa, facing the sea, in a place where the noble family clans owned no houses.[88]

At the urban level, as in all manifestations of social life, the noble unit, or more generally the unit of the powerful family clan, retained an evident originality: this, firstly, in the high density of households and their close links. Their houses, often arranged in disorder or crowded around a few common buildings or the leaders' palaces, often formed an inextricable tangle crossed by narrow, tortuous alleys, with passage-ways above them – some of which were simply cul-de-sacs serving a single back-courtyard or garden. The present lay-out of Lucca, in many quarters, still has a large number of these interior courtyards, obviously of medieval origin, which were once the courts around which several houses of a single clan were disposed.[89]

The houses of a single clan very often communicated conveniently with one another by means of these courts and open spaces, or directly by doors, or again by the cellars or by stone arcades above the streets, and even by wooden galleries, light structures which were easily removed. M.V. d'Addario refers to a large series of cellars in the vast zone between the Via Lambertesca and the Piazza della Signoria in Florence; they were linked by doors, and formed a network of veritable underground passages following the plan of the streets.[90]

These urban units of clans and family federations, with their close-packed houses and cohesive members, must have become well individualized at this period; they formed small, separate, well defined worlds, bearing the name of the group; the Genoese called them *contrade*.[91] Their houses, imposing in the case of the heads of clans and much more modest or communal in that of the dependants, and often isolated from the rest of the city, turned the backs of their lofty, windowless walls to the other quarters, inhabited by strangers if not by enemies. All these houses opened onto the main streets of the *contrada* or the little square, twin centres of communal life. Here were the *gentilizie* church (the church of the *gens*),[92] the *loggia*, central meeting-place of the menfolk at all hours of day and night, and sometimes the garden of the cloister. The *Liber estimationum*, drawn up between 1260 and 1266, provides a very interesting picture of the distribution of landed wealth in Florence; it offers some remarkable examples of family units or quarters. Every property that was destroyed, be it palace, tower or simple house, is classified here by *popolo*, and on each occasion the scribe indicates the nature of neighbouring properties, as well as their ownership. A study of these adjacent properties shows firstly how the houses of a single family were arranged around the family square and crowded close to one another. In fact, the most frequent indications of close proximity are: *domus eorundem* or simply *ipsius* or *eorundem*. Here are three particularly evocative examples out of several dozen characteristic of such proximity.[93]

In the *sestiere* of Borgo and the *popolo* of Santa Trinità, the brothers Ugonis and Manetti Spina are listed as owning six houses. This entry refers to about twenty adjacent houses, only two of which are owned by different families. Nine of these references involve the Spina's street, square or common land (*classus*); all the others, a dozen, concern other properties belonging to the family.

In the *sestiere* of Porta San Pietro and the *popolo* of San Pietro Maggiore, Masio de Uccellino owned:

medietatem cuiusdam turris Masi dñi Vinciguerre de Uccellinis pop. S. Petri Maioris, j platea dicte ecclesie, ij et iij ipsius et consortum.
medietatem alterius domus lingnaminis iuxta dictam turrim in dicto pop. cum dictis confinibus.
unum palatium ipsius dicto pop. ad Pinti extra civitatem, j via ij et iij et iiij ipsius et fratrum.
quandam aliam domum ipsius ibi prope, j via ij et iij et iiij ipsius.
alteram domum dicto pop. ad Pinti ipsius, j f: orum Ferrantini ij et iij et iiij ipsius et fratrum.

In the same *popolo* the five Guidallotti brothers ruled a whole vast quarter where a considerable number of buildings were listed:

a palace on a corner (*in Balla in angulo*), adjoining strangers;

seven neighbouring houses (*ad unum se tenentes*) at another corner (*in alio angulo Balla*); on both sides, strangers;

one corner house, with strangers on one side and their own property on the other;

six houses around a corner, two being joined (*ad unum se tenentes quatuor domus et alie due pro se*), with the properties of two strangers adjoining;

one house adjoining another of their properties and three belonging to strangers;

one palace with warehouse (*cum fondaco*) and a house with a cloth stretching shop (*de tiratoriis*), having five shops at street level; three houses with dyers' shops and four further houses *in quibus recondabuntur scope*; all this, the palace and eight houses, in a single group (*omnes in uno residio*); on one side their own property, on the other, strangers;

one house (*domum terranam in qua recondabantur arnesia dictorum tirotorium*) situated in their garden, having eight cloth stretching shops; this was round a street corner, adjoining their own property on each side;

an oven with another house and a stretching shop; all this in a single building, on a corner; on each side, their own property;

one house outside the walls;

one house in the *popolo* of San Piedro Celorum.

So, of two palaces and twenty-seven houses, only two houses were outside the family quarter. This was only the legacy of a single family head, left to five brothers who remained together. This quarter therefore included a very large number of buildings of all kinds: residences, workshops for the drying and dyeing of cloth, an oven, a warehouse and shops; it included at least one open space, which they called a garden. It was at once a place of residence and an exchange, a kind of industrial enterprise.[94] Normally, the buildings were grouped into compact blocks at the meeting of two streets.

In the course of time the originality and isolation of these social units probably tended to become attenuated. But in Genoa they were still strong right at the end of the Middle Ages, especially in the case of the greatest families, each of which had its own square and dominated a whole quarter. The plan of the San Matteo *contrada*, which was very successfully reconstituted by Jacopo d'Oria,[95] shows just what this quarter of the Doria consisted of at the beginning of the sixteenth century. It has not greatly changed. The plan emphasizes the almost geometrical arrangement of streets and blocks; but it also reveals very clearly great inequalities of size between these blocks. Some streets were mere cul-de-sacs; the north-south gradient demanded the use of steps. Yet all life was ordered around the small, narrow square, nestling in front of the church; right beside it the cloister was at that time surrounded by tiny gardens, planted with trees. The houses of the southern part, a little further from the square, probably did not all still belong to the Doria; there, we find allies, and even strangers such as the Spinola or the Lomellini. But the real heart of the *contrada*, the approaches to the square, remained exclusively in the hands of the Doria, of the clan's leaders.

The social consequences of this very unusual form of medieval town planning are noticeable in at least two areas.

On the one hand a considerable fragmentation of all human activity, of social life in the most general sense of the word, occurred. This fragmentation appeared very clearly in Byzantine Constantinople, where more or less specialized open or covered markets were scattered

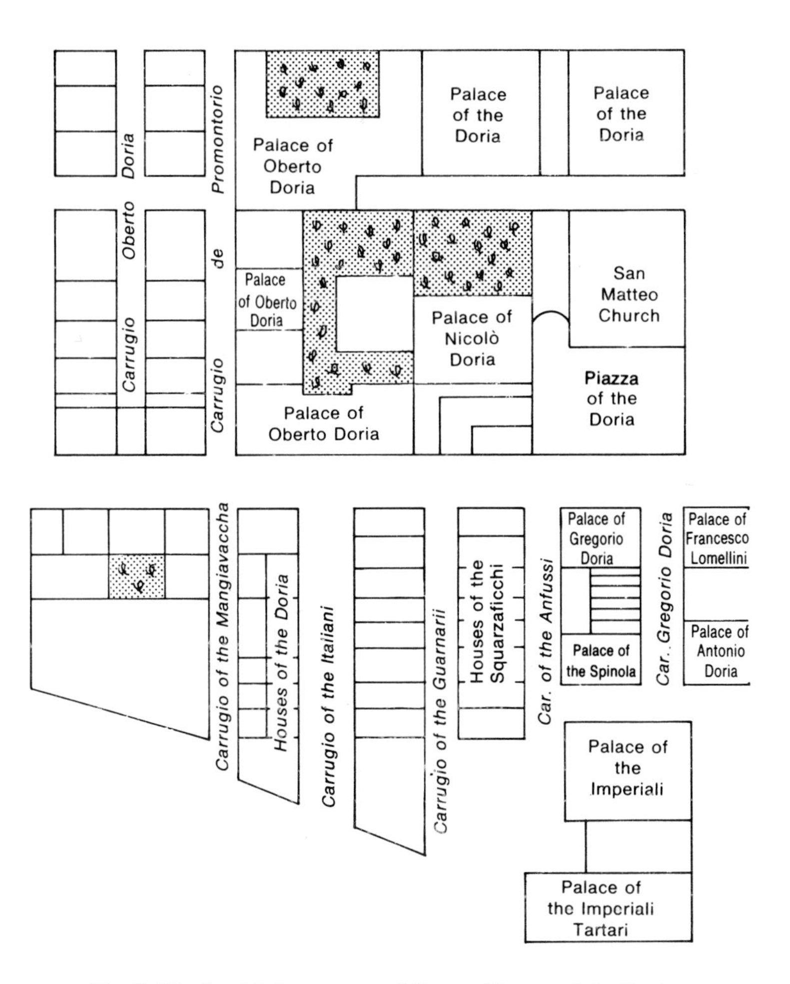

Fig. 2. The San Matteo quarter of Genoa. Houses of the Doria.

in several parts of the city: markets of furriers, druggists and writers, coal-markets, corn and barley markets. Constantinople had no large thermal bath in the manner of Roman cities, but small public baths (about thirty in the fifth century, but less than ten under the Macedonians) and more than 150 private baths.[96] Thus the urban civilization of Byzantium, like that of Islam which in many respects seems to have been similar, was resolutely opposed to that of ancient Rome. It was the same in the West where, in contrast to the cities of the ancient world, a medieval town would only very rarely see a meeting of all the citizens. Each large town probably possessed a cathedral, and one square which was larger than the others; but the inhabitants came only on a few solemn occasions: they came to the cathedral for services and the liturgical ceremonies of high days, and to the square to witness games and jousts, precisely on the occasions when different quarters confronted one another. The rest of the time, for all the activities of daily life, people remained in their own quarters, and the members of a clan lived alone together. On every occasion they met in small, private enclosures. Here was no forum, no vast space open to all citizens, but rather a multiplicity of meeting places, small markets,[97] family warehouses, the benches of notaries and money-changers, and above all the small squares of families – tiny squares, tightly enclosed between the houses, or simply squares in front of churches.

The men of the clan or of the family also met inside the seignorial houses, either in the main room or in a *loggia*. This was a very ancient tradition; the wooden keep built by the count of Guines in the town of Ardres around 1120 included, at this early date, a *loggia* in which, according to a writer who describes this in detail, the lords would happily sit in pleasant conversation; the same author therefore asserts that the word *loggia* (*loge*) came from *logos* (speech).[98]

In Genoa throughout the Middle Ages, an *albergo* or *consorteria* often had a *loggia* for the use of its members; these people also held their meetings in the cloister of the church, or in the great hall (*caminata*) of their finest palace, a residence which at that time served as a communal home in the manner of the hall of English manorial houses. Anselmo Adorno notes that in Genoa: "Generally all the members of a *parentate* or lineage live together in a single quarter or around a single square. There they sometimes own in common a church and a house with a *loggia* where, every day, the members of the family meet to discuss trivial or serious matters".[99] This *loggia*, which allowed relatives, friends and even dependants to meet, thus demonstrates tangibly the clan's social importance; it was a mark of power and even of nobility; in the towns of Tuscany the *loggia*, placed beside a palace, signified prestige and nobility; texts speak, in referring to a "noble" line, of a *famiglia di loggia.*[100]

Far away from Genoa, on the other side of the Apennines, although in a very different political context, the anonymous author of the *Chronicle* of Pavia also notes: *Quasi omnia parrochie civitatis et nonnulle progenie nobilium singulas porticus habent, ubi conversantur nobiles et multi alii cives.*[101] The *popolani* conversed and discussed their affairs in the parish *loggia*;[102] the nobles and their dependants in that of their clan, of their tribe.

At a very early date in Florence, before 1200, at a time when urban architecture had not yet reached its highest development and when stone houses were certainly not yet the norm, at least thirteen great families already owned their own *loggie*, which were at once refuges for the members of the clan and meeting-places for holidays, weddings and funerals. This social life, which was thus linked to the daily meetings of relatives and allies in the *loggia* every day, or those on high days when they would sport festive costume, arms and livery, was maintained unchanging for a long time; the *Cronaca de Monaldi*, describing the funeral of Jacopo degli Alberti, in 1319, says that *tutti i consorti e parenti stretti della casa comparvero a sanguigno, tutte le donne entrate e uscite di lor case vestite a sanguigno, e molte famigli, i servi e i garzoni di nero.*[103] The leaders wore the clan's colour, dependants the black of mourning.

Medieval cities in the West built no more large-scale thermal baths but, as in Constantinople, very small bath houses, private establishments where, again, only the members of a single family met. This was true of all aspects of daily life: the fountain fed by a spring or a branch of the communal aqueduct which had been monopolized, or the well, or the handmill, the oven or the winepress. In spiritual life, too, the church or the chapel within the church and their patronal festivals were more important than the cathedral with its great public ceremonies.

A second important consequence of this family structure in the medieval town was the absence of any real social segregation. The town where family clans, and especially noble clans, retained such power does not display any specially aristocratic quarter to the visitor. Of course the very poor, the newcomers, the criminal types were always contained within a few remote areas, outside the walls as far as possible; it was so for foreigners, and often for Jews. But inside the city itself the real citizens were not at all distributed according to their wealth. As we shall see, these social units formed by family clans included men of all stations. The leaders of a noble clan necessarily lived close to their dependants, protégés or attendants, who were sometimes lodged in their own houses, or in small houses close by. Such promiscuity, such intimate proximity of men of greatly varying conditions, are characteristics of medieval towns and contradict the *a priori* idea of class conflict between the powerful and the weak. The plans of the towns demonstrate a vertical division of society into different clans or federations of clans, much more than a horizontal division into economic classes.

These very special characteristics were asserted above all where nobles remained powerful and much attached to the old traditions, keeping their protégés close by. The burgesses for their part had no such dependencies. In Genoa, the *contrada* of the Giustiniani contained far fewer lesser men than any noble *contrada*; from the 1430s this essentially 'bourgeois' quarter seems to have been more homogeneous, more generally aristocratic: this is one of the rare examples, the only example perhaps, of social segregation in the whole city.

In the West these neighbourhood links remained for a greater or lesser period of time, depending on regions, and on social structures, in short, on the type of civilization. For example in the cities of France lineages did not assert themselves with as much vigour, especially in the north; the rich lived in quarters which were more restricted than elsewhere, and the large houses of aristocrats surrounded the main square in lordly fashion (texts sometimes refer to influential men as *placiers*), so that their houses became more and more isolated from the rest of the city. This development seems characteristic of the last years of the Middle Ages. In Bristol the rich merchants first lived in the old commercial quarter, surrounded by walls; their houses, tightly crowded, lined the two main streets which intersected at High Cross in the centre of the business quarter, where the Guildhall was built. At street level these residences contained booths, for the businessman did not cut himself off from the commercial world, from passing customers, from artisans and lesser men. Only later, during the fifteenth century, did other families, apparently ship-owners rather than simple merchants, build very opulent residences right away from this world of business, of populous, noisy streets. Their houses, such as that of the Canynges, stood then on the bend of the Avon, to the south of the old town, where extensive open spaces enabled them to isolate themselves, to surround their residences with large gardens, lawns and all sorts of outbuildings. These eminently aristocratic houses were really only rich residences; they show a clear desire to live apart, to be really segregated.[104] In the 1300s Bordeaux built a *Rue Neuve*, totally aristocratic, lined with fine *oustaus*, large noble houses, with gardens.

It seems that in Italy the idea of town planning evolved much more slowly. In his celebrated work *De re aedificatoria*, completed in 1450 and published in 1485, a book which some hold to be the first 'modern' architectural treatise, breaking with 'medieval' traditions, Leone Battista Alberti is still hesitant to commit himself; but at least he notes the divergence of opinions among his contemporaries, mostly Florentines:

> There may perhaps be some who would like better to have the habitations of the gentry separate by themselves, quite clear and free from all mixture with the meaner sort of people. Others are for having every district of the city so laid out, that each part might be supplied at hand with every thing that it could have occasion for, and for this reason they are not against having the meanest trades in the neighbourhood of the most honourable citizens.[105]

This was why in Italy neighbourhood ties lasted much longer and the aristocratic quarters asserted themselves only at a time when the cohesion of the great noble lineages was weakening, when dependants were decreasing. In Genoa the great families built a *Strada Nuova* only in 1560.[106] This wide thoroughfare cut through the close-built houses of a very old quarter, and was then lined with the new palaces of the nobles, in their new style; the nobles' opulent residences were aligned close to one another, but without any neighbourhood links, without any social basis of any sort. This triumph of pure wealth is like a symbol, and points to other ways of life, to very different social ideas; from this point of view it marks the end of an era, of a certain style of social relations.

Notes

[1]Alberti, L.B., *Opere volgari*, 295–296.

[2]Alberti, *Opere volgari*, 42–43, quoted by Tamassia, N., in *La famiglia*, 117.

[3]For examples in France, see: Aubenas, R., "Le contrat d'*affrairamentum*", in *R.H.D.F.E.*, 1933; "Tendances archaïsantes et famille artificielle en pays de droit écrit au Moyen Age", in *Annales du Midi*, 1941, 113–141; "Réflexions sur les 'fraternités artificielles' au Moyen Age", in *Études d'histoire à la mémoire de Noël Didier*, Paris,

1960, 1–10; Chassaigne, A., *Les communautés de famille en Auvergne*, 1911; Destray, P., "Études sur les vieilles associations nivernaises", in *B.P.H.*, 1920; Saint-Jacob, P. de, "Études sur l'ancienne communauté rurale en Bourgogne", in *Annales de Bourgogne*, 1941; Lugnier, A., "Les communautés familiales de Roche du XIVe siècle à nos jours", in *Bulletin de la Diana*, xxxi, 205ff.; Dussourd, H., *Au même pot.*

[4]For some observations on this subject, with reference to demographic studies taking the house as their basic unit, see Heers, J., in *Annales D.H.*, 1968, 59–62.

[5]Stiehl, O., *Der Wohnbau des Mittelalters* (*Handbuch der Architektur, Zweiter Teil, 4. Band, zweites Heft*), Leipzig, 1908, 130–176.

[6]Schneider, J., *La ville de Metz*, especially figs. 17 and 22, and p. 58.

[7]Quenedey, R., *L'habitation rouennaise. Étude historique de géographie et d'architecture urbaine*, Rouen, 1926.

[8]Le Mené, M., "La construction à Nantes au XVe siècle", in *Annales de Bretagne*, 1961.

[9]Louvre, *Book of hours of Étienne Chevalier*, c. 1450.

[10]Paris, Bib. Nat., MS. fr. 247, f. 248 (c. 1450).

[11]Paris, Bib. Nat., MS. fr. 247, f. 89.

[12]Tafur, P., *Travels and adventures 1435–1439*, London, 1926, 27.

[13]Lille, Bib. Mun., MS. 330, f. 3 (b) and f. 5 (a).

[14]On this picture by Grasso, see above, p. 103, and Volpicella, L., in *Atti della società ligure di storia patria*, 1924.

[15]Giustiniani, A., *Annali della Republica di Genova*, Genoa, 1935, ii, 145.

[16]Lupi, C., "*La casa pisana e i suoi annessi nel medio-evo*", in *A.S.I.*, xxvii, 1901, 264ff.; xxviii, 267–270.

[17]Benjamin ben Jonah, of Tudela: *The itinerary of Benjamin of Tudela.* Critical text, translation and commentary by Marcus Nathan Adler, Oxford, 1907, 480.

[18]Bonvicinus de Rippa, *De magnalibus urbis mediolani*, ed. Novari, F., in *Bolletino dell'Istituto storico italiano*, 1848, 67–114.

[19]Robin, F., "Sestri Levante", 134.

[20]Jeancard, R., *Les seigneuries d'Outre-Siagne*, Cannes, 1954, 48–51; Aubenas, R., *Chartes de franchises et actes d'habitation*, Cannes, 1943 (140 Ligurian families who settled in the region between 1461 and 1470, especially in Cabris, Le Tignet and Vallauris).

[21]Kolodny, Y., *Géographie urbaine de la Corse*, Paris, 1963.

[22]Arbos, P., "La maison corse: raisons historiques et sociales", in *Revue de géographie alpine*, 1933.

[23]Heers, J., "Un exemple de colonisation médiévale: Bonifacio au XIIIe siècle", in *Anuario de estudios medievales*, 1964, 561–571.

[24]Balard, M., "Caffa, colonie Génoise à la fin du XIIIe siècle", unpublished thesis, Paris-Sorbonne, 1968, 60ff.

[25]Quoted by Goldthwaite, R.A., in *Private wealth*, 255.

[26]Goldthwaite, R.A., *Private wealth*, 257–258; see also Goldthwaite, R.A., "The Florentine palace as domestic architecture", in *American Historical Review*, 1972, 977–1012.

[27]This explanation is provided by Arbos, P., in *Revue de géographie alpine*, 1933.

[28]Torres Balbas, L., *Resumen historico del urbanismo en España*, Madrid, 1954.

[29]Bourlet-Poisson, C., "La justice à Mantes au XVe siècle", unpublished dissertation, University of Paris X, 1972, 66 (Mantes, Archives Communales, F.F.1, court records (1380)).

[30]Stahl, B., *Adel und Volk*, 95–101.

[31]Thiriet, F., *La Romanie vénitienne au Moyen Age*, Paris, 1969, 125–126.

[32]Balard, M., "Caffa", 64ff.

[33]Balard, M., "Caffa"; Heers, J., in *Anuario de estudios medievales*, 1964.

[34]Racine, P., "Les Placentins à Gênes à la fin du XIIIe siècle", unpublished thesis, Strasbourg, 1970, 112, 219.

[35]Bongi, S., *Cronache di Giovanni Sercambi*, Rome, 1892, 11.

[36]Villani, G., *Cronica*, vi, 1, Chapter 39, ed. Dragomanni, 1864, 261.

[37]Larchey, L., ed., *Journal de Jehan Aubrion bourgeois de Metz avec sa continuation par Pierre Aubrion*, Metz, 1837; at the end of the book is an Appendix entitled *Topographie Messine*, which includes a plan of the town in the years 1465–1412; on this plan there are many other towers which are unnamed.

[38]*A.S.G.*, Notaio Giovanni Vernazza, filza 1, no. 85; for the part played by the *vicinia* in the formation and political life of the Italian commune, see: Sella, P., *La vicinia come elemento costitutivo del Comune*, Milan, 1908.

[39]An infringement carried the heavy penalty of a fine of fifty florins.

[40]The famous and all-powerful Qurayshite clan, which occupied the immediate environs of the Caaba, was itself divided into about ten clans, one of which was that of Umayya; each clan held its own street or square.

[41]Robin, F., "Sestri Levante", 165, 171.

[42]Raymon, V., "Les villages perchés d'Outre-Siagne. Étude de leur structure. Les maisons anciennes", in *Actes du XC[e] congrès national des sociétés savantes. Section archéologie (Nice 1965)*, Paris, 1966, 139–155.

[43]In the Alpes-Maritimes Department, Grasse *arrondissement*, canton of Coursegoules.

[44]Bouches-du-Rhône, Archives départementales, 396, E, 18, f. 278; the Latin text and its French translation are to be found in Roncière, C. M. de la, Contamine, P., and Delort, R., *L'Europe au Moyen Age*, Paris, 1971, iii, 283–284.

[45]Roncière, C.M. de la, and others, *L'Europe au Moyen Age*, iii, 140.

[46]Fournier, G., "La défense des populations rurales pendant la guerre de cent ans en basse Auvergne", in *Actes du XC[e] congrès des sociétés savantes (Nice 1965)*, Paris, 1966, 157–199.

[47]See Fournier, G., in *Actes du XC[e] congrès*, 166–167 and plate facing p. 168, for a remarkable plan and aerial photographs.

[48]On poultry-yards and dwellings, see also: Charbonnier, P., *Guillaume de Murol. Un petit seigneur auvergnat au début du XVe siècle*, Clermont-Ferrand, 1973, 126, 130–131.

[49]Stiehl, O., *Der Wohnbau*, 120–121.

[50]Brattö, O., *Liber estimationum*, 74.

[51]Amadei, E., *Roma turrita*, Rome, 1943, 27, 67.

[52]Poleggi, E., "Le contrade delle consorterie nobiliari a Genova tra il XII e il XIII secolo", in *Urbanistica, rivista dell'Istituto Nazionale di Urbanistica*, nos. 42–43 (15–20), 18. Although in Venice the central power of the state was forcefully asserted at an early date, the layout of the city was not really different from that of any other Italian city. For many years, probably into the thirteenth century, Venice possessed only one public square large enough to be called a piazza; the city was constructed without any overall sense of direction, and was formed entirely of *campi*, which were seignorial squares, each controlled by a great family. The four sides of each *campo* were taken up by the canal, the leaders' house or houses, their church and their dependants' houses, which were separated by *calli* or *corti*. Subsequently, when the municipality took over the

planning of the city and added a system of public roads to the arrangement of *campi*, the seignorial *domus* and their *corti*, surrounded by nobles' houses and dependencies, remained the principal element of this new townscape. See Pavan, E., "Maisons, urbanisme et structures", 37, 47, and plans on pp 50, 77, 79.

[53]D'Addario, M.V., "La casa", in *Vita privata a Firenze nei secoli XIV e XV*, Florence, 1966 (53–74), 59–62; the author gives no reference, but in his own text he cites register no. 862 (perhaps in *A.S.F.*?) of the Congregazione di Gesù Pellegrino.

[54]Roux, S., "L'habitat urbain au Moyen Age: le quarter de l'Université de Paris", in *Annales E.S.C.*, 1969, 1196–1220.

[55]Janin, R., *Constantinople byzantine. Développement urbain et répertoire topographique*, Paris, 1950, 286.

[56]Lehman, E., "Bemerkungen zu den baulichen Anfängen der deutschen Stadt im frühen Mittelalter", in *Settimane di studio del Centro italiano di studi sull'alto medioevo*, vi, Spoleto.

[57]Bongi, S., in *A.R.A.L.S.L.A.*, 1886, 481.

[58]Tamassia, N., *La famiglia*, 113; the author gives several bibliographical references.

[59]Lupi, C., in *A.S.I.*, 1901, 78–79.

[60]See Zdekauer, L., *Il constituto del Comune di Siena*, Milan, 1897; Mandolfo, *Il populus a Siena fino alla riforma antimagnitizia (1277)*, Genoa, 1911. In contrast, there are to be found, in Verona, several family clans which bear names proving their geographical roots in the town: *Quelli da Palazzo, Quelli di capo di ponte, Quelli dal Merca novo, Quelli dal bel di porto* (see Gaspard, M.H., "Une chronique véronèse inédite (1115–1405)", unpublished thesis, University of Paris X, 1972, 117–119).

[61]Bongi, S., in *A.R.A.L.S.L.A.*, 1886, 471.

[62]Lupi, C., in *A.S.I.*, 1901, 79–80; quoted by Cristiani, E., *Nobiltà e popolo*, 81, note 36.

[63]Melis, F., *Aspetti della vita economica*, 61–63.

[64]Goldthwaite, R. A., *Private wealth*, 33–34.

[65]Bernardi, ii, 66; quoted by Tamassia, N., *La famiglia*, 120.

[66]*A.S.G.*, MS. 88: an exhaustive list of the noble *alberghi*, classified in geographical order of *compagne*; fiscal records are more precise and enable us better to situate the settlements of these *alberghi*: see Heers, J., "Urbanisme et structure sociale à Gênes au Moyen Age", in *Studi in onore di Amintore Fanfani*, Milan, 1962, i, 371–412.

[67]*A.S.G.*, Sala 42/65, Possessionum Gabella, Anno 1463, Nobili. In Venice, however, a list of citizens who had taken part in a communal loan in 1379 shows clearly that the aristocratic families were scattered over the city's six *sestieri*: for example, the Badoer, the Contarini, Dandolo, Morosini and Sorzano families. See Pavan, E., "Maisons, urbanisme et structures", 169–170. So apparently, although the structures of family and city seem to have been identical in Venice and Genoa over a long period, in Venice family groups were dispersed towards the end of the 'medieval' period, although they were still very numerous, and they lost all cohesion resulting from physical proximity.

[68]Heers, J., *Gênes*, 570–571 and map no. 8: distribution of country houses of four large federations of Genoese clans.

[69]*A.S.G.*, Possessionum Gabella, Anno 1477, Nobili, Sala 42/65, B.

[70]Brattö, O., *Liber estimationum*, 74.

[71]Grandjean, B., "Étude du cartulaire de Renier Acorre (1258–1288)", unpublished dissertation, University of Paris X, 1971 (a study of MS. fr. 8593 in the Bibliothèque Nationale, Paris). See especially the purchase made of Jehan Ribueide, of "his house

with all the vaults and all the appurtenances above and below, situated in the street of the late Evrart de Joi, between the gate of the said Renier on one side and the stables of the said Renier on the other side" (f. 108).

[72]Schneider, J., *La ville de Metz*, 124, 125, 128.

[73]Velluti, *Cronica di Firenze*, Florence, 1731, 10; quoted by Tamassia, N., in *La famiglia*, 113.

[74]By a process which is almost completely unknown to us.

[75]Heers, J., *Gênes*, 579–580; according to the records of the *Gabella possessionum*.

[76]Ascheri, A., *Notizie*, 7: *Nomi delle famiglie aggregate agli alberghi nei secoli XIV e XV, e che, avendone assunto il cognome, fecero pure parte di quelli del 1528 senza più ripiglare, da pochissime eccezioni in fuori, la primitiva loro appellazione.*

[77]*A.S.G.*, Notaio Risso Baromeo, filza 1 (2), no. 3, 3 May 1449.

[78]The coincidence of dates is most striking; the Grimaldi admitted the Ceba, then the Oliva, after an interval of a few days, in December 1448 (see Ascheri, A., *Notizie*, 74); the initiative of the other four families of the parish was obviously their reply.

[79]*A.S.G.*, Archivio di San Giorgio, Cartularii delle Colonne, S (Nobilis).

[80]On this point, see below, p. 230.

[81]*A.S.G.*, Sala 42/66, B, no. 612, focagiorum (1465), *contrada* of San Siro.

[82]Ascheri, A., *Notizie*, 7.

[83]Mundy, J. H., *Liberty and political power*, 11.

[84]Schefer, C., *Le voyage d'outre-mer de Bertrandon de la Broquière*, Paris, 1892, 148.

[85]See Schneider, J., *La ville de Metz*, 49–50; the author studies a very fine example of this new town development, but it is later and, without doubt, less characteristic of the medieval period.

[86]Schneider, J., *La ville de Metz*, figures 5 and 6.

[87]Schneider, J., *La ville de Metz*, 57.

[88]In Florence it was only in 1350 that the Commune was able to open up the Via del Pozzo Toscanelli, which gave access to a gate in the walls without the necessity of *andare sotto la forza de'Rossi e de'Bardi, e fu ben fatto per lo popolo*: Villani, *Cronica*, xii, 25.

[89]See the various plans of the quarters of Lucca in Pierotti, P., *Lucca; edilizia urbanistica medioevale*, Milan, 1965, for example 108, 113, 116.

[90]D'Addario, M.V., in *Vita privata a Firenze nei secoli XIV e XV*, 1966, 56.

[91]Poleggi, E., in *Urbanistica*, nos. 42–43.

[92]On this point, see below, pp. 239ff.

[93]Brattö, O., *Liber estimationum*, 50, 73.

[94]Villani, *Cronica*, xii, 8, writes of the *casolare de'Tebaldini de porta san Piero ch'è uno grande compreso*, and (xii, 10) of the judges of the duke of Athens, who *teneano corte nelle case e cortili e logge de'figliuoli Villani di san Brocolo.*

[95]D'Oria, J., *La chiesa di San Matteo in Genova*, Genoa, 1860; see Figure 2, p. 159.

[96]Janin, R., *Constantinople byzantine*, 280.

[97]As an example, see the very full and detailed enumeration of all the markets of Pavia in the description of the town by Anonymi Ticinensis, in *R.R.I.S.S.*, xi (1), 48–49.

[98]"Lamberti Ardensis Historia comitum Ghisnensium", in *M.G.H.S.*, xxiv, Hanover, 1879, Chapter 127, p. 624; quoted, with a French translation, by Roncière, C. de La, and others, 155–156: *in logium, quod bene et procedente ratione nomen accepit – ibi enim sedere in deliciis solebant ad colloquendum – a 'logos', quod est sermo, derivatum.*

[99]*Itinéraire d'Anselme Adorno*, f. 5 (a).

[100]Fleury, G. Rohault de, *La Toscane au Moyen Age*, Paris, 1870; see also Kent, F.W., "The Rucellai family and its Loggia", in *Journal of the Warburg and Courtauld Institute*, 1972, 397–401.

[101]Anonymi Ticinensis, in *R.R.I.S.S.*, xi (1), 49.

[102]This *loggia* was often situated in the church itself, a part of an outside wall, as for example that of San Pietro in Banchi, in Genoa.

[103]Quoted by Tabarrini, M., in *La vita italiana nel Trecento*, 1904, 171.

[104]Carus-Wilson, E.M., "The overseas trade of Bristol", in *Studies in English trade in the 15th century*, London, 1933.

[105]Alberti, L.B., *Ten books on architecture*, translated into Italian by Cosimo Bartoli and into English by James Leoni, London, 1965, vii, Chapter I, 134.

[106]Poleggi, E., *La strada nuova*, Genoa, 1968.

CHAPTER 5

The military power of family clans

The lineages, especially those of the nobles, which were solidly rooted in the heart of a medieval city, always commanded great military power; they threatened their enemies or their neighbours and had an important influence upon the fortunes of the city. This dangerous situation was not only a source of disturbance and constant civil war: it also went so far as to inhibit the very existence of the state. In many countries, and especially in Italy, the political life of medieval cities was merely a long struggle on the part of communes, or sometimes of princes, to impose their will and to weaken the forces of the great families. In this we also, obviously, note great chronological differences in Italy itself where, for example, the commune asserted itself in the thirteenth century in Tuscany and much later in Genoa, where the pope mastered his city only very late in time. In any case, the clans' forces, their men-at-arms and their fortresses, long affected certain aspects of life, and especially the townscape.

Dependencies and armies

In Italy the armies of rural vassals, of all kinds of dependants, were certainly the main strength of the great noble families in the early years of the communal period, in the twelfth and thirteenth centuries in Tuscany, and apparently later in Pisa than in Florence. Later, chroniclers still felt this threat and spoke of the armies of highlanders that such and such a clan could raise in its Apennine fiefs. The most turbulent families probably lived outside the city, where they had no roots, and threatened it from their distant castles.

However, in Tuscan towns the structure of the armies and all military organization bore for a long time the marks of the seignorial and family origins of military power; this was another aspect of the movement from the countryside to the town. The idea of a strictly 'communal' army formed by the 'people', recruited by the magistrates and established in the earliest years of the commune in affirmation of its independence must be greatly modified or even totally re-examined. Here, D. Waley's study of the Florentine army at the time of the defeat at Monteaperti (1250) makes a decisive contribution and emphasizes indisputably the permanence of family and seignorial institutions.[1] The famous companies of *pedites* which the chroniclers are fond of describing, and which were recruited by the *popolo*, served only to maintain internal order and intervened only in civil war. The real Florentine army was raised and organized by *sestieri*, that is, by geographical areas which were still subject to the influence of the great families. The cavalry, for the most part, was recruited on a strictly family basis: each group of relatives (*consorti*) was charged to supply and keep one or several horses. So, in the single *sestiere* of San Pancrazio, 116 of 185 horses enumerated belonged to a group of *consorti* (twenty-four to brothers, sixteen to fathers and sons, and the others to more distant relatives). The same traditions and the same system of cavalry recruitment had obtained in Siena in the 1250s.[2] These customs obviously strengthened the cohesion of noble groups and ensured their military power. The amalgamation into a commune of the seignorial families established in the city occurred only slowly, more slowly than seems to be indicated by formal texts, texts of a strictly political nature. Meanwhile, the 'communal' army was by no means an army of 'people's' militia.

Similarly, in coastal towns, the commission and command of warships and the recruitment of crews were very often left to social groups, whose military power was thus strikingly asserted. G. Volpe writes that in Pisa the 'tower associations' which linked the heads of families who jointly owned a fortified keep in the city were also, very frequently throughout the thirteenth century, 'ship associations' which commissioned vessels for the 'communal' fleet.[3] The Genoese fleet which conquered the Pisans in 1285 in the naval battle of la Meloria entered the fray according to a strict geographical order of the city's noble *compagne* and *contrade*.[4] Much later, the famous picture by Grasso shows the same Genoese fleet, in the year 1481, leaving the port to fight the Turks; the Genoese are led by enormous vessels, each bearing the colours of the family responsible for its commission, in addition to those of the admiral and the commune.[5]

This tradition was not necessarily weakened by the use of paid armies. The recruitment of mercenaries often led the commune to seek the services of the warrior clans of the mountains, who still survived without difficulty in their adherence to a 'feudal' way of life, away from the political hold of the city. It was in the mountainous areas of southern Tuscany, in the Apennines, on the borders of Romagna and the Marches, in all those areas which were still highly feudalized, that the commune of Florence found its mercenaries. Thus, from 1290 to 1293, Count Manete of Sarteano was paid by Florence in return for the service of an armed band varying between forty and a hundred men; these warriors were all mounted, which probably implied a greater number of grooms and servants; they were the count's own vassals and attendants.[6] Thus the *route* or *condotta* of mercenaries paid for by the communes of Italy was very often only a troop of feudal origin, which mustered relatives, vassals and allies around their leader, showing the undiminished military power of these family clans which were solidly established in the countryside.

Two centuries later, at the very end of the Middle Ages, the slow increase of communal power had still not taken all military power from the clans of the nobles, in the mountains or in the cities. True, in Venice the urban nobles no longer had fiefs or power of command over men; Machiavelli well said that the *gentilhuomini* of Venice were *nobili più in nome che in fatto; perchè loro no hanno grandi entrate di possessioni, sendo le loro richezze grandi feudate in sulla merchanzia e cose mobili; e di più, nessuno di loro tiene castella, e ha alcuna juridizione sopra gli huomini.*[7] In the Quattrocento the Venetian noble had no more military power than the ordinary great merchant of Florence, the burgess.

Elsewhere in Italy the position was completely different. We have already noted that the great *alberghi* of Genoa included two very distinct categories of 'nobles': on the one hand, a good many of those established in the heart of the city were employed in commerce and banking; but on the other hand there were real noblemen owning large fiefs and holding solid strategic positions,[8] who were capable of raising large armies. Even after 1450 the Genoese noblemen of the Apennines built new fortresses, or repaired old ones, and demanded that their peasant vassals maintained a watch over the walls of the township and the seignorial keep. These 'nobles of castles' were probably rarely the same as the nobles of commerce; often they did not bear the same name before their amalgamation in a vaster confederation. Thus we may distinguish, inside the clan, two types of Genoese aristocracy, and it seems difficult to appreciate to what extent the federation of family groups caused any real social mixing. Yet all the members of a given clan remained closely linked by the strong suprafamily alliance of the *albergo*, the cohesion of which is undoubted. Some amalgamations, some reinforcements of *alberghi* had, we have seen, no other aim than to unite men of fiefs with men of commerce.[9]

Even the most rapid examination of a few great families of Genoese nobles confirms the importance of these seignorial armies in the life of the city, and allows us to measure the extent of their intervention – or of their threat. True, in the Quattrocento, the families of the great leaders, of the Genoese doges, the Adorni and the Fregosi, were interested only in castles, armies and seignories; but the Fieschi who, it was said, could raise 4,000 armed highlanders in the hinterland of the Riviera di Levante, had several allies, bearing their name and subservient to their clan, who were established in the commercial metropolis, in its business quarters and in its trade. For many years the Fieschi led a harsh armed struggle against the commune itself, in an attempt to seize from it some coastal areas close to their fiefs; and in the city they instigated many disturbances, frequently causing the fall of doges and leading street riots, with the help of their own men and dependants. Thus the army of a seignorial clan remained a force which had a great influence on the fortunes of the urban state, of the city itself.

Great families such as Grimaldi, Doria and Spinola were perhaps less hostile, but nevertheless all-powerful and sometimes threatening; through the connections of their *alberghi* they controlled at once the most important commerce and banking and, nearby, fiefs rich in man-power. In contrast to the Fieschi family, these three *alberghi*, dominated by real feudal lords (having lands, fiefs, serfs, the rights of justice and banishment), also put themselves, through several of their number, in control of the *Casa di San Giorgio*, the newest institution of the city, the most free from archaic feudal influence, in some measure the most bourgeois; it was a powerful institution which tried in many respects to assert the peace of commerce and promote a city administration very different from that of previous times. This did not prevent the Doria and Spinola from raising their own armies. When the commune, under the command of the doge, gathered the soldiers of its district to defend its lands, it counted the men brought by Doria and

Spinola separately, after those of the city and the Rivieras. For example, in 1447, to attack the marquess of Finale, Genoa and its immediate environs sent 800 'men' and 400 bowmen, the eastern Riviera 1,000 'men', the western Riviera up to Noli 1,000 'men', the western Riviera beyond Noli 4,000 'men' and finally, listed separately, the Doria and Spinola sent 250 bowmen. For the second sector of the western Riviera the clerk added "including Doria and Linguiglia" (a fief of the Doria);[10] this leads us to think that the basis of recruitment here was the seignorial fief, and that the Doria *albergo* recruited its own men and led them to battle. Thus the Genoese army was by no means exclusively an army of militia; neither was it solely formed of mercenary troops raised and led by *condottieri*; it remained in large measure a 'feudal' army. This army was able to serve the commune because of the integration of several noble lineages. But this very service and these battles also reinforced the clan's political cohesion. This was also true of the fleets of warships, whose methods of recruitment are unknown to us, but whose large vessels, as we know from Grasso's picture, were put under the command of the leaders of the principal noble *alberghi*.

The private armies of nobles established in cities were undoubtedly retained in many regions outside Italy: most definitely so in Germany where, in the last 200 years of the Middle Ages, the most powerful lineages of central and southern towns (for example Mainz, Trier, Frankfurt and Regensburg), who enjoyed possession of political power, in order to maintain their positions, gathered numerous dependencies of *Muntmannen*, constituting their armed followings.[11] These protégés, recruited from the weak and the poor, rendered all kinds of services, often wearing the livery of the lineage, and they armed themselves and fought as occasion arose. Of course, they repeatedly threatened the peace of the cities, but the numerous attempts of the civic authorities to prohibit them were without great effect.[12] These bellicose practices were at times also rife to quite a late date in the towns of Flanders.[13]

In south-west France, where the cohesion of noble lineages remained strong for a long period, the great families also included dependencies of lesser men, who were often armed. Y. Renouard notes that in Bordeaux in the 1290s the chiefs of clans, constantly involved in bitter struggles, surrounded themselves with men of all ranks "wearing their livery, kept and paid by them, blindly devoted to their cause", and that these "mercenaries soon occupied as much room in these *mesnies* as the family."[14] Great numbers of small dependants of varied social origins, who were kept at the lord's table and who followed and served him, were also present in Iberia, and especially in Castile. Indeed, well beyond the fifteenth century the social structures of the cities of the interior were characterized, in an unusual way, by bands of *criados*, protégés and dependants of greatly varying status.[15]

Urban fortresses

The other factor of power, in the town and in the countryside, was the ownership of a fortified residence or of a refuge where relatives, all the members of the clan, protégés and neighbours, might be sheltered. Such a fortress alone allowed the clan to defend itself against its enemies and against the authority of the state; it thus gave the clan the opportunity to assert itself and to welcome new members. It would certainly be easy to establish a close parallel between the existence of such urban fortresses and the survival of complex social structures characterized by the presence of vast family or suprafamily groups.

First, noble families very often inherited, and used, ancient Roman monuments, which they converted and modified to a greater or lesser degree. We know the extent, in all circumstances, on all occasions, of the re-use of stones, or quite simply of the re-occupation of the buildings of ancient cities. In this way, in the very first years of the communal period, that is, at the time when feudal structures were still in the ascendant, the nobles, using ancient monuments in their own defence, held solid centres of resistance, solid stone fortresses which they had converted with little effort.

This process was probably not equally common everywhere. Several writers show that it was rather more frequent in the south of France, where the scale of urban development inherited from Rome was relatively high, and where the weakness of the economy and the low level of wealth, at least up to the twelfth century, frequently encouraged nobles, through lack of money and workmen, to use old buildings. In Aix-en-Provence they entrenched themselves inside the gates of the ancient walls and in the mausolea of the great Roman families on the Via Aurelia, beyond the eastern gate.[16] Elsewhere, they took possession of theatres, and especially amphitheatres, which offered a circular enceinte which constituted in itself a continuous bastion of stone; thus did they cut themselves off from the rest of the city.

In Narbonne the nobles established themselves in the old Roman capitol which they had transformed into a stronghold; they entrenched themselves there and defended it jointly.[17] The story of the knights of the 'castle of the arena of Nîmes' is much better known.[18] It appears that from the sixth century families of warriors, who had established themselves similarly in the *Tour Magne*, which was of Roman origin, had turned the arena into a community fortress. The arena, protected by a high outside wall in which were four gates, was surrounded by a moat (*vallatum arenarum*) and topped with two or three square towers, often mentioned in texts of the twelfth and thirteenth centuries. There were many houses in the porticos and galleries or built in the arena itself;[19] in these houses lived the families of the nobles and of their dependants. Two chapels, one with a tower, completed this rather unusual arrangement of a Roman monument. Thus the arena at Nîmes was the seat of a veritable seignory, in which each knight had his own fortified dwelling in fief from the viscount. Individually, the knights also owned, around the town, lands and fiefs, the names of which they bore: for example, Langlade, Clarensac, Aramon. Deeds of enfeoffment and oath-takings show that the numbers of families of knights of the arena constantly increased: there were about thirty in 1100, fifty in 1174 and nearly a hundred in 1226.

So in all the towns of Mediterranean Languedoc these groups of knights formed a clearly privileged social category; as masters of the only fortified parts of the city, they imposed their power and political influence on the whole town. Their strength was in their geographical concentration: at the time of the Albigensian Crusade the French occupation was immediately expressed, at least in Nîmes, in the seizure of the arena and the dispersal of the nobles, whom Louis VIII sent to different parts of the town.

Much evidence leads us to believe that in other towns of Provence amphitheatres were also fortified and used as 'castles' by several different groups, who must have shared them according to some unknown formula. This was for example the case in Arles.[20] A very curious drawing, of uncertain origin and difficult to date, shows strikingly the use which knights once made of the fortified arena of Arles.[21] This monument, which the Arabs had already turned into a fortress by topping it with four towers,[22] still, much later, presented the picture of a conglomeration of various buildings, solidly protected and isolated from the rest of the city. The external arches had all been completely blocked up, but apparently with quite light material, then in some cases pierced by very few narrow windows. This veritable fortress was guarded by three thick square towers, but on the drawing one of them seems already to have been demolished. Finally the stone houses, with their tiled roofs, and a few offering to the outside only tall, windowless walls, were arranged in three concentric rows on the old tiers, leaving a central open space. Other houses, probably of later construction, clung to the outside walls; the church too was built against this improvised enceinte. Thus, in Languedoc as in Provence, the amphitheatre is a perfect example of a great urban fortress, used and dominated by families of knights in association. This is reminiscent of the Italian tower associations of the same period;[23] it is also an example of the migration of nobles into and around existing fortifications.

Were such uses of ancient monuments much less common in Italy? Probably, like so many other Roman mausolea, the mausoleum of Hadrian was transformed into a medieval fortress. In any case the city of Rome offers almost innumerable examples which are highly characteristic of the occupation and fortification of ancient Roman edifices by warring noble families. Despite the absence of precise references and the confusing speed with which it is developed, the book of Emma Amadei[24] supplies some very interesting information on this point. The powerful and turbulent federations of nobles in medieval Rome had a considerable number of towers, some of which, apparently the most imposing and the most solid, were built with the materials and even on the sites of ancient towers or ancient monuments of all kinds. Such were the *di Mecenate* tower, which rose from the *Circus Maximus*, and especially the *Manilia* tower, which dated from Roman times and was built in the centre of the Suburra. Fourteenth-century texts refer to a *turris posita super arcum Septimi Severi* (it was demolished only in 1636). At that time the *Miranda* tower, which belonged to the Arcioni in the 1500s, still rose over the ruins of the temple of Jupiter; it served as a customs-house for cattle. Finally, the enormous and very famous *dei Conti* tower, probably dating from the early thirteenth century, was also built on a large base striped in black and white, among the ruins of another Roman temple, probably the Temple of Tellus.

It would be interesting to know whether noble families in central and northern Italy also appropriated amphitheatres and took refuge there with their dependants: in Verona, for example. We may believe, in any case, that the arena of Lucca was used in this way, for an engraving of 1820 still shows it clearly, transformed for occupation, with its arches blocked up, although relieved by a few windows; in our own time aerial photography still shows very clearly that the tall houses, some of which were five storeys high, were arranged right round the amphitheatre in two perfectly concentric rows following the plan of the ancient exterior wall; moreover this plan also included the whole of another row of houses, further out.[25]

At a later period noble family clans occupied and kept one or more parts of the city enceinte: ancient Roman walls brought back into use, or even new walls; above all, these clans sought to possess a tower, which they would have to maintain and defend in case of attack. Those towers were rarely inhabited, but served rather as refuges; they were no less important an element of power for that.

This was probably the case throughout the Mediterranean world, in the whole of southern Europe. It certainly went back to an old tradition; in Constantinople, throughout the Middle Ages, the internal wall of the ancient ramparts of Theodosius had ninety-six towers of different shapes; most were entrusted to the owners of neighbouring land, who had the use of them.[26] The cities of southern France offer several examples of this. In the 1230s the Barravi 'clan' of Toulouse owned communally a tower in the 'Saracen wall' of the city, situated right at the end of a street which also belonged to them and where their houses stood.[27] In Bordeaux the large houses of the nobles, the *oustaus*, mostly stood next to the outermost ramparts of the city, and these families had usurped possession of the nearby towers.[28] For example, the north-east tower of the walls rose from inside the d'Arsac *oustau*, and the tower near the church of St Pierre was in the Martin *oustau*. In the eighteenth century there were still three Gallo-Roman towers thus enclosed in the precinct of the *Intendance* building, which had replaced the old medieval *oustau* of Puy-Paulin, the residence of the famous Bordeaux family. It was the same, at that time, in Dax and Bayonne.[29] In Carcassonne, knights often held one of the towers or even one of the gates of the city walls in fief from the viscount.[30] In Nîmes, too, knights had built strong keeps in the Porte d'Arles; several held a tower or a gate of the castle in fief from the viscount and there too, men's names, which later became family names, bore witness to their possessions: Bernardus of Portaveteri or of Portavetula, Bertrandus of Turre, Petrus of Porto-rades.[31]

The nobles' seizure of the city walls appears to have been more rare, or is at least less definite, in Italy; especially in Tuscany where the commune itself attempted to take the responsibility for ensuring the protection of the city. Associations of *popolani* and their militia normally held the fortified gates of ramparts and could thus supervise their total defence. In some towns, however, it is uncertain whether or not noble families controlled one or other of the towers of the enceinte; sometimes these towers bore their names. In any case, nobles held the towers of the walls in places where the state had not been able to weaken their power; they also claimed towers in the oriental cities which they had conquered in the great armed expeditions of the crusades.

In the time of Martin V, about 1420, the ancient enceinte of Rome had a considerable number of towers which were still well maintained or had been rebuilt: forty-nine were in the section of the ramparts between Porta Appia and Porta Ostiense, twenty between Porta Metronia and Porta Latina;[32] as in Constantinople, most were in the hands of the great families.

The nobles of Bologna who answered Pope Honorius III's call to the crusade were drawn up in two bodies led by the Geremei and the Lambertazzi, the two most powerful families in the city; in 1219, after the capture of Damietta, the buildings of the city, and especially the many towers around its walls, were equitably distributed among the nobles of these two bodies.[33]

It seems that in the whole of the medieval West, the great families attempted to secure control of the principal fortifications of a town, especially where there were remains of Roman ramparts. This was very probably true in Germany, in the Rhineland and the southern provinces, especially in Regensburg. Even in the towns where other ramparts were built much later, on no ancient foundation, by the sovereign or by the commune of burgesses, certain families were entrusted with the maintenance and defence of one of the towers, which in that case would bear their name; it appears that this was so in Paris, at least for the enceinte of Philip Augustus.

In Rouen, in the eleventh century, one of the richest aristocrats, named Clarus, lived in the *Turris Rainerii*, which was part of the external fortifications, and which he had obtained from the abbey of Jumièges. In Bayeux, around the 1080s, two families of knights lived in fortified houses near the enceinte: one of them, occupied by the head of the lineage and his five sons, was referred to as *castellum nobile, cum turri fortissima.*[34] In Bristol, much later, in the fifteenth century, merchants still lived in towers which dominated the city's outer ramparts.[35]

Apart from the occupation and usurpation referred to above, family clans erected lofty towers, veritable keeps firmly rooted in the centres of cities; they were certainly refuges, but were also the tools of military power and domination. These towers, almost always built of stone, seem to have been the distinguishing feature of cities where noble lineages asserted themselves; here the private towers of the great families generally stood in opposition to the city gates, which were held by associations of *popolani.*

These keeps certainly date from feudal times: they were built in periods of unrest and civil war. In Rome, when the ever precarious peace was threatened by some individual conflict or other, the nobles would hurriedly erect towers of wood and brick from which defenders could hurl stones;[36] these were of course ephemeral structures, purely engines of war which could offer refuge to a few people only.

In cities, noble towers were, in any case, only a particular type of those fortifications which all powerful men erected in town or country. T. Saraina, author of a history of Verona in the Middle Ages, established a very significant parallel between the construction of urban towers and that of rural castles: in the 1180s, he says, *In breve tempo furono edificate in Verona bene settecento torri congiunte alle propre case e palagi de'cittadini . . . similmente nel territorio fecero molti e molti castelli, e roche munite di fosse e bastie, di modo tale che in ciascuno villagio vi era una fortezza murata.*[37] The armed conflicts of the city were prolonged in these country areas, and family clans everywhere built their private fortresses. In those insecure times the pride and power of a group were first asserted in a lofty, imposing, arrogant tower; in Verona again: *Questa (famiglia) che Lamberti si chiamava, per esser . . . richissime vole lasciare di se onerata memoria a posteri e percio l'anno 1173 edifico a sue spese la Torre grande chi è posta su la piazza del Mercato.*[38]

Some crude keeps were probably still being built in the second half of the eleventh century in northern Italy, especially in Tuscany. At this time, inside the walls of Padua, many of the wooden dwellings were replaced by stone houses which were fortified and topped with towers; a chronicle tells us that in this remote era there were a hundred towers in Vicenza.[39] The years 1170–1190 show a great burst of tower building throughout Italy; at least, the most significant documents date from these years. Certainly, the Lamberti built their massive tower in Florence in 1172 and the Bevenzini built theirs in 1180.[40] In Siena, in 1186, the Gallerani family were granted the right to build towers (they were to own two) and a text which probably dates from a little earlier notes an agreement between four heads of families in the city to share a piece of land and to build a tower upon it.[41] This land was the *Poggio di San Pellegrino*, and as in the case of a certain type of feudal country castle, it was a natural eminence.

The first known agreements of tower associations date from 1177 in Bologna, and from 1178, 1180 and 1209 in Florence.[42] Later, many more towers were built: families ceased to associate with one another and built, not just a single tower, but several. This was for centuries one of the important concerns of town life and a main preoccupation of noble clans.

In Italy, there is no doubt of the omnipresence and power of seignorial towers in northern and central towns, as far as Rome, although in Lombardy and Tuscany the rapid and superficial observer could be misled, by the fact that these great keeps have now practically all disappeared, into ignoring this essential part of all medieval townscapes. Bologna has retained only a few towers, although it is true to say that some of them are magnificent, quite exceptional and indisputably the finest of their time. In Tuscany the small city of San Gimignano, seen from the surrounding countryside, still gives an idea of the extraordinary spectacle offered to the traveller from afar by medieval towns bristling with slender towers which rose high above the crowds of houses. But in other towns there are only very few examples left.

We must therefore rely on documents, texts and pictures which all go to prove the existence of great numbers of towers in Italian towns. It would, I believe, be to no purpose to make a catalogue; this would certainly be tedious and could not be exhaustive. It would also be pointless to attempt to map these towers; all the towns of the ancient *Regnum Italiae*, at least up to Rome, would appear on such a map.

It is difficult to place geographical limits on this very characteristic townscape in Italy. Towards the south, or rather towards the ancient Byzantine territories, there is some uncertainty; we still lack detailed studies of urban environment and planning in the towns of southern Italy and Sicily, in Naples or Palermo for example. Travellers who passed through Naples at the end of the Middle Ages did not refer spontaneously to fortified houses with towers. One could doubtless point to the long tradition of centralized, monarchic power which may from early times have prevented family clans from entrenching themselves in fortifications: the Byzantine Empire, then the Norman kings, then the German emperors, and finally the Aragonese kings. We could possibly draw a parallel between this situation and that of Venice, which was also affected by Byzantine traditions, and where a strong state, municipal in this case, also imposed its rule. However, that is perhaps merely fanciful, and this hypothesis is not entirely satisfactory[42A] Indeed, we are ignorant of many aspects of the civilizations of the south. The great families of Ravello had *gentilizie* towers and churches. On the outskirts of Palermo, in the garden area, there were at the end of the Middle Ages many private towers rising "in the centre of the suburban estates of the great families". In the fourteenth and fifteenth centuries some land-owners built "towers which still corresponded to defensive needs": towers between eight and twelve metres high, square of base, with thick walls, solidly built and topped with *merguli quadrati.*[43]

We must also reject a different kind of limit for Italy: the demographic size and economic importance of towns. In effect, every group of dwellings, even the smallest village, necessarily had one or more fortified houses, with a tower close by. The tower was by no means a specifically urban characteristic, but rather a factor of seignorial power, which is found everywhere: simple rural estates (*poderi*) in Tuscany, bought by Florentine merchants, had their own towers.

When we investigate the extent of this phenomenon in available documents, in an attempt to establish the density of towers in medieval Italian towns, the result is surprising. It is probably not possible to take at face value some of the figures which we are given; these reflect the enthusiasm of chroniclers or amazed travellers more than their concern for precise and accurate information. Thus we must approach with circumspection the 900 towers mentioned by Gregorovius in his *History of Rome,*[44] or Verona's 100 towers,[45] although these are less improbable. On the other hand it does seem useful to emphasize that all writers and artists dwelt, normally without giving detailed figures, on the very large numbers of towers in their cities and on their astonishing density. There are two significant examples of this point of view: the anonymous author of the *Chronicle of Pavia,* having enumerated the campaniles of the churches and expressed his admiration for their fine bells, continues his enthusiastic description of the town saying: *Ceterum autem turrum super laycorum domibus excelsarum mirabiliter maximus est numerus;*[46] the highest towers could be seen from afar by any man arriving over the plain. In a similar way Lupo di Castiglionchio tried to characterize the place of towers in the countryside and social life of Florence:

E dentro alla detta piccola città ebbe in poco tempo appresso di cento cinquanta torri di Cittadini d'altezza di CXX braccia l'una, senza le torri delle mura della detta città; e per l'altezza delle molte torri che erano allora in Firenze, si dice qu'ella si dimostrava di fuori di lungi, e d'appresso la più bella e rigogliosa terra del suo piccolo sito che si trovasse.[47]

This is the traditional picture which attracts all writers: a proud city, visible from a great distance thanks to its numerous lofty towers.

The same impression is given by iconographic documents. In drawings[48] or in paintings, if they have any concern for detail, artists all give prime importance to the tower in the urban scene, often making it the main element.

This appears very clearly in the backgrounds of all the pictures by Tuscan and even Lombard painters from the thirteenth to the fifteenth century. We see the town as belonging to a part realistic, part idealized landscape; it is surrounded by strong walls and dominated by tall private towers which are far higher than those of the ramparts and even of the churches. In his 'Expulsion of the Demons from Arezzo', a fresco in the upper church of Assisi, Giotto (1267–1337) provides a remarkable example of a city bristling in this way with stout keeps; in the same church there is a similar example, a town in the background of another fresco, painted before 1300, depicting St Francis giving his cloak to the poor; this is more in the background and therefore less detailed. Ghirlandajo naturally painted the fine towers of San Gimignano in the collegiate church of the Augustinians in the town (in the fresco: 'The Funeral of St Fine'). The 'Deposition' by Fra Angelico in the convent of San Marco in Florence (about 1435) also shows in the background a fine fortified town with several towers, albeit squatter than normal, rising above the houses. Perugino (born 1448–1450) painted for the banner of the *Giusticia* a beautiful 'Madonna and Child' with a very detailed view of his city, where we can count a dozen tall and narrow towers (Perugia: Umbrian National Museum). Finally, a little-known fresco by Altichiero in the Oratory of San Giorgio, Padua, depicting the 'Beheading of St John the Baptist', also represents the city surrounded by high ramparts and dominated by several seignorial towers.

Artists' intentions are much more evident in pictures where a town is not merely a part of the background, but is represented for its own sake and studied in the details of its design, its general aspect, the arrangement of its important buildings. Such descriptive pictures or illustrated plans sometimes provide striking views of medieval Italian cities. There is thus no doubt that one of the favourite themes of painters attentive to contemporary reality was the town dominated by its seignorial towers. From this point of view there is great interest in Lorenzetti's famous fresco expressing the political and social ideal of Siena's masters; not only has the artist not forgotten his city's tall, slim towers, but a detail of the vast and complex composition symbolizing 'Good Government' also depicts a town by the sea (Talamone, it is thought), surrounded by walls and dominated by its seignorial towers.

Jean Fouquet, who stayed in Rome in 1444 and 1445, retained a very specific idea of Italian towns: fortified cities dominated by keeps. One of his miniatures illustrating the *History of Livy* represents the 'Foundation of Rome'; two companions cut blocks of stone on one shore; on the other side of the river rises the almost completed city, tightly enclosed within high ramparts of white stone, the whole dominated by a few church towers and especially by the slim, square, very tall, very closely packed towers which form a multitude of seignorial fortresses.[49] The city of Rome seems equally well provided with towers in an anonymous miniature, probably of the French school, illustrating the 'Rape of the Sabine Women', in another *History of Livy*.[50]

In the case of Genoa, a city of a quite different artistic tradition, the picture by Cristoforo Grasso, which seems to me to be one of the most authentic and characteristic, perhaps also the most detailed, of surviving medieval paintings of towns, depicts the lofty houses of the fortified city dominated by the slender, tall, crenellated towers; these square keeps, of such proud aspect, vie with the square campaniles of the cathedral and churches, striped in black and topped with pointed roofs.[51] Some of these Genoese towers, but far fewer and of more modest aspect, can still be found, presented as poor remains, on the plan published in 1573 in Rome by Antonio Lafreri.[52] In the space of a century, here, strong towers disappeared almost completely from the townscape, at a time when the large family clans were taking on a quite different nature.

Artists apparently held longer to this theme – throughout the sixteenth century – for other towns. The fresco painted towards the middle of the Quattrocento in Castiglion d'Olona by Masolino da Panicole[53] shows the towers of Rome beside fortified houses. It should be compared with the sketches of two northern artists who travelled through Rome: Martin Heemskerk in 1534 and Anton van der Wyngaerde in 1530; their work provides some very interesting representations of the seignorial towers maintained by the great Roman families.[53]

On an oblique projection plan of Orvieto, dated 1600, a large number of houses stand in the shadow of tall, slender towers, which usually rise from street corners; on this plan nearly every block of houses has its tower, and these private towers are much more numerous than church towers.[54] The collection edited by L. Benevelo shows that these observations are also true for Siena, according to a very beautiful engraving which also dates from 1600 and which represents the siege of the city by Charles V in 1555.[55] This time, the artist does not give a plan but presents a real picture of the city, embellished with a few rather naive, but certainly spontaneous scenes; above all, he emphasizes the trappings of war: the emperor's camp, the detachments of cavalry and the square formations of infantry, the ramparts with their crenellated gates and the citadel. He takes even more care to show the city's fine, lofty towers: exactly twenty slim keeps, rising high over the houses in their protection. This picture of Siena still conjures up the same image of an Italian town dominated by its towers. Noble towers can also be seen in fine positions on a small wood-cut of the sixteenth century, which gives a much more schematic picture of Pisa.[56]

Stylized, in a way symbolic, representations of towns reduced to their essential elements seem to me to be of even greater significance than these rather late overall pictures and detailed plans. Several writers have maintained that the burgesses of the Middle Ages proudly asserted their independence and autonomy by proliferating pictures of their ramparts; on seals, for example, city gates appeared symbolically to demonstrate the strength of the commune. This was so in the north, in France and especially in Flanders; but in Italy the ramparts were always accompanied by the lofty towers of seignorial residences. Thus the stylized pictures of the cities of Tuscany and Lombardy presented a double symbol: in the foreground, the gates of the political and military societies of the *popolani*; then, arrogantly dominating the whole city, the towers of the noble family clans. Such was the ideal picture of an Italian town, where the nobles demonstrated their own power for a long time, family by family.

For Lucca, often called the city "of great towers", two clear and significant stylized sketches of this type have survived; one, really very simple, illustrating the *Cronaca* of Giovanni Sercambi, dates from 1450–1460;[57] the other, more elaborate, was reproduced at the head of a page in a book printed in Venice in 1477.[58] Both show clearly, above the outer wall with its fortified gate and half-dozen towers, and rising over the houses which are sketched in more or less detail, the city's lofty towers: on the left the cathedral tower and the tower of the communal palace; on the right and all over the city, the square, slim seignorial towers. There are nineteen towers in the second picture, and they rise as high as the towers of the public buildings.

An engraving of the battle of Pavia in 1525 presents a very fine picture of the town, astonishingly foreshortened. The town is surrounded by circular ramparts in which are two solid fortified gates, but it is dominated by nine very tall, slim towers, built beside the houses.[59]

There were two other types of painting which tended to idealize towns, reducing them to the same symbolic elements. On the one hand, there were Madonnas of Mercy which protected the town with the hems of their cloaks; on the other hand were pictures of dedication to the Virgin, in which a bishop was portrayed offering the city, which he held in his outstretched hands. The best known example of the former is probably the famous fresco of the Loggia del Bigallo, still well preserved in the Palazzo della Signoria, in Florence.[60] Three examples of the bishop's offering also seem to me to be very interesting: one in the church of San Nicolo di Pisa dating from the end of the Trecento;[61] one by the painter Taddeo di Bertolo, showing San Gimignano bearing his own town;[62] and finally, the much more famous and more important fresco by Lorenzetti in the room known as *della Madonna* in the communal palace of Siena, where the artist depicted a Dominican friar offering up the city.

These reductions of towns to such a small scale conform well to our idealized picture. They emphasize particularly well the tall fortified family towers: slim and lofty, and isolated from each other in San Gimignano; wider, forming compact blocks, in Pisa. The anonymous painting of Pisa, especially, forcefully asserts the idea of a strong and noble city: within the ramparts, just behind the cathedral and baptistery, higher even than the pillared leaning campanile, is a crowning group of narrow and severe stone towers, unadorned, their walls pierced only by two or three windows; they completely dwarf the houses and the other churches.

In Italy the townscape was long thought of in terms of tall towers. From the social point of view, these often marked off the ancient noble city, the residence of the foremost clans of the founders and masters of the city, from the outer parts where newcomers had established themselves. One of the illustrations in the *Cronaca* of Giovanni Sercambi shows the construction of a wall to protect the outer districts

Fig. 3. City towers and the construction of a *rocca* (after the *Croniche* of Giovanni Sercambi, i, 23, for the year 1222) (see above, p. 204, n. 57).

Fig. 4. The towers of Lucca about 1400 (Biblioteca Governativa di Lucca. Archivio Capitolare, incunable 157, published by R. S. Lopez in *La naissance de l'Europe*, Paris, 1962, 241).

of Lucca: the towers are in the already enclosed part, and there are none in the new area.[63]

These superb keeps took on a definite symbolic value. In Lucca the most imposing towers, those which increased the pride of their owners and of the whole city, had nicknames: *Lancie, Guardamonte, Torre del Levre.*

After the harsh quarrels between factions and families, after the harsh struggles between the clans and the commune, which of course tried to assert the rule of its law against these private fortresses, the city constantly gloried in its towers, seeing in them one of the causes of its pride and beauty. Chroniclers all praised the great quantity, the height and the strength of their cities' towers: Villani and Malespini in Florence,[64] Sercambi in Lucca.[65] In 1342, in Perugia, the commune itself prohibited the sale or destruction of any tower in the inner city or in the outlying parts of the town; on this occasion the magistrates asserted: *Cun cio sia cosa la citade, casteglle e fortezze de le terre avere grandissima consegaescano bellezza e alcuna fiade utilità delle torre e essere sarcare en alcuno modo paia laidezza de la citade.*[66]

This impression of medieval cities, in northern and central Italy, dominated by numerous towers, is fortunately confirmed by detailed texts and by historical studies giving unassailable estimates of numbers. Davidsohn was able to count 135 towers in the Florence of 1180 and thought that the true figure for the city was three times greater.[67] Santini has put together two very interesting items of information: on the one hand an extract from Villani's *Chronicle* asserting that immediately after 1248 the Ghibellines *feciono disfare da 36 fortezze de' guelfi, che palagi e grandi torri . . .*; on the other hand, a statement of property lost by the Guelphs when they were exiled in 1260–1266; this was drawn up for the *estimo* and reports, among other things, the destruction of fifty-nine towers in those years.[68] On this basis Santini thinks that the number of towers in Florence, around 1250, might have been about 300.

In Rome, the *Turrigius* numbered forty-four towers in a single *borgo* of the city,[69] and several other quarters also held a considerable number. The Orsini owned several close to each other in the *Rione* no. VI, and one of the streets in this city district bore the very significant name of *contrada turri.*[70] In the neighbouring *Rione* (no. VII), Pietro delli Cosciari, doctor of law, personally owned five palaces with towers, in the fourteenth century.[71] Finally, in the *Rione Monti*, the prime area of towers within the walls of Servius, a quarter at the foot of the Oppian hill was named *Campo Terrechiano* in the Middle Ages.[72] Between the church of Santa Agata dei Goti and the famous tower *delle Milizie*, in the valleys of the Argileto and of the Suburra, rose *una vera selva di torri*.[73]

In a remarkable study of Bologna, the only exhaustive study based on all kinds of archival documents which enables us to reconstruct the townscape of a medieval Italian city from this point of view, G. Gozzadini provides information on this subject which is particularly valuable.[74] Besides extracts from the statutes of the commune, he has used and published 240 post-1300 notarial acts which mention towers: deeds of sale, of sharing, and wills. We should note that this period is already late and that by this time some noble families must have demolished or lost their private fortresses, increasingly threatened as they were by the activities of the commune. Nevertheless, Gozzadini's investigations have enabled him to identify with complete certainty 194 family towers. In fifty-four of these cases he is able to give their width and the thickness of their walls. A street-by-street summary clearly shows the astonishing density of towers in some quarters of the city: eighteen seignorial keeps in the Strada Maggiore alone, ten in the Via Porta Nuova, and thirteen in the Via Castiglione, although it was much shorter.[75]

All these figures are indisputable and it would be possible to investigate other cities with similar success; the figures reinforce our impression of the medieval Italian town – *torrita*, private fortresses dominating all townscapes.

In other countries there are fewer clues. Specific architectural traditions intervene and, in many parts of Europe, even towns where strong noble lineages were established probably possessed neither private stone fortresses, nor, *a fortiori*, stone towers. All traces of lighter, less strongly built fortresses have been lost. Yet, in at least two large regions, the lofty forms of towers did rise above the mass of city dwellings.

Information for the south of France is scarce and sketchy; but it is no less significant for that. One of the quarters of Aix-en-Provence was long known as the 'city of towers'.[76] In 1226 when he seized Avignon, Louis VIII ordered the moats to be filled in, 300 turreted houses within the town to be demolished, and the walls to be completely razed.[77] Throughout eastern Languedoc nobles still joined, in the early thirteenth century, into large groups of knights living together in country castles or, inside towns, very close to one another. Rural nobles gathered in this way in the castles of Calvisson (150 knights, it is said), le Cailar and Aubais; in Béziers, in the high part of the town, near the castle, rose several fortified and crenellated residences.[78] In Toulouse, not only did the knights hold towers on the ramparts in fief from the count; they also built other towering fortresses in the heart of the city, to protect and watch over the clan's quarter. J.H. Mundy notes several examples of such seignorial towers mentioned in different documents of the thirteenth century, especially the large tower and fortified house which the Maurandi family owned in Toulouse.[79] Most of these towers, in every town in Languedoc, were probably destroyed at the beginning of the occupation by the French, who strove from the first to weaken the power of the noble clans. Yet despite this determined action, this persistent tradition was maintained for a very long time in different towns of south-west France; it is even found in the famous tower of what is erroneously known as the Templars' house, in the *bastide* of Sainte-Foy-la-Grande. This house, dating from 1280–1300, was merely a large fortified residence; we do not know who were its first owners or what its real social function was, but it seems very comparable to the houses of the great seignorial families in older towns, a century earlier.[80]

There is no doubt that very many private towers existed in the towns of central and southern Germany, and E. Lehman has well described the role of seignorial fortresses in the development of the medieval German town.[81] After the construction of the town walls these stone towers, which were then contained inside the town, played an important part in street fighting and firmly asserted the elevated social position of the families which owned them. In short, in early times every seignorial house in a German town was a fortified house, a *festes Haus*, and towers seem everywhere to have been plentiful. At an early date Regensburg had between sixty and eighty towers; almost half were to survive for centuries, throughout the 'modern' period. The situation in Geneva was similar.[82] In certain towns further to the north, even though they had been much more extensively rebuilt, there were still many towers standing before the Second World War: as many as, or even more than, in Italy. For example, there were thirteen in Magdeburg and eight in the little city of Meissen. Similarly, there were certainly towers in the towns of the Rhineland,[83] especially in Trier and much further to the west up to Metz, where J. Schneider believes that there were large numbers of private towers; he cites the fact that towers might only be built with the authorization of the count or bishop.[84]

Thus three vast zones, central and northern Italy, the south of France and central Germany, seem to confirm that there was in the Middle Ages a special townscape, characterized by the numerous fortresses and stone towers of the nobles. It would be interesting to have information with respect to other countries, which probably had the same social structures and similar civilizations: for example, in the north of the Iberian peninsula and in different parts of northern Castile.

Finally, there is nothing to say that the towns of north-west Europe did not also witness the construction of fortified towers, as the residences of lords and notables, either close to their ramparts or in the town centres, though admittedly the prince's power, which was more evident and effective here than elsewhere, could not long tolerate such fortified houses. Unfortunately, lack of documents and detailed studies prevents us from forming an accurate idea of the townscapes of these regions. A few indications allow us to build up only a very imperfect impression, as we have noted, for example, in Rouen and Bayeux in Normandy.[85] The *Chronicle* of Gislebert of Mons refers to towers erected in Ghent by the city's powerful families.[86] In Chartres,[87] Provins[88] and Rennes,[89] powerful families lived in towers on the ramparts.

The nobles' towers and society

These towers were probably not the same in every place; their appearance depended on the townscape over which they rose, taking from it their essential characteristics and traditions: materials, general aspect, colour, the shapes of windows and battlements. We can gather sufficiently precise impressions from the often very detailed notarial acts mentioning Italian towers, and from archeological studies of German towers.

In Florence, Lupo di Castiglionchio asserted that the 150 towers which were built at the beginning of the thirteenth century were at least 120 spans high – that is, about 70 metres.[90] The highest known tower reached a height of 130 spans or 76 metres.[91] The towers which still stand in San Gimignano, although imposing, do not exceed these heights. They all appear to have been quite wide, on firm foundations. A slightly different tradition was perhaps established in Siena, where towers were slimmer and apparently higher, like the Mangia tower which rose over the communal palace; similarly too, according to our pictures, in Lucca. So we see already that there were two different townscapes in Tuscany itself.

In northern Italy these slim, lofty towers, which were always square, certainly rose higher over the houses. The finest example is of course the famous Asinella tower in Bologna, which reaches the height of 97 metres. Much less well known is the Embriaci tower in Genoa, hidden from sight by the houses which gather close round, but whose tall profile dominates the city seen from the sea; this tower is a very fine example of those slender seignorial keeps rooted in the heart of the old city; it is perched on the Sarzano hill, and its walls of thick, dark stone, without a single window, rise uninterrupted to a height of 78 metres.[92] So much for surviving buildings; but G. Gozzadini provides figures which give the exact measurements, at ground level, of the old towers of Bologna which have now disappeared: very thick walls, often 3 metres and even more; at the base, a square section varying over about fifty cases studied between 4.5 metres and 11 metres wide.[93]

German towns, for their part, had much more bulky, squat towers. They were wide and much less tall. The *Hochapfelder Turm* in Regensburg, although it was one of the tallest, seems to have been quite characteristic of southern German towns. At its base it measured 7.4 metres by 9 metres, but it rose only seven storeys high. Another tower in Regensburg, the *Heidenturm*, was only 28.5 metres high although it was 13 metres wide at the base. In Trier, too, the *Frankenturm*, with a base measurement of 6.80 metres by 14.20 metres, had only two storeys, the second being furnished with battlements.[94]

These towers were originally places of refuge in times of conflict; they were rude shelters, lacking comforts. Later, when they became reserved for single families rather than for several allied families or whole bodies of dependants, some storeys were converted into habitable rooms and the towers were used in a more permanent way.

Interior conversions of this type recall the arrangement of wooden or stone keeps of the feudal period brought to light by recent archeological research; a long passage in the *History of the counts of Guines* gives a very detailed description of this, which is remarkable in every aspect. The author, Lambert of Ardres, describes how in 1120 the count had built in the fortified town of Ardres, in Artois, a wooden house (*domum ligneam*); it was built by a carpenter of Bourbourg, *in huius artis ingenio parum discrepans a Dedalo*. He compares this keep, with its numerous rooms, offices, corridors and staircases, to an inextricable labyrinth (*Et de ea fere inextricabilem Laberintum*). On the ground floor were cellars and granaries, with all their stores. Above were the residential premises where the household gathered (*habitacio et communis inhabitantium conversatio*); they consisted of the large chamber, another chamber for the maid-servants, a small room separate, a store room and an adjoining kitchen separated into two levels, one of which was given over to the rearing of pigs and poultry. Lastly, the third storey contained the upper chambers for the children – one for sons, another for daughters – and the chapel.[95] All these rooms clearly show that in this case the 'feudal' keep was a residence for the master and his family, and for his servants.

In towns, especially in Italy and more precisely in Tuscany, heads of lineages willingly lived either in the towers themselves, or in houses with adjoining towers. In Florence, the *Liber estimationum* (1260–1266) very often uses the expressions *turrim sive palatium* or conversely *palatium sive turrim* when referring to dwellings which had been destroyed, in the town or in the countryside. This evolution of the tower between the twelfth and fourteenth centuries and later, from strict fortress to residence, can also be seen in the considerable modifications of its external appearance. Yet its defensive function, which was still of the greatest importance, imposed a pattern which we find everywhere. At ground level a single room took up the whole space. This room, protected by very thick walls and almost always having a stone vault, served as a store for victuals and munitions; later it became a meeting room where relatives and friends gathered and where men practised using weapons. This lower room was practically inaccessible from the street; its walls had very few openings, and these were narrow, easily defended. Normally, there was no special entrance at ground level.

Access to towers was through the upper storeys, either by easily withdrawn wooden ladders, or by bridges slung across from neighbouring or adjoining houses. A Genoese illustration of the thirteenth century clearly shows a sort of wooden drawbridge hanging by a chain, linking a house to a window of the upper storeys of the neighbouring tower.[96]

Inside, there were light stairs which gave access to the lower room; other stairs led to the upper storeys, and up to the flat roof. This rested on a slightly corbelled cornice and was protected by battlements. From here, at least in the early years following the construction of the first towers, stones, cannon-balls and all kinds of projectiles were hurled onto the enemy, and defenders built rudimentary catapults here. Archers positioned themselves on the different floors and shot through windows or loop-holes. At first these smooth, high, narrow walls had only very few openings, which were all narrow and purely rectangular, broached through broad slabs of stone. Tuscan painters and draughtsmen depict them thus: only two or three very narrow openings on each side, very high up. Then, when the residential function of towers became established, these slits grew in numbers and sometimes made up a kind of elegant decoration: windows with rounded arches, now much wider and in pairs, separated by more or less thick pillars, as can be seen in German towns. All the storeys of the *Hochapfelder Turm* in Regensburg were embellished with pretty windows of unusual shape, often in pairs, surmounted by a perfect rounded arch or a trefoil; they bore the arms of the family. Even the lower room was extensively lighted, on at least two sides, by two groups of these elegant windows.[97] This is an example of a tower, although it was probably built very late – most probably in the fourteenth century – in which the exclusive concern for defence faded before the quest for comfort: one of the rooms even contained a vast fireplace.

The first towers were not built by single families, but by several; apparently the cost was beyond the means of a single group. This communal construction and use of a tower offered one of the main opportunities for strengthening neighbourhood links. These tower associations, which were also formed to consecrate peace between two or more families, marked thus the beginnings of more or less artificial, certainly more extended, family clans. They played an important part in the social, political and even economic life of the medieval cities of Italy, especially in Tuscany.

The first Florentine tower associations brought together very large numbers of people, or rather of heads of families. The first agreement referred to by P. Santini, dating back to 1178, mentions fifteen or sixteen names of families involved in the erection of two or more towers. A more detailed contract of 1180 agreed between the *socii* of two towers situated in Por Santa Maria indicates at least thirty heads of families (part of the parchment containing this list has been destroyed); these men belonged to several groups and bore at least seven different names. This agreement provided for the election of *Rectores* empowered to oversee the building of the towers, to spread the cost and to decide cases in dispute. So these towers were common property divided into a certain number of shares; each share was hereditary, passing in case of death to the eldest son of each associate. For a time, one of these two towers was temporarily transferred to an associate who was engaged in an external conflict and requested the use of the tower. Moreover, the pact provided for real mutual assistance in preparation for the eventual integration of the contracting families: if one associate were driven from his house by an enemy, the others were bound to receive him in their own houses.

Another pact, dated May 1209 and concerning a single tower built near the Piazza Orsanmichele, contains other interesting provisions, especially concerning the communal use of the fortress. In this case, eleven men belonging to three different family groups took joint ownership of a piece of land for this tower to be built; the tower was divided into three equal parts and was to have three doors – one for each family, who could use only their own entrance.[98] Similar pacts were concluded in several Italian towns, at different times, for example in Bologna, in 1177.[99]

Although the statutes of these associations rarely emerge from the archives, many notarial acts which more or less marginally concern them show that they had become established very early on, and that they remained united, sometimes to a very late date. In 1174 a noble of Florence sold a quarter of a tower belonging to him and some of the terms of the contract show indisputably that a kind of tradition, or at least a precise set of customs, had become established in much earlier times, and had legal force: *Et ita ut adimpleas et observes omnia pacta et conventiones inita inter socios.*[100]

Other contracts of sale reveal greater fragmentation: for example a twentieth of a tower was sold in Florence in 1183;[101] and there was even subdivision of the original shares: in 1181 the *Rectores* of the *Torre delle Pulci* sold two thirds of a share to one Arrighetto,[102] and the *Rectores* of the *Torre del Leone* sold half a share to the descendants of the Ugocione di Nucio.[103] In 1227 a Roman notary drew up a contract entitled: *Instrumentum venditionis trium unciarum turris de Amatisiis.*[104] Above all, the Florentine *Liber estimationum* of 1260–1266 gives much information on the subdivision of towers in Florence between the leaders of a single group or between several associated groups. In the *sestiere* of Porta del Duomo, eight groups of people (joint heirs, sons or brothers) owned eight of the thirteen shares of a tower situated near the city walls, and Gerio de Sitio was compensated for two of the forty shares of another tower.[105]

The strength of this tradition is shown by the election of *consules* of a tower association at a very late date: in Lucca, in 1286.[106]

We see that a great number of people had an interest in towers. These people were closely linked by the concern to protect and defend themselves and each other, and they were also linked by family or even close blood relationships. The tower rose from the very middle of the clan's *contrada*; it dominated and protected the leaders' palaces and their dependants' houses, just as in the countryside the seignorial fortified keep dominated and protected the manorial court.

At first, families attempted to erect at least one tower immediately beside their main residence, so that they could go easily from one to the other through an inner passage which was easily walled up; thus they avoided passing through the street. This absolutely classic arrangement with the tower at the side of the house can still, now, be seen in San Gimignano, where the *Torre degli Oti* is precisely at the side of the Oti Palace, which is itself high and narrow. Here too, in an even more striking picture, the twin Salvacci towers exactly frame a narrow building which shelters between them.[107]

When several families owned and administered a tower, it would rise equidistant from the houses of all the associates, for greater ease of refuge. The clerks charged with estimating the value of the property of the Guelphs exiled from Florence in 1260–1266 frequently wrote: *unam turrim cum palatio* . . ., or *quandam turdomum juxta turrim*, or again *unum palatium sive turrim cum tribus domibus iuxta dictum palatium.*

Associates and members of tower-owning families could often enter their tower directly by means of wooden galleries. Often, too, the towers of a family clan protected a whole group of houses, a complete social unit, as can be seen from the plans of cities. Texts do not refer to the tower of such and such an individual, but to that of a whole family group; the name of the tower was in the plural; the property was manifestly common to all, as also, and especially, was the use of it. The more powerful clans were distinguished from the others by the fact that they owned several towers, but these were all in the same quarter close to their houses. In Florence, for example, the Tornaquinci belonged to an association which owned a *turris maior* and a *turris minor* built on the Mercato Vecchio, right against the family clan's houses. In the *sestiere* of San Pier Scheraggio, the Uberti ruled over a large complex of houses and towers, the highest tower being very close to their main residence. The brothers Brunetto and Gerardino degli Uberti also had a tower each in the neighbourhood of the Badia.[108]

These groups of houses belonging to the same family clan, tightly clustered around their tower, appear clearly on schematic pictures of cities as late as the sixteenth century; indeed this pattern appealed irresistibly to artists of the time. On a plan of Siena drawn up in 1555[109] the town as a whole is represented in a particularly detailed way as a rather anarchical juxtaposition of family units and their towers. This arrangement gives way to individual houses only close to the walls and in the immediate neighbourhood of the communal palace and the great religious buildings; everywhere else the houses of the nobles are clustered together; usually in groups of three or four, and climbing the slopes of the hills right up to the very tall tower against which the last house was built. On the plan of Orvieto dating from 1600[110] we can equally clearly see a very different arrangement, but it is quite as significant. Throughout the town the houses are grouped together, this time in tighter bunches of different sizes and shapes, generally around a large garden; the outside walls, on the street side, show severe façades, broken only by a few windows in the upper storeys. These houses all face the space which they enclose. On this plan, although it is of a late date, many towers are seen to rise, each over a group of houses, apparently at the most exposed point – on the street, or often at one of the corners.

The urban tower's social and military function of providing refuge and protection meant that it was for centuries one of the essential elements of social life in cities, of the communal life of the noble family clan, and of the clan's cohesion. At once symbols and causes of the nobles' power, these towers obviously opposed the authority of the state and the progression from a 'feudal' political regime to a different, more centralized system. This hostility and the use of seignorial towers as fortified keeps, explain the systematic destruction ordered by sovereigns when, after revolt or siege, they reimposed their authority; a king or prince would have city towers razed and countryside strongholds demolished. This was true of the German emperors in Lombardy: Frederick Barbarossa even destroyed the campanile of Milan cathedral. In the towns of southern Languedoc most towers disappeared during or immediately after the royal campaigns against the Albigenses.

In central Italy noble towers were especially threatened by the activities of the communes. If we read the chronicles or even the various civic ordinances and statutes, we have the impression that the attack on these fortresses was one of the main aspects of the action of municipalities against the military and political power of family clans. Yet this attack on towers, symbols of strength and arrogance, began more or less early and enjoyed unequal success; any notion of the systematic destruction of towers by the actions of an all-powerful commune must be greatly modified.

It seems that at first the commune, which was in fact a commune of consuls of the noble aristocracy and was dominated by these great noble families, guaranteed the cohesion of tower associations, and attempted to protect them. It sought to prohibit, or at least to restrict, transfers of property which might disorganize the group and cause shares to fall into the possession of opposing or non-noble families, or into the hands of strangers. In some Tuscan towns, for example in Pistoia, the municipal magistrates themselves forbade the division of towers.[111] Elsewhere, division and sale, when they were finally authorized and had become normal practice, were nevertheless subjected to all kinds of restrictions. Thus the cohesion of these social groups was maintained for many years in all these towns; and it was greatly increased in times of danger and conflict. The intrusion of strangers was avoided because associates were forbidden to dispose of their shares. In Pistoia again, the very statutes of the commune, decreed between 1191 and 1217, forbade any man to sell a share of his tower without first offering it to all the members of the *consorteria*; under no circumstances might this share be allowed to go to an open enemy of the clan.[112] In Lucca, a clause in the municipal statutes, entitled *De consortatu turrium*, gives the exact form of the oath which the *consorti* who were co-owners of a tower were to swear to each other; it also gives the precise rules which had to be observed in order to maintain joint ownership.[113] The commune of Pistoia accepted and enforced adherence to oaths sworn between individuals inside a family clan. This commune of aristocratic nobles also tolerated, and even encouraged, defence associations, against which no action was taken. In other places, if the commune did not directly intervene, strong traditions ruled. Normally, shares in towers could be sold only if one of the families lacked a male heir; even then the sanction of the *Rectores* was generally demanded.

At first, in fact, the Italian communes wished only to restrict the number of towers, to regulate their use and control their power. Above all, they ordered the destruction of fortresses belonging to rebels and exiles; this sometimes happened very early, for example, a number of nobles' towers were destroyed in Rome, in 1144.[114]

Communes often took steps to reduce the height of towers, for example in Genoa in 1143;[115] apparently the Embriaci were only allowed to keep their lofty tower, which was much taller than the others, as a reward for distinguished services rendered on the occasion of the conquest of the Holy Land (they had also been entrusted with the seignory of Giblet). Similar action can be traced through the centuries in other, very widespread cities: in Bologna in 1245, in Viterbo in 1252 and in Lucca in 1308.[116] In Lucca the municipal statutes included no less than thirteen clauses affecting towers: it was forbidden to throw stones from them and to shoot arrows from the windows.[117]

In Florence, although the power inherent in towers had long been denounced as a danger to peace and a threat to the commune's authority, the commune nevertheless struck directly and formally only very late, through the statutes of the *podestà*, which were decreed in 1324 or 1325 – well after it had begun to take measures against the magnates. These statutes ordered, first, the destruction of all towers which were badly maintained, in bad repair, more or less in ruins, and whose stones threatened to fall into the streets; then they prohibited the construction of towers higher than 50 spans (a little less than 30 metres) and the installation of catapults; towers were to be of square section. Further, these same statutes also provided for arrangements to settle conflicts between *consorterie* which might make the towers less useful.[118] The height limit on towers, which were thus reduced to such a low level, dealt a cruel blow to the pride of families and the power of their fortresses. There was therefore violent resistance to the application of these ordinances, and in Florence towers were destroyed or reduced in size only with great difficulty and very slowly.

In fact, in most Italian towns, seignorial towers resisted long and successfully the often very diffident and belated activities of communes, which found it easier to attack the specifically political power of the family clans than to abolish their military strength and the outward signs of their pride and might. Rather, towers disappeared through lack of money, as a result of neglect or desertion,[119] or else because of the evolution of methods of combat and even more of ways of life. This change in the townscape occurred slowly, often imperceptibly.

By the end of the Middle Ages the towns of Italy and even of Germany had greatly changed, but many of them still possessed their crowns of towers. Siena and Lucca, for example, still seemed to be dominated by their very tall, severe, stone keeps, although most were in bad repair, without battlements, their upper storeys threatening ruin. It seems very difficult to quantify this persistence in Genoa; yet here, where in the thirteenth century the *podestà* had ordered the destruction of private towers, several dozen such towers could still be counted in the records of the *Gabella possessionum* in the Quattrocento. They belonged to the great noble families such as the Spinola, or to other, much more modest families, some of which, truth to tell, were so unobtrusive as to have practically disappeared from the hierarchy of honour and wealth: for example, the Claritea, Scipioni and Malocelli families. The "houses with towers" were even sometimes owned by rich *popolani* such as Andreà de Rocca in 1447, or the heirs of Nicolino Sauli living in Canetto in the quarter of the Giustiniani.[120] Giovanni Piccamiglio, a businessman who between 1456 and 1460 was principally occupied in banking, in lending and changing money, belonged to a family who, despite their great antiquity, were real city 'burgesses', for they had neither fiefs nor military power. As late as 1437 this family built, or restored, a tower rising in the very centre of their *contrada*, near the *fons Piccamiglium*.[121] These towers were perhaps not all survivals, anachronisms; some, on the contrary, show a desire for power, to give a concrete and distinctive indication of high social rank.

The tower beside a noble house, the remnant of past dominance over the quarter or the assertion of a new rise in status, was for long probably much less lofty, reduced to a very modest size, sometimes only a rough imitation; but it was always very significant, and one of the most characteristic aspects of urban architecture in numerous towns: for example, in all the communes and seignories of Italy, in Corsica[122] and Germany, in eastern France and the whole of southern Languedoc up to Auvergne. It is also found in Italian country districts, in simple country houses such as those near Genoa or in the magisterial houses which evolved from seignorial fortified houses, as in Tuscany. When they bought rural estates, Florentine merchants kept the old seignorial tower if there still was one; in all cases the leaders' large houses, surrounded by all kinds of offices and *case di laboratori*, were embellished by a squat, square, not inelegant tower, which was pierced by wide windows. This was also the case near Palermo.[123]

Even if they lacked towers, from the earliest times and throughout the Middle Ages all nobles' houses were like fortresses. Italian texts, in Bologna, Siena and Rome, distinguish between towers and houses with towers,[124] *case-torri*, which were at least fortified houses, each topped by a watch-tower. In any case, in all the areas where family clans were established and to which we have referred, the military function of a noble's house imposed on it for centuries a very special appearance. The little Tuscan town of Sovana, situated remarkably well for defence at the meeting of two steep valleys, still to this day possesses a very large number of fine houses with tall, narrow towers. It is a magnificent and well-preserved example of civil architecture of the Middle Ages, although far removed from the great economic centres.[125] In Metz, one of the old noble houses of the Rue des Trinitaires, the *hôtel Saint-Livier*, which O. Stiehl has described and depicted,[126] is a very fine example of this highly characteristic style: a narrow building of at least four storeys, the whole façade topped by battlements, and having a tower of about two storeys above the main house; this tower, which was apparently used as a dovecot and to keep a look-out, contained a staircase which ensured access to the different floors of the house.

Even when there was no lateral tower, or when it had shrunk to the level of the rest of the building, the ancient characteristics of the noble house still remained very clear: the height of the house, its narrow frontage (normally only two windows on each floor) and above all the stairs at the side giving access to every floor, which recall the fortified towers with their external ladders or internal staircases. All this shows the previous, and perhaps even continuing, desire to isolate and protect the living rooms. This very characteristic arrangement was found in all the fine noble houses of Metz, although they no longer had towers.[127] In the south, the side stairs at the front are also found in Italy, and most clearly in Genoa,[128] and otherwise in many other cities, towns or even villages of eastern Provence[129] and Corsica. It would be instructive to seek in Italy and Provence, and indeed in the whole of the south, houses of this pattern belonging to a much later tradition, and to study their geographical distribution, contrasting these lofty houses with side stairs with the more squat houses whose stairs are either central or rise from one of the rooms. This difference could conceal others which I have already mentioned, between the towns where the traditions of noble clans long prevailed, and those where such traditions were not so strong.[130]

Notes

[1]Waley, D., "The army of the Florentine Republic from the twelfth to the fourteenth century", in Rubinstein, N. (ed.), *Florentine studies*, 70–108; see especially 74, 75.

[2]See *Libri dell'Entrate*, xii, 49–58, quoted by Waley, D., in *Florentine studies*, 75, note 4.

[3]Volpe, G., *Medio Evo italiano*, Florence, 1904, 85–86.

[4]Sant'Angelo, C. Imperiale de, *Annali genovesi*, Rome, 1929, ii, 54; these two facts are referred to by Poleggi, E., in *Urbanistica*, nos. 42–43, 13.

[5]The sixteenth-century copy by Cristoforo Grasso is kept in the Naval Museum of

Pegli; the original was painted at the end of the fifteenth century; it represents the city of Genoa and an armed fleet setting out against the Turks in 1481. See Volpicella, L., *Genova nel secolo XV.*

[6]Waley, D., in Rubinstein, N. (ed.), *Florentine studies*, 92–93.

[7]Quoted by Renaudet, A., in *Machiavel*, Paris, 1956, 137.

[8]See Heers, J., *Gênes*, for a political map of Liguria (Appendix) and comments, pp. 592–596.

[9]This was true of the alliances between the Grimaldi and Ceba families, and between the Grimaldi and the Oliva; see above, pp. 79–80.

[10]*A.S.G.*, Diversorum Registri, 21 November 1447.

[11]Glass, O., *Die Muntmannen*, quoted by P. Dollinger in *Recueils de la Société Jean Bodin*, vii.

[12]Dollinger in *Recueils de la Société Jean Bodin*, vii.

[13]Espinas, G., in *R.H.D.F.E.*, 1899.

[14]Renouard, Y., *Bordeaux sous les rois d'Angleterre*: volume ii of Higounet, C. (ed.), *Histoire de Bordeaux*, Bordeaux, 1965, 80.

[15]Miss M.C. Gerbet is at present engaged on research on social structures in the nobility of Estremadura.

[16]See Laphand, J., *Aix-en-Provence, Son histoire, son destin*, Marseilles, 1950; Pourrière, J., *Aix-en-Provence; rues et monuments*, Aix, 1953; Pourrière, J., *La ville des tours d'Aix-en-Provence*, Aix, 1958.

[17]Divic-Vaissette, *Histoire du Languedoc*, i, 123–124; iii, 353–354; iv, 672, 824.

[18]Michel, R.A., "Les chevaliers du château des arènes de Nîmes aux XIIe et XIIIe siècles", in *Revue historique*, 1909, 45–61.

[19]Ménard, *Histoire civile, ecclésiastique et littéraire de la ville de Nîmes*, i, 75; iii, 26; quoted by Michel, R.A., in *Revue historique*, 1909.

[20]Anibert, *Mémoires historiques et critiques de la ville d'Arles*, ii, 266; quoted by Michel, R.A., in *Revue historique*, 1909.

[21]A drawing of the arena at Arles was published by Anibert in *Mémoires d'Arles.*

[22]On these alterations see Benoit, F., *Arles*, Lyons, 1907.

[23]See below, pp. 194–195.

[24]Amadei, E., *Roma turrita*, 5, 17, 19; we should also note that the Theatre of Marcellus became the fortress first of the Pierleoni, then of the Savelli, then of the Orsini; the Caetanni established their tower upon the tomb of Caecilia Metella; and the Francigani quarrelled with the Annibaldi over the Coliseum and turned the arches of Titus and Constantine into fortified bastions.

[25]Corsi, D., *Statuti urbanistici medievali di Lucca*, Venice, 1960, Plates 16, 17.

[26]Janin, R., *Constantinople byzantine*, Paris, 1950.

[27]*Et in fundo illius carrerie erat turris rotunda in clausura civitatis que turris erat predicti domini Arnaldi (Barravi) et fratrum suorum*; Toulouse, Bibliothèque Municipale, MS. 490, f. 113; quoted by Mundy, J.H., in *Liberty and political power in Toulouse, 1050–1230*, 11.

[28]Drouy, L., *Bordeaux vers 1450*, Bordeaux, 1874.

[29]Renouard, Y., *Bordeaux sous les rois d'Angleterre*, 465, 496.

[30]Devic-Vaissette, *Histoire du Languedoc*, v, cols 919–926.

[31]Michel, R.A., in *Revue historique*, 1909.

[32]Amadei, E., *Roma turrita*, 3.

[33]Gozzadini, G., *Delle torri*, 286.

[34]Musset, L., in *Annales de Normandie*, 1959, based on the *Vie de Geoffroy, abbé de Savigny*, ed. Sauvage, E.P., *Analecta bollandiana*, 1882.

[35]For Bristol see Carus-Wilson, E.M., in *Studies in English trade in the XVth century*, 1933.

[36]Amadei, E., *Roma turrita*, 9.

[37]Saraina, T., *Le historie e i fatti de' Veronesi nei tempi del Popolo e Signori Scaligeri*, Verona, 1542, 3.

[38]Dalla Corte, *Storia di Verona*, Verona, 1590, 286; quoted by Gaspard, M.H., in "Une chronique véronèse inédite (1115–1405)", 190.

[39]Gozzadini, G., *Delle torri*, 8.

[40]Santini, P., "Società delle torri in Firenze", in *A.S.I.*, 4th series, no. 20, 1887.

[41]Bigwood, G., and Grunzweig, A., *Les livres de comptes des Gallerani*, 27.

[42]Santini, P., in *A.S.I.*, 1887, 46–55.

[42A]There are very few texts from which we can build up an accurate picture of Venetian aristocratic palaces, and the towers themselves have not survived; but despite appearances it seems certain that these palaces were protected by towers up to a relatively late period, perhaps up to 1200 or 1250. Proof of this is furnished in many toponymic details. The palace given to Petrarch, long after his stay there, bore the name *palazzo delle due torri*, given to it by the *geminas angulas torres* referred to in other texts. See Pavan, E., "Maisons, urbanisme et structure", 50.

[43]Bresc, H., "Les jardins de Palerme (1290–1460)", in *Mélanges de l'École française de Rome*, lxxxiv, 1972, 84. Perhaps the Italians borrowed from the Orient these systems of defending gardens and orchards or irrigated fields; at any rate the fields around the towns in the Holy Land were guarded by fortified towers (see Prawer, J., "Colonisation activities in the Latin kingdom of Jerusalem", in *Revue belge de philologie et d'histoire*, 1951); this was especially so in Acre; see Rey, E., *Recherches historiques et géographiques sur la domination des Latins en Orient*, Paris, 1877. In the kingdom of Granada at the end of the fifteenth century, shortly before the Christian reconquest, peasant houses in the *vega* (irrigated plain) and in the outlying parts of cities were still protected by a tower which rose one or two storeys above the main house. This Mediterranean tradition of a fortified rural house whose walls surrounded a central courtyard and a single tower for defence was perhaps the heritage of the Roman *villae* of large estates, as may be seen in North African mosaics, especially in present-day Tunisia. This tradition was also maintained in the Visigothic *villae* around Cordoba.

[44]Amadei, E., *Roma turrita*, 3.

[45]See Saraina, T., *Le historie e i fatti de' Veronesi* and Dalla Corte, *Storia di Verona*.

[46]Anonymi Ticinensis, in *R.R.I.S.S.*., xi (1), 17.

[47]Messer Lupo di Castiglionchio, *Epistola o sia ragionamento*, ed. Meur, L., Bologna, 1753, 72; quoted by Santini, P., in *A.S.I.*, 1887, 25.

[48]Volpe, G., and Volpicelli, L., *La città medievale italiana nella miniatura*, Rome, 1960.

[49]Paris, Bib. Nat., MS. fr. 273, known as the *Tite-Live de Versailles*, f. 7 (about 1475).

[50]Paris, Bib. Nat., MS. fr. 20071, reproduced in Piponnier, F., *Costume et vie sociale: la cour d'Anjou (XIVe–XVe siècles)*, Paris, 1970, Plate XXIVa.

[51]See Volpicella, L., *Genova nel secolo XV*; the picture of the port quarter is reproduced in Heers, J., *Gênes*, Plate 3, facing p. 322.

[52]Reproduced in Benevelo, L., *La città italiana nel Rinascimento*, Milan, 1969, Plate IX, p. 64.

[53]Reproduced in Amadei, E., *Roma turrita*, Plate I, pp. 4–5, 10.

[54]Benevelo, L., *La città italiana*, Plate XVI, p. 82.

[55]Benevolo, L., *La città italiana*, Plate XXVI, p. 107; this picture is also reproduced, in a larger format, on the dust jacket of the book.

[56]Reproduced in Tolaini, E., *Forma Pisarum*, Pisa, 1969, Plate IV, b.

[57]*Archivio capitolare di Lucca*, Incunable no. 157; reproduced in Pierotti, P., *Lucca; edilizia urbanistica medioevale*, Plate I (see also Fig. 3, p. 186). See also the drawings presented by Bongi, S. (ed.), in Sercambi, G., *Croniche* (Archivio di Stato di Lucca, MS. 107). This illuminated manuscript, written in 1424, is illustrated with numerous figures in watercolour, which Bongi's edition reproduces as sketches. The town appears several dozen times, and is always stylized as outer walls dominated by the seignorial towers – generally six or seven. One very fine picture of Lucca (i, 84) shows the town crowned by fifteen towers and other fortified palaces from which fly oriflammes (but there are only two church towers). When other cities are represented, it is in a similar way; such is Bologna, with six towers, one of which rises high and leans (i, 98); such also are Pistoia (i, 54), Petrasanta (i, 91) and Motrone (i, 169).

[58]See Pierotti, P., *Lucca; edilizia urbanistica medioevale*, Plate 9.

[59]This engraving is reproduced without a precise reference in *Journal de voyage de Montaigne*, Paris, Club français du livre, 1954, facing p. 326.

[60]This fresco dates from 1340–1350; the detail which is most characteristic for our present concern is reproduced in Mèlis, F., *Aspetti della vita economica medievale*, Plate LXXVI, facing p. 378.

[61]Tolaini, E., *Forma Pisarum*, Plate XXVI.

[62]Reproduced on the dust jacket of Fiumi, E., *Storia economica e sociale di San Gimignano*, Florence, 1961; the picture is in the Civic Museum, San Gimignano.

[63]Sercambi, G., *Croniche*, i, 221.

[64]Villani, G., *Cronica*, ed. Gherardi-Dragomani, Florence, 1844–1845, cap. 45.

[65]Sercambi, G., *Croniche*, ii, 101.

[66]Statute of 1342, Perugia, Lib. IV, Rubr. 93, ed. Giustiniani degli Azzi: "Lo statuto del 1342 del Comune di Perugia", in *Corpus statutorum italicorum*, i, Rome, 1913; ii, Rome, 1916; quoted by Braunfels, W., in *Mittelalterliche Stadtbaukunst in der Toskana*, Berlin, 1953, 179.

[67]Davidsohn, R., *Forschungen zur älteren Geschichte von Florenz*, Berlin, 1896; Stahl, B., *Adel und Volk*, 78.

[68]Santini, P., in *A.S.I.*, 1887, 26, 28.

[69]*Crypt. Vatican*, part 2, p. 407, in Muratori, *Ant. Ital.*, i, 364; quoted by Gozzadini, G., in *Delle torri*, 8.

[70]Amadei, E., *Roma turrita*, 79, 83.

[71]Amadei, *Roma turrita*, 102.

[72]Amadei, *Roma turrita*, 15.

[73]Amadei, *Roma turrita*, 10.

[74]Gozzadini, G., *Delle torri*.

[75]Gozzadini, G., *Delle torri*, 59f.

[76]On the city towers of Aix, see Laphand, J., *Aix-en-Provence*, Pourrière, J., *Aix-en-Provence* and Pourrière, J., *La ville des tours d'Aix-en-Provence*.

[77]"Gesta Ludovici", *Historiens de France*, xvii, 310a.

[78]Michel, R.A., *L'administration royale dans la sénéchaussée de Beaucaire*.

[79]Mundy, J.H., *Liberty and political power in Toulouse, 1050–1230*, 11; the Caraborda family also had a tower in the town.

[80]Rouville, J. de, "Les bastides dans la région de Sainte-Foy-la-Grande. Urbanisme et peuplement (XIIIe–XVe siècle)", unpublished dissertation, University of Paris X, 1970, 46–47.

[81]Lehman, E., in *Settimane di studio del Centro italiano di studi sull'alto medioevo*, vi.

[82]Babel, A., *Histoire économique de Genève des origines au début du XVIe siècle*, Geneva, 1963, 515–516. In the sixteenth century a Genevan pastor described the outskirts of the city: "Built of churches, rich houses and towers".

[83]Uslar, R. von, "Turris, Curtis und Arx im Mainz des frühen Mittelalters", in *Kölner Jahrbuch für Vor- und Frühgeschichte*, 1967–1968.

[84]Schneider, J., *La ville de Metz*, 118.

[85]See above, p. 178.

[86]Gislebert de Mons, *Chronique*, ed. Vanderkindere, 192; quoted by Schneider, J., *La ville de Metz*, 118.

[87]Chèdeville, A., *Chartres et ses campagnes du Xe au XIVe siècle*, Paris, 1973, 417–418.

[88]Bourquelot, F., *Histoire de Provins*, Paris, ii, 379.

[89]Leguay, J.P., *La ville de Rennes au XVe siècle d'après les comptes des miseurs municipaux*, Rennes, 1968, 276.

[90]Quoted by Stahl, O., *Adel und Volk*, 78.

[91]Gozzadini, G., *Delle torri*, 10.

[92]Grassi, L. I., "La torre degli Embriaci", in *Giornale ligustico*, Genoa, 1878, v.

[93]Gozzadini, G., *Delle torri*, 10.

[94]Stiehl, O., *Der Wohnbau des Mittelalters*, 117–118; the *Frankenturm* was probably built in the eleventh century with materials from the ruins of Roman buildings; the parts of the walls which were built of brick were reinforced with cornices and bands of large, rectangular stones; for the groins of the façades, large ashlar-stones were used.

[95]See "Lamberti Ardensis Historia comitum Ghisnensium", in *M.G.H.S.*, 1879.

[96]"Annales génoises de Caffaro", Paris, Bib. Nat., MS. Latin 10136, f. iii v°.

[97]Stiehl, O., *Der Wohnbau des Mittelalters*, p. 118, fig. 107.

[98]Santini, P., in *A.S.I.*, 1887, 46f.

[99]Gozzadini, G., *Delle torri*, 8.

[100]Bellomo, M., *Ricerche sui rapporti patrimoniali tra coniugi.*

[101]*Documenti di storia italiana*, x: *Documenti dell'antica-costituzione del Comune di Firenze*, ed. Santini, P., Florence, 1895, 527; quoted by Stahl, B., *Adel und Volk*, 80.

[102]*Documenti dell'antica costituzione del Comune di Firenze*, 526.

[103]Santini, P., *Studi sull'antica costituzione del Comune di Firenze*, 535; quoted by Stahl, B., *Adel und Volk*, 80.

[104]Amadei, E., *Roma turrita*, 103.

[105]Brattö, O., *Liber estimationum*, Porta del Duomo, 78f., nos. 419, 438.

[106]Santini, P., in *A.S.I.*, 1887, 55.

[107]For two remarkable photographs see Fiumi, W., *Storia economica e sociale di San Gimignano*, figs. 7, 8.

[108]Stahl, B., *Adel und Volk*, 79.

[109]See Benevolio, L., *La città italiana nel Rinascimento*, 107.

[110]Benevolio, L., *La città italiana nel Rinascimento*, Plate XVI, p. 82.

[111]Braunfels, W., *Mittelalterliche Stadtbaukunst*, 180.

[112]Stahl, B., *Adel und Volk*, 79, note 38.

[113]Gozzadini, G., *Delle torri*, 28.

[114]Braunfels, W., *Mittelalterliche Stadtbaukunst*, 179, note 601.

[115]Braunfels, W., *Mittelalterliche Stadtbaukunst*, 179, note 601; based on *Cod.*

Diplomatico della Republica di Genua. Fonti italiani di storia patria, Rome, 1936, i: *Breve Consolare.*

[116]Braunfels, W., *Mittelalterliche Stadtbaukunst,* 179, note 601.

[117]Gozzadini, G., *Delle torri,* 26.

[118]Santini, P., in *A.S.I.*, 1887, 28, 37; for all these measures taken by the communes against towers, see the many examples quoted by Gozzadini, G., *Delle torri,* 33–49.

[119]In Lucca, in 1196, two badly-maintained towers collapsed into the street, causing deaths; see Sercambi, G., *Croniche,* i, 11.

[120]*A.S.G.*, Possessionum gabella, Anno 1447; two registers: Nobili and Popolani, incomplete.

[121]Heers, J., *Le livre de comptes de Giovanni Piccamiglio,* 7.

[122]Mérimée, P., has provided an excellent description of these towers in the small towns and villages of Corsica, as they were when he visited the island in 1839: "It is a square building about forty feet tall . . . The narrow door opens eight feet above the ground, and access is by a very steep staircase. Above the door there is a window which has over it a kind of balcony like a machicolation, from which unwelcome visitors may safely be felled . . . I should add that the residential buildings adjoin the tower, often being linked to it by an internal passage". *Colomba,* Paris, 1964, 82–83.

[123]Bresc, H., in *Mélanges de l'École française de Rome,* 1972, 84; on this matter the author quotes La Duca, R., "Sviluppo urbanistico dei quartieri esterni di Palermo", in *Quaderno dell'Istituto di elementi di architettura,* Palermo University, Faculty of Architecture, iv, 1964, 6.

[124]Gozzadini, G., *Delle torri,* 29–31; Nardi, L., and Molteni, L., *Le case torri lucchesi,* Florence, no date. In the very late Middle Ages, in Italy, towers were still regarded by some theoreticians and practising architects as a fundamental and indispensible element of a leader's house. In his famous architectural treatise of 1537 Sebastiano Serlio (1475–1554), who was admittedly a native of Bologna, the city of towers, but left to live in Rome and Venice before going to work at Fontainebleau, states that the "leader of a party" must live in a fortress which possessed a corner tower where he could take refuge and defend himself for long periods. See Colombier, P. du, and d'Espezel, P., *L'habitation au XVIe siècle d'après le 6ème Livre de Serlio,* Paris, no date, 37–38.

[125]There is a very interesting photograph in Bautier, R.H., *Civilisations, peuples et mondes,* Paris, 1967, iii, 329.

[126]Stiehl, O., *Der Wohnbau des Mittelalters,* 119.

[127]Schneider, J., *La ville de Metz,* 380.

[128]Belgrano, C., *Vita privata dei Genovesi,* Genoa, 1876; Pandiani, E., "La vita genovese nel Rinascimento", in *Atti della società ligure di storia patria,* xlvii, 1915.

[129]For example, the house which I believe is very characteristic, which still stands in Grasse, near the former church of the Franciscans; in this house we see very clearly all the characteristics of houses which developed from the fortresses of the nobles: on the ground floor a large vaulted room (now a garage); a very narrow frontage, three storeys high; a very distinct lateral staircase. In villages high up in mountainous areas, too, upper storeys were reached by means of a steep staircase at the side of the house; see Raymon, V., in *Actes du XC[e] congrès des Sociétés savantes (Nice 1965).*

[130]Domestic architecture of this kind is found, although it is less characteristic, in several towns of the north; for example in Paris: see Bruel, A., "Notice sur la tour et l'hôtel de Sainte-Mesme nommé l'hôtel du Pet-au-Diable", in *Mémoires de la Société de Paris et de l'Ile-de-France,* 1887, 239–256.

CHAPTER 6

Family clans: total communities?

The strength of the cohesion of family clans varied according to circumstances and areas; it did not depend solely on the desire for defence or vengeance, and was not asserted only in vendettas and towers. These groups also took on economic power; they became communities, governed sometimes very strictly. They had a clear sense of social responsibility and all their members often also shared the same faith and belonged to a single religious community; in the heart of a city, they would all belong to a particular parish, which was characterized by them. All these factors enable us to focus on the group; they show the life of a medieval city, and men's activities and devotions within it.

Economic communities

The family societies or companies which engaged in commerce, industry or banking, even in their most diverse and developed forms, were the direct heirs of the collective exploitations of landed estates. In the towns, these societies were the result of continuing rural habits and organization, the attitudes of peasant owners of small properties as well as of nobles who possessed large fiefs. Brothers who were business associates never forgot the old ways of collective exploitation of land, indeed they nearly always stayed together in the collective management of their country properties.

From this point of view, too, we can see important contrasts if we study the law and administration of rural property. Even leaving aside the artificial communities (tacit communities, brotherhoods) which R. Aubenas has so rightly brought to our attention,[1] certain parts of the West long held to indivision of inheritance; in these regions there were many associations of heirs or brothers. Yet it seems that in other regions each child, or at least each son, was quick to claim his own portion; family cohesion had weakened, and could not prevent the division of inheritances.

A study of how the restrictions applying to lineages were observed or broken in different regions and levels of society would reveal serious variations in the development of laws and customs. These restrictions, whose purpose was to keep intact and undivided at least the landed part of patrimonies, were most evident when inheritance or sale took place. Often, they attempted to limit the freedom of the testator and the privileges of his main heir. We are not here concerned with the extraordinary diversity in laws or customs of succession applying to nobles, even in France at the end of the Middle Ages; this very diversity shows the greater or lesser resistance of lineages to the idea of the rights of the individual, of the head of the family, and to the notion of equality between heirs.[2] Even in areas where the right of the eldest son was established, the portion which was allotted to him, normally by custom, varied greatly.

Whatever happened, clans sought to prevent any property from passing out of the family. This was done either, in the case of inheritance, through the *réserve* (the testator was prevented from transferring a certain proportion of the patrimony outside the family, especially through charitable donation), or, in the case of sale, by the invocation of *laudatio parentum* (the consent of the relatives)[3] or of the *retrait lignager* (the right of any relative to buy back, at the price paid, property sold to a stranger).[4]

At the end of the Middle Ages, in Franche-Comté, a noble could still not dispose of his property at will; he could appeal to his overlord and to the courts of the archbishop or of the duke of Burgundy, but he had to take account of the rights of all his relatives. These preoccupations are brought out in wills: testators made all those of their relatives who were present swear to respect all their provisions, and not to oppose the fulfilment thereof; or testators would attempt to buy off their relatives by giving them all a sum of money.[5]

In the heart of the Ile-de-France, in Mantes, in the 1380s, the consent of 'kindred friends' and neighbours was still necessary for the property of a minor to be disposed of: for example, two guardians "summoned their kindred friends and neighbours to know their opinion" on the sale of a ruined house;[6] in this case the friends and neighbours were numerous: eight men, bearing different surnames.

This custom demonstrates the strength of tradition and the weight of restriction on the freedom to dispose of property, although here community customs had suffered considerably from the encroachment of royal power.

Rather than fiscal records or lists of hearths, we must study land registers and cadastres to see whether the ancient tradition of indivision was long retained in any particular region. Usually, we lack documents; or else what documents we do have have not been examined with this in mind.

More detailed work has been done on this subject in relation to Italy; in it we again see the diversity of social milieux and structures. D. Herlihy has studied, not cadastres but private documents concerning lands in Tuscany; he notes that lands held in common, usually indicated by the phrase "sons of" or "heirs of", formed 15 per cent of the total between 976 and 1000 and 21 per cent between 1001 and 1025, although they had been only 7 per cent in the eighth century.[7] So, economically speaking, the great noble family in Tuscany seems to have been, not a survival from ancient times, but rather an ever-increasing consolidation of an original nucleus. Herlihy also says, however, that this same family community was rapidly weakened between the twelfth and the fourteenth centuries, that is, mainly during the time when the commune was in the ascendancy. There was a barely perceptible recovery at the very end of the Middle Ages, probably due to disasters and upheavals of all kinds.[8] However, it must be added that these last, rather pessimistic conclusions of Herlihy, on the decline of the common ownership of property among family clans, especially in Florence in the so-called 'communal' period, rely on provisions found in legislation against the magnates, and also on several passages in Villani's *Chronicle* which describe, in decisive terms, the decline of particular families; this is in contrast to his conclusions for earlier periods, which are based on statistics. It is difficult to compare results arrived at from such different sources and by such different methods, and in truth, the second method is less persuasive than the first.

There is no evidence that decrees against the magnates were successful; and the disappearance of several clans, sometimes for accidental reasons, does not necessarily imply a general break-up of all the Tuscan *consorterie*. In fact, there is a detailed document which allows us to correct, or to modify, this point of view. This is the *Liber estimationum* which gives an interesting picture of the damage suffered by the Guelphs during their exile from Florence in 1260–1266.[9]

For each *sestiere* of the city I have tabulated the number of heads of families which are mentioned with some indication of common property: *et consortum* or *et nepotum*; *heredes* or *filii*:

Sestiere	*Total number of entries*	*Uses of* 'et consortum'	*Uses of* 'et nepotum'	*Uses of* 'Heredes' or 'filii'	*Total number of communal properties*	*Per cent of total*
Oltrarno	46	3	2	4	9	20
San Piero Scheraggio	47	4	3	11	18	38
Borgo	31	7	2	11	20	65
San Pancrazio	23	0	2	6	8	34
Porta San Piero	28	1	4	7	12	42
Porta del Duomo	27	1	0	5	6	22
Total	202	16	13	44	73	36

These percentages are very high, and very surprising; they affect only the Guelph aristocracy, and vary quite remarkably according to area.

These evaluations of property in thirteenth-century Florence always give exact details of neighbours, as well as descriptions of the properties themselves. It is more difficult to study these neighbours, but such a study of each quarter throws light on a much larger number of property owners belonging to more diverse families and greatly differing social circles. Of all landowners who were neighbours of the Guelphs, 48 per cent in the *sestiere* of Oltrarno are referred to (normally by the words *heredes* or *filii* or *fratrum*) as having communal property; the comparable figures are 52 per cent in San Piero Scheraggio, 56 per cent in Borgo and up to 73 per cent in Porta del Duomo.[10] These figures are far higher than those given in the table above, and they show beyond all doubt that the economic cohesion of family clans and indivision of property were maintained in Florence, even if their political power and autonomy might have been eroded;[11] this state of affairs is observed quite late in time, and much more clearly than D. Herlihy has indicated.

Such cohesion was not peculiar to Florence or even to Tuscany; it was evident, and sometimes for much longer, in other parts of Italy. The few examples which C. Rotelli has transcribed from the cadastral registers of Chieri, in Piedmont, indicate that the terms *et fratres* or *heredes* were still in use in 1437, 1466 and even 1514; and so, therefore, was common ownership, at least between heirs.[12]

This was also the case in Liguria: 1,069 properties are listed in the cadastre of Sestri Levante, on the Riviera di Levante, in 1467, and about 31 per cent of these were owned communally; they are either described in detail or referred to by the simple formula *heredes quondam* or *et fratres*.[13] So here, family cohesion was as strong as in the Tuscan countryside, two centuries previously – perhaps even stronger. Here again is that close cohesion which has been found so often in the Ligurian Riviera and Apennines – that rural archaism so typical of all mountainous or simply isolated areas. From an economic point of view, indivision of inheritance was reinforced, or clarified, through *affrairamentum*, by which men provided, in the presence of a notary, for communal possession of all property, for a communal way of life, and for joint responsibility for taxes; this would be for a long period, twenty-five years for example. In contrast to other regions, such as Provence,[14] this arrangement (called here, a *fresca*) involved only brothers or very close relatives – uncles and nephews – but never, apparently, sons-in-law. In fact these communities which were formed by legal contract were not very different from the many others which arose and were maintained purely through the tacit agreement of all those who jointly inherited indivisible property. The only difference is that in the *fresca* the community included not only the property from one legacy but, without exception, all the property of the contracting relatives.[15]

It appears that the situation was exactly the same in Genoa in this period, although here the commune was undoubtedly more restrictive. According to the extensive records of the *Gabella possessionum*, 23 per cent of the Spinola di San Luca owning buildings in the city, in 1447, owned them communally (they are referred to as *heredes* or *filii quondam*); for the Doria, the corresponding figure is 33 per cent.[16]

Another indication of the persistence of the economic community in family clans, or at least of the strength of the restrictions which they imposed on individuals, is the number of female heads of families. J.C. Russell[17] and D. Herlihy[18] have both noted that on every tax, hearth or cadastral register the proportion of women (generally widows) who were responsible for a hearth or were property-owners in their own right, is an interesting indication of the cohesion of family clans. When the figure is low (5–10 per cent), these widows were not isolated, not counted separately from their young children; they held their dead husbands' families together, and this proves that family links were strong. If on the other hand the figure is high (15–20 per cent) the fact is that widows lived alone and family ties were weak. It must be added, however, that the proportion of women who were responsible for their own hearths seems to have been very unstable even inside any one area, so this variation may have been due to special circumstances.[19]

In this detail, as in others, the countryside of Liguria differs considerably from Tuscany. The proportion of hearths ascribed to women around Pistoia is 12 per cent (J.C. Russell) or 9.8 per cent (D. Herlihy) in 1244, and 7.6 per cent in 1427 (D. Herlihy).[20] In every case the figure seems to have fallen, so family links, which were already relatively strong in 1244, became even stronger in the following two centuries. This confirms the previous evidence which D. Herlihy obtained from other sources. We should also note that many fewer hearths were attributed to widows in country districts than in towns; which implies much closer family ties in the country. The two figures for the Arezzo region in 1427, for example, are 6 per cent and 17.6 per cent.[21]

In Liguria the situation is much clearer. In Sestri Levante there were practically no women listed in the cadastre of 1467: only four, in fact, all widows, out of a total of 1,069 heads of family. Matrimonial law, especially concerning dowries, confirms this slight but important statistic. Normally a married woman could dispose of property which had been her dowry only with the consent of her father or brother; if she died without issue, the dowry reverted to her family; if she were widowed, she lived with her husband's heirs until the dowry was returned, at which time she went back to her own family; but she never lived alone.[22] In the eastern part of the Ligurian Riviera, although it was conquered by the city of Genoa at a very early date and the landed aristocarcy seems to have totally disappeared, in this land of peasant or 'bourgeois' landowners, family groups still exhibited strong cohesion, even at this late date; in the economic sphere, the property which daughters were given as dowries even had a chance of reverting to fathers or brothers, and returning to their communal holdings.

In the case of aristocratic families the indivision of fiefs led to military solidarity and sometimes to deference to a kind of suprafamily control. But it also often implied a really communal use of the resources, of land, and more frequently of seignorial rights, which had been inherited.

This was so in the case of forests, which often remained undivided. The Orlandi *consorteria* owned and exploited jointly the Selva

Palatina, a vast stretch of wooded hills between the sea, the lower reaches of the Cerchio, and the hills of Lucca.[23] Close by, the Ripafratta *consorteria* had, around 1000, received several substantial grants of land from the emperor; these included *selve* and three *monti*, over which the newly established lords had civil and criminal jurisdiction.[24] Common ownership of this property lasted for a long period: only in 1362 did the *communitas* of lords lease the *Monte Maggiore* out *in perpetuum*, with the reservation only of a few particular rights of usage for the nobles. This transfer of land from the nobles to the *homines*, to the *fideles*, was apparently the beginning of the institution of communal ownership of woodlands by the peasants around Pisa and Lucca.[25] It is surely significant, moreover, that the nobles who left the countryside to settle in the city of Pisa, towards 1200, were called *nobili selvatici*.[26]

Ownership and, sometimes, communal use of forests and *monti* – mountain pastures – very often made it easier for the nobles to control pasture, especially transhumant grazing. For example around Pisa the most thoroughly entrenched seignorial right, and the most jealously guarded, seems to have been that of *pascuum*, in the forests of their estates and in their fallow fields.[27] Some nobles used these pastures for their own flocks: in April 1284 several members of the Masca *consorteria* of Pisa joined with a native of Lucca to form a 'Sheep company'; the beasts were to graze for six summer months in Gafargnana and for the rest of the year, throughout the winter, in the Pisan plain.[28]

Throughout southern Europe the use of mountain pastures kept social links close. In Cáceres in Estremadura, one of the city brotherhoods – the Santa Olalla, founded in 1467 – recruited its members only from among the co-owners of the Aldeyuela pastures; one of the aims of this religious association seems to have been the control of this pasture. Members met regularly in the hermitage of Santa Olalla, a long way (about six kilometres) from the city, to pray and hear mass; the hermitage was built of Roman stones, found on the *heredad* of Aldeyuela itself.[29] Such brotherhoods of livestock owners, controlling communal pasture, a *dehesa*, can be found without difficulty in Estremadura and throughout Old Castile.[30]

Aristocratic rights remained in common ownership much longer than did landed estates. The whole organization and geography of trade in western Europe point to the nobles' demands for tolls. At first, at least on the less important roads, tolls became established despite the attempts of princes and then of municipalities to take over these feudal taxes, or more often to replace them by royal or municipal ones. As a result, away from towns and the main markets, subsidiary routes and secondary markets developed or expanded; these were able to divert a proportion of trade and thus introduce a significant element of competition.[31] There is no orderly documentation, and no study has been made, so these markets and routes are naturally much less well-known than those laid down by state or city; but they were not without importance. In Italy the commercial communes were obviously hostile to such aristocratic rights over the transport of goods, and conflict between the two sides led to a continued and strengthened cohesion of rural noble clans. In 1184 the decision of an arbitrator between the commune of Pisa and the Ripafratta clan acknowledged that the family had the undoubted right to levy tolls on the carts and beasts of burden which passed through their land, and at least throughout the thirteenth century the *consules* and *rectores* of the Ripafratta *consorteria* continued to levy tolls, retaining a quarter as their own remuneration.[32] Much later in Pisa, some *consorterie* did not take their names from vast rural estates, but from particular entitlements which were their property, and which they exploited jointly; this explains the *consorteria delle Stadere*, which was mentioned in 1320. The name was taken from the *stadera*, the scales used to weigh and tax merchandise. The same explanation goes for the *consorteria Bullia* or *de Bullis* or even *Buglia*; apparently this family levied a private tax on the practice of placing seals (*bulle*) on some cloths.[33]

In Genoa the great noble families continued to administer and levy tolls on Apennine roads up to the end of the Middle Ages and sometimes later. Here, the commune seems to have been powerless to guarantee an overland passage free from restriction by the nobles. At this time the movement of merchandise to Lombardy and the fairs of Lyons or Geneva was still hazardous, subject to attack by brigands; there was in fact only one very difficult route, the Bocchetta road which ascended to 772 metres; the Via dei Giovi was much easier, ascending to only 470 metres, but could not be used for commercial traffic to and from Genoa because it followed the Scrivia valley, through the fiefs of the Spinola family.[34] This is an obvious example of the importance of aristocratic rights, enjoyed jointly by the members of noble family clans, for the geography and economy of trade.

In Genoa itself, up to 1539, merchants had to pay a tax, which is ill-defined in available documents, called the *introitus vicecomitatus*. It was obviously of feudal origin, and was the distant, but still respectable, relative of a tax which the great families of the city, the *visconti*, had once levied. The commune made many attempts to abolish this tax, both under the 'popular' doge Simone Boccanegra and much later under French administration; but these efforts were vain. In 1425 this private *drictus* belonged to thirty-two persons, who owned between them, albeit very unequally, the 288 *denari* making up the whole. In this period these shares could be sold or otherwise disposed of, and there is proof that this *drictus* was a very old heritage shared between a number of individuals; for it had been subdivided to as little as 1/80 of a *denaro*, or 1/23,040 of the whole! For example, one family head's share was reckoned as four, 2/9 and 1/60 *denari*, and another share as twenty four, 1/10, 1/6 and 1/80 *denari*. Yet, despite dispersal and sale, the *introitus vicecomitatus* remained mainly in the hands of the great families, the noble *alberghi*, which were of feudal character and ancient origin. These families organized the tax through consuls, collectors and subordinate officials, some elected from among the joint holders, others, strangers, salaried.[35] Thus, to the imposts of the commune, the *carati maris* for example, was added a tax of essentially feudal nature and origin, which remained practically unassailable for centuries despite much dealing in shares (the list of participants in 1126 is known to us). The fact of jointly enjoying this tax and the need to administer it strengthened cohesion within each family clan; they also caused and encouraged the growth of understanding and cordiality between several *alberghi* which had an interest in the joint exploitation of this privilege.

By maintaining their aristocratic heritage the great noble families were thus able to enjoy considerable riches and power in the very heart of the commercial quarter. These family clans held sway over lands, shores, markets, ports and bridges, and thus had in their power important or strategic places, the very bases of commercial expansion. At the beginning of the period when these families conquered the seas and opened up new markets, their properties were the foundations of their great wealth.[36] In this sense, at the time of the western Mediterranean crusades and the expeditions to the Holy Land, Italian commercial towns were noble towns. The advantages of the nobles were long evident; in Genoa, in the fifteenth century, three of the six moles, simple wooden or stone jetties where ships tied up in the inner port, bore the names of great noble families: Cattaneo, Spinola, Calvi. These *alberghi* owned land in the neighbourhood, and even on the shores; they had built these moles, and were for many years in charge of the unloading of cargo. In addition, these *alberghi* owned warehouses where they unloaded the bales brought on mules, stored goods and lodged travellers.[37]

All these associations of families concerned with rural property, or the joint exploitation of estates, forests or seignorial rights, emphasize the continuation of family customs in old and traditional spheres of economic activity. Real commercial, financial or banking associations are also often seen to have been based on such customs. Throughout the West, in the Middle Ages, commerce and banking depended ultimately on the family. At first, and sometimes for several generations, the most usual type of commercial association was quite naturally one in which brothers joined, and where nephews were subsequently included. This fact is easy to prove, in any region, throughout the Middle Ages, whatever the size and standard of the enterprise, or the nature and variety of its activities.

When we come to examine financial institutions, it is once more with reference to Italy that the most detailed work has been done, and conclusions can most easily be drawn for this country. In Siena and Florence the earliest banks which changed and lent money were normally close associations of brothers. The first company of the Gallerani, who were Sienese merchants and were active money-lenders in London, Paris and the fairs of Champagne, originally consisted of two brothers: a little later there were six associates, four of whom were very closely related (this was in 1260). The company became more and more complex as it became involved in increasing numbers of markets and wide-ranging business affairs, and it was reorganized in Paris in 1296 by means of a contract, signed and sealed. It still bore the name *Societas Galleranorum*, but now incorporated nine merchants, all citizens of Siena; among these associates were three distinct groups, each of two brothers. Here the strength of family links is clear; for each associated pair of brothers held a single share of the capital, which was therefore divided, not nine ways, but into only six parts.[38]

The infamous *casane*, the money-lending offices which were run in numerous western cities by usurers who were known as 'Lombards', but who were in fact probably Piedmontese or Tuscans, were not the shady, almost clandestine enterprises of isolated individuals acting alone, of outcasts from family and city; these 'Lombards' joined together to form stable companies for commerce and money-lending – companies which often united large numbers of relatives. The

Piedmontese family of Vagnon, originally from Trofarello in the diocese of Turin, were a veritable breed of money-lenders. Richard Vagnon had an office in Montbrison in 1330 and his brother Jacques had one in Saint-Étienne-de-Saint-Geoirs, in Dauphiné. Richard's three sons were at Voiron, Saint-Laurent-du-Pont and Saint-Marcellin; there were cousins similarly occupied in and around Die, and in Lons-le-Saunier and Château-Chalon. We see here a network of a dozen related 'Lombard' money-lenders, who evidently kept in close touch, and who covered between them the areas of Forez, Dauphiné and Franche-Comté.[39] Similarly, six of the Bonnet family from Chieri were established in various towns in Dauphiné.[40] All the households which owned *casane* in the valleys of Savoy always included numerous heads of family; in fact, they formed veritable tribes. For example, in less than half a century, between 1317 and 1363, twenty-three Pelletta were acting alone or in association with another equally wide-spread clan, the Bergognini, in nearly fifty different places; in 1400 there were still twelve Pelletta running fifteen money-lending offices in the valleys of Savoy.[41] In all the rather insecure and diffuse activities of these 'Lombards' in commerce and usury, exposed as they were to frequent reversals of fortune, the decisive bonds seem to have been those of the family.

In Florence, the structure of the family remained established for many years in every type of association – modest companies[42] or the wider-ranging enterprises made up of branches and subsidiaries in the main market centres of the western world. In 1344, at the age of twenty, Matteo dei Chorsini went to London to trade in woollen cloth, herring and Bordeaux wines, and he worked there with his brothers Duccio and Bartolomeo, who were to die of the plague in 1349; at the same time his marriage was being negotiated in Florence by two other brothers, Neri and Giovanni. Matteo returned to re-establish himself in Florence in 1361, was married, and in the next two years bought a considerable number of estates, farms and plots of land in the *contado* as well as houses in the city. In every case purchase was made jointly with Giovanni, the only surviving brother to remain in business (Neri was a priest and Matteo's other brother, Andreà, was bishop of Fiesole).[43] So this commercial company also formed a real community of property, even of land, which was bought jointly by the two brothers and exploited to their common advantage.[44]

Despite the important role of branch managers, and later of associated friends, who provided their own capital, the great

Florentine companies retained a very pronounced family structure in the Peruzzi period, as well as in the time of the Medici. This is evident in the names of compaines, which were always family names. This same structure was forcefully maintained for many years. Florentine companies allowed each member little initiative; they were often 'exclusive', that is, no major associate, not even a branch manager, was permitted to invest capital or take on business outside the company. It follows that it was impossible to spread investment and risk over several types of business, and that each associate was highly vulnerable: whence some repercussive bankruptcies. Thus, at this late period, respect for family cohesion, for a special idea of community of property, led to a lack of flexibility in business.

Such economic partnership between all the associated members of Tuscan companies seems, moreover, to have included the very honour of the family name. When, on 4 April 1488, at the age of sixty-eight, Francesco Sassetti drew up his will in Florence, he first of all strongly exhorted his three sons to accept his legacy, "even if they receive more debts than wealth"; he also compelled the two eldest (the third being a priest) to retain joint ownership of their property: "I wish all to be common to you both"; moreover, the three sons formally agreed to respect their father's last wishes, for they endorsed the will, each in his own hand.[45] This acceptance of the will by the heirs, which was definitely an old tradition, is in itself a good indication of the solidarity of the family group and of the continuing existence of some kind of community of wealth.

A century later, Tuscan companies which above all comprised members of a single large family or of a single family group were still commonly established throughout Europe; for example, the Bonvisi, merchants and bankers, originally natives of Lucca. Their six companies legally established in Lyons between 1575 and 1629 were made up solely of members of their large family; among its associates the Genoa subsidiary counted eight businessmen who bore the name of Bonvisi; there were also eight Bonvisi in Venice and twelve in Piacenza. These various branches of the same great enterprise maintained close links with the parent company in Lucca.[46]

Family communities of this kind were most strongly established, as part of commercial life, in Venice. Here the *fraterna*, whose profound originality has been well emphasized by F.C. Lane, arose from the communal ownership of property and way of life of two or more brothers, who lived in the same house and jointly, together with their wives and children, enjoyed the fruits of their lands. In Venice, too, every commercial fortune ultimately derived from the ownership of vast estates. Venetian law clearly stated that those members of a family who lived in the same house were necessarily business associates, without needing to draw up any documents of association. Throughout the Middle Ages this *fraterna* was the most normal form of business association in Venice. The city's most important members, its richest merchants, dealt within the framework of the *fraterna*, a strictly family-based association, although it might occasionally be enhanced by fleeting arrangements with strangers. In Venice, *fraterne* retained, so to speak, their original purity; they did not expand to become companies in the Florentine mould. F.C. Lane sees in this the Venetian need to adapt to a highly diversified trade which was in constant flux, and in which there was no specialization; hence it was impossible to introduce the rigid structures of the company with its stable associates. The primacy of the *fraterne* as bases of business demonstrates the respect of the state, which was incompatible with the emergence of groups of great economic power in the city, and underlines the strength of the family ideal. These *fraterne* were still real communities in the sixteenth century; brothers pooled all they possessed: houses, lands, furniture, even jewels, ships and merchandise. In their accounts, domestic expenses for food or the upkeep of the house were entered side by side with disbursements for goods purchased in far-off markets for business purposes.

Between 1509 and 1528 the three Pisani brothers lived together in the family palace, the Palazzo Pisani-Gritti; the wealth of these Venetian merchants was estimated at the enormous sum of 250,000 ducats. Their income accrued from many varied business affairs: the Terra Ferma estate near Rovigo, mills near Treviso, public bonds, the sea-borne trade, especially with Constantinople; and they supplied local industry with wools and dyestuffs. The group's cohesion and commercial restrictions were so strong that the brothers could not invest on their own accounts in other enterprises, except by using money obtained from their wives' dowries or borrowed from the *fraterna* itself; even then, such concerns were more or less linked to the *fraterna* by all kinds of economic connections; they would employ the same broker as the *fraterna*, and would be of constant assistance to it.[47]

Businesses in every Italian town probably manifested their own structural eccentricities; but it would be strange if this kind of family cohesion, in the economic sphere, were much less apparent in Genoa, especially as all other forms of clan solidarity remained strong in that city. Yet in this case historians have invariably emphasized the triumph of individual initiative; the Genoese businessman is represented as a man acting alone, who eschewed partnership and avoided lengthy contracts of association; rather, he invested his money in numerous enterprises which were all totally unconnected. Now, this schema is not completely inaccurate, but it is naive and requires some modification.

At the highest level, that of the largest enterprises, Genoese businesses did not rest on family bases. They were joint-stock companies named, not after families, but according to their products: salt, alum, cork, coral and others. Shares in these companies were infinitely divisible, and could be bought or used as securities in units or fractions. This led to large and highly variable numbers of associates who, increasingly, were strangers to one another. Although initially a business might have been floated by one or two families, sales and transfers of shares quickly introduced completely new elements. So any businessman could avail himself of these Genoese businesses *a carati* (referred to thus because in theory their capital was divided into twenty-four parts, called *carati*) in order to invest his capital where he wished, outside family circles, to spread his risks, buy and sell shares – in short, to speculate.[48] This attitude is perfectly typical of a man acting alone.

This peculiarity of Genoese business can perhaps be attributed to the considerable extent and complexity of the family group, which admittedly prevented all the members from active participation in joint business matters; but we should rather look to the extreme specialization of these companies, which were generally formed to exploit the monopoly of a single commodity; and obviously such specialization called for the investment of capital from greatly varying sources.

Yet the primacy of individualism was not total in Genoa. In refutation of this popular theory we should note first of all that the members of the most powerful company, which traded the alum from Chios – a company which in its capital and in the extent of its undertakings far outweighed all others – felt the need to unite to form an artificial *albergo*; this was the very cohesive Giustiniani clan.[49] But above all, though, at a lower level, the structure of Genoese business fairly closely resembles the organization of companies in that other maritime city, Venice: large numbers of ephemeral associations supported by firm, stable family organizations. If we turn to contemporary documents we are unavoidably led to the conclusion that the normal frameworks of economic activity in Genoa were companies formed by two or more brothers; but an almost total lack of private documents means that we are unable to obtain a satisfactory idea of the structure and activities of these fraternal companies. However, I have been able to examine two companies in some detail, thanks to a relatively large number of notarial deeds; and both were formed by brothers. These were the Centurioni and the Grimaldi de Oliva.[50] The brothers Federico and Filippo Centurioni, the most active bankers in the city, traded goods and currency with Pisa, Milan, Geneva, Barcelona and, even more, throughout Castile; they were succeeded by Federico's one son and the three sons of Filippo. Emmanuele and Leonello de Grimaldi de Oliva were more modest traders, retailing spices, wool, leather, dyestuffs and salted fish; they owned several shops, stalls and a warehouse, were very united, and lived together in a house by the harbour. Without exception, in every notarial deed concerning them, their names are linked.

There is even more significant evidence: associations of brothers also appear in great numbers in the records of the *avaria*, which listed not landed property but personal wealth. In 1479, 26 per cent of the Spinola listed, 29 per cent of the Doria and 38 per cent of the Lomellini were accounted for by associations of brothers or heirs;[51] these proportions are considerable, and show the strength of family tradition even in business matters.

So, in Genoa as in Venice, the family was still the basis of economic organization late in the Quattrocento, not only in associations restricted to commerce, in which each member would have retained control over his own fortune, but also in veritable communities of wealth and ways of life. In Genoa, such communities were transcended or broken only in particular and highly specialized transactions in which the vicissitudes of finance called for individual investment. Such 'capitalism', indulged in through joint-stock companies, was far removed from the family framework as too, in all the large cities of northern and central Italy, were investments in state 'banks' such as the famous *Casa di San Giorgio.*

Thus in Italy, at any rate, economic cohesion was still, at the end of the Middle Ages, expressed through families, and this is probably true of many countries and cities in the western world. Men rarely acted alone in business; 'family' associations still often shared their wealth together, just as they had also jointly exploited the undivided property of their heritage.

Family clans in town or countryside often contained men of greatly varying condition, and certainly of very different levels of wealth. Even ignoring the slaves and servants, or *fideles*, there was great inequality between the rich, who controlled the lineages, the men of middle rank and the weakest, who were more or less total dependants. Such social conditions are easily discerned in the use of certain adjectives in ordinary speech and, occasionally, by notaries themselves.

In Genoa, vocabulary was complex and subtle, and was doubtless linked to an individual's profession, wealth or prestige; the fine distinctions between words are not easy to pin down. They are however clearer, and can almost be reduced to statistics, in fiscal registers which show the amount of tax on property or chattels. Inside any particular clan, according to these documents, men bearing the same name were distinguished by considerable variations in wealth. This is true in cities as well as outside them, for example in the region around Sestri Levante.

At Sestri Levante, the cadastre of 1467 refers only to landed property. Each *albergo* listed included men of all levels of wealth. The following table shows the estimated wealth of each head of family in two of the principal *alberghi*, in cadastral pounds:[52]

Costa albergo

Martino and Lansaloto	3,400	Tommaso*	660
Paolo	2,035	Antonio	587
Martino†	1,685	Luciano	560
Giovanni	1,540	Bonania	500
Angelino	1,520	Faciolo	345
Honorata	1,045	Bartolomeo	337
Heirs of Marco	1,030	Heirs of Tommaso	296
Andreà	870	Marino	78

*Obviously another man with the same name as the late Tommaso referred to in this table. It should also be noted that of the four women listed as heads of household in Sestri Levante, two were members of the Costa *albergo*.

†Either the same man as before, listed here according to his personal property, or another member of the *albergo* bearing the same name (this cadastre does not indicate relationships).

Musso albergo

Jacobo	1,723	Emmanuele	775
Bartolomeo and brothers	1,720	Antonio and brothers	638
Heirs of Quilico	1,700	Stefano	390
Nicolo	1,000	Heirs of Remedio	360
Giovanni	970	Antonio	200
Heirs of Domenico	901	Andreà	110
Monimo (?)	850		

In these two *alberghi* the most highly taxed belonged to the principal families of Sestri by virtue of their landed wealth; the least taxed, on the contrary, took their place not with the poorest, but in the middle ranks, with those who had little wealth.

In Genoa the *Gabella possessionum* taxed mainly houses of more or less luxury and, very unusually, open spaces or land in the immediate vicinity of the city. Genoese merchants did not invest their money in vineyards, land or métairies; so, *a priori*, the range of landed wealth might seem narrower than in Sestri. Yet this is not so, for there is a clear hierarchy of differences of wealth. We may take the Doria clan as an example: in 1447 the clan's eighty-six landowners declared estimated property values ranging from £9 (Genoese) in the case of the least well-endowed to £2,638 for the most well-off.[53] Such a spread of wealth emphasizes the great diversity of social standing inside the *albergo*, which was one of the most powerful in the city. These insignificant properties were few: gardens, ramshackle buildings, demolished houses; but apart from this, there were two easily discernible groups: on the one hand the owners of large estates, with more than £500 worth and often even more than £700 worth of property; on the other hand a large number of modest, even mediocre fortunes;[54] the houses of those who lived in dependency in the shadow of their great relatives, were worth little – no more than the houses of the small artisans who were classed with the *popolani*.

This dependent element can be seen even more clearly if we study taxes on chattels in the *avaria* registers. Here there is a greater spread: in 1479, for example, the Spinola ranged from 10 sous to £233. Figure 6 shows a considerable number of the Spinola to have had a very low income, at the lowest limits for taxation, and infinitely less than the incomes of their leaders.[55] The lower level would certainly be even more common if tax registers listed every head of family; but we know that they did not, for in the case of the *avaria* on chattels, only those who enjoyed a certain level of wealth were listed and taxed.

According to this register and others of the same period, these

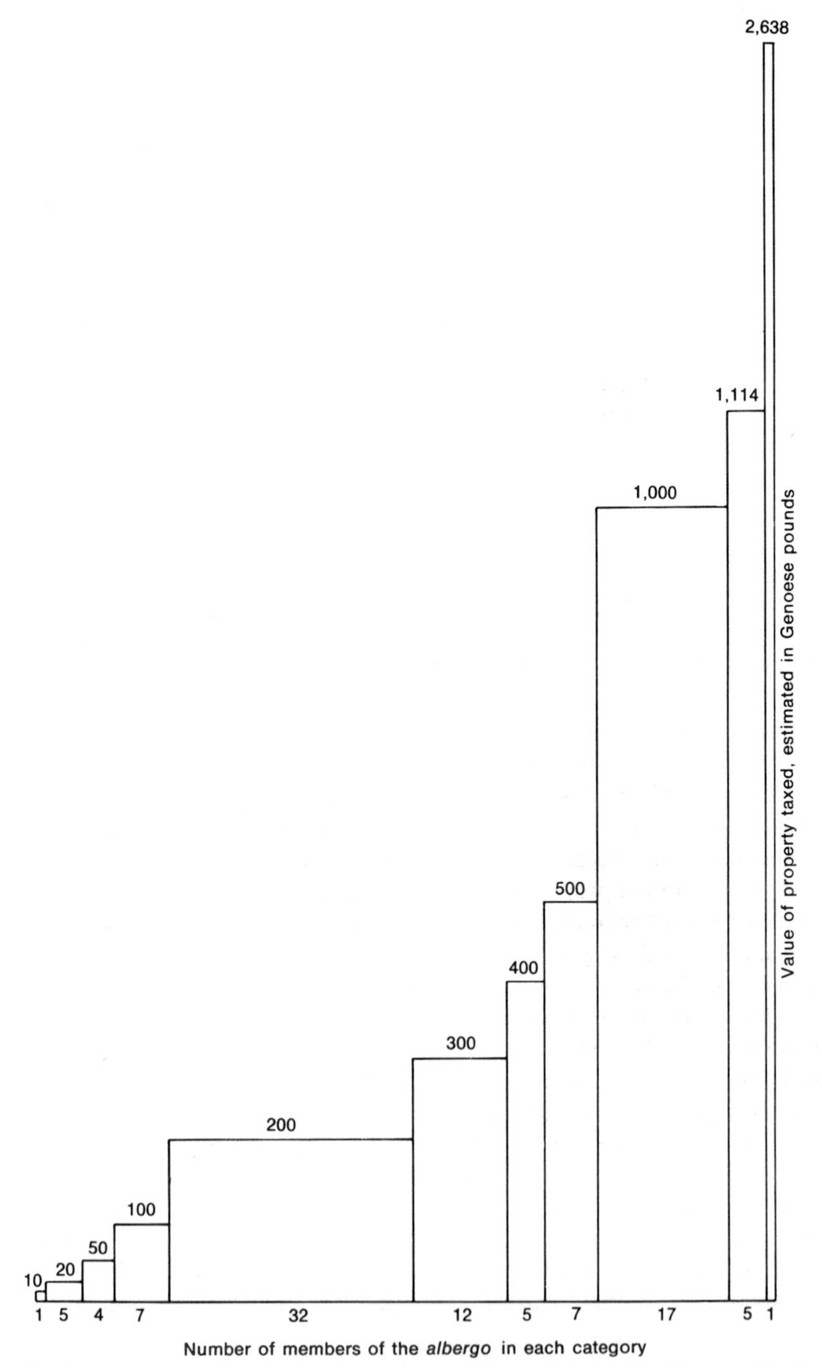

Fig. 5. The property of the Doria clan in Genoa, in 1447 (*A.S.G.*, Antiche Finanze, Sala 41, Gabella possessionum, 1447).

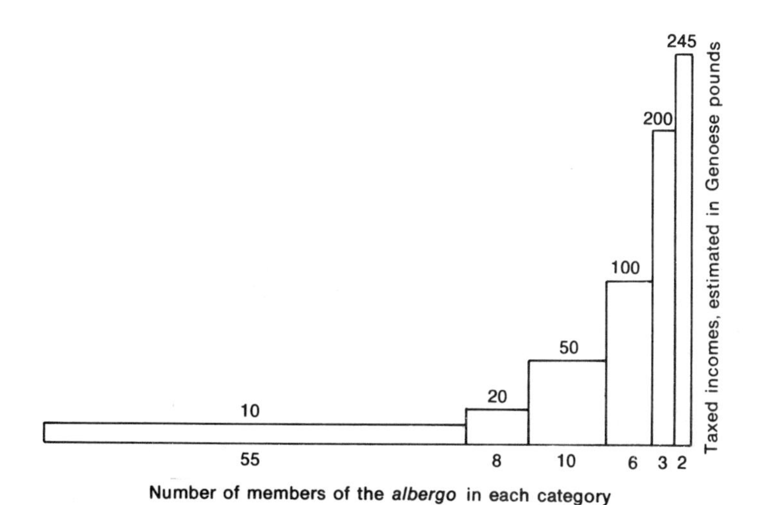

Fig. 6. The incomes of members of the Spinola *albergo* in Genoa, in 1479 (*A.S.G.*, Sala 41/sg. 103, Bancone, Avariorum, 1479).

observations apply also to all the noble *alberghi* of Genoa, although there were some important distinctions which should be emphasized. The range of social levels was even more obvious and seemed to be wider in the case of populous households which had economic and above all political power, than in those establishments which had failed to keep the limelight, which no longer had an important part to play in political life, and seemed threatened by an inevitable decline: in the former case there was a large dependency; in the latter, an old but decayed family of aristocrats, without dependants. In addition, the *alberghi popolani*, especially the Giustiniani, did not exhibit the same spread of wealth inside their clans. In 1465 fifty-four Giustiniani were listed in the *Focagiorum* register,[56] and there was much less variation between the richest and the poorest. But it seems certain that in the Quattrocento the great noble households of Genoa still kept large numbers of dependent relatives who were much poorer than the leaders of the clans. The *popolani* did not gather so many dependants to themselves, and nobles whose wealth and influence had decreased failed to retain such a group, which was undoubtedly a sign of power, an essential criterion of social and political success.

It is difficult to discern the existence of dependencies in other cities where the cohesion of social groupings was weaker, and especially where the diversity of names means that the informal ties between different families cannot be identified. In fact, patronage extended not merely to men who rejoiced in a direct blood relationship and bore the same name, but also to all other relatives and allies, to 'kindred friends' and *voisins*, to servants and the 'kept'. This tutelage was exhibited and strengthened at every opportunity that clans had to show themselves as cohesive groups, at public, municipal ceremonies and, more, at private celebrations. It is for this reason that we should attach importance to the study of private festivals, the outward and corporate expressions of a social life which united leaders and dependants. The great sporting events – horse-races such as the *Palio* at Siena, regattas in Venice and Pisa, ball games in Florence – were decisive factors of social cohesion, for they exacerbated group rivalry, seemed to reflect in peace-time the passions aroused in civil wars, and even maintained an atmosphere of vendetta.[57]

In Italy these violent diversions usually set different parts of cities (parishes, *sestieri* or *contrade*) against each other; but we have seen that these geographical areas also constituted strong social groups, frequently led by noble lineages. Sometimes family clans were even directly involved. Montaigne describes with some passion the carriage race which took place in Florence, in midsummer 1581, in the great square of Santa Maria Novella. The race was in fact simply a contest between the carriage of the grand duke and that of the Strozzi. Montaigne writes: "I noticed that the people broke their silence as they saw Strozzi approach, applauding the prince with all their might with loud cries as he appeared". A little later, "from the middle of the throng there suddenly arose a unanimous cry of public approbation directed at Strozzi, who finally won the prize".[58] This example of the social and political role of festivals shows a distinct rivalry between bodies of dependants, who here sided with the two great rival families; and the presence of the clan at these occasions is one sign of its fidelity.

Documents of 'aggregation', which were drawn up by notaries to receive new members into Genoese *alberghi*, imposed on the newcomers the obligation to appear all together, bearing the arms and insignia of the household, as proof of the strength of the group, on any occasion when a ceremony brought the notables of the city together in the presence of the doge.[59] On public holidays all the members of clans, relatives and dependants, thronged the streets, their *gentilice* square and especially their *loggia*, crowding into their arcades and in front of their houses. This tradition was maintained throughout the Middle Ages, even after the consolidation of a commune which was less subservient to family groups. The *Annali genovesi* report that in 1227, at the celebration of a decisive victory over Albenga and Savona, crowds thronged the arcades of the large aristocratic houses,[60] and much later, in 1502, crowds of relatives, neighbours or dependants, especially women, still poured into these arcades to watch Louis XII and his retinue as they passed.

In town and countryside throughout the West, marriage was an opportunity to show the power of a family clan over all its neighbours; this was brought out in the richness of the ceremony itself, in invitations to celebrations and feasts, and by the giving of presents or alms. In this way marriage played an obvious social role; it was the most notable occasion of recreation and charity.

When, in June 1466, Bernardo Ruccellai married Nannina, the daughter of Piero di Cosimo de' Medici, the celebrations lasted for three whole days and involved their entire quarter of the city. For the wedding day itself, that is, for the entertainments, and especially the balls, the family had a vast platform erected. Its area was about 1,600 square spans, and it *teneva tutta la piazzuola ch'è dirimpetto alla casa nostra*; it was covered with cloth in the colours of the two families' arms. For the meals, 170 people sat at the top table *tra parenti e amici e uomini de' principali della città*, and more than 500 sat at the other tables. The leaders of the clan distributed sweetmeats at these collations; in all, they purchased 2,800 white loaves, 120 casks of wine, 2,966 fowls and four calves *per dar mangiare a' contadini.* These celebrations and this liberality were accompanied by distributions of various alms, which further indicated the primacy of the clan. The bride was given 100 handfuls of small coin (*grossoni*), which she threw to those present; the chronicle of her father-in-law, Giovanni Ruccellai, states: *donammo a più parenti, servidori e amici della casa paia 70 di calze di panno alla divisa.*[61] The number of liveries is a clear indication of the size of the dependency.

Marriage ceremonies thus ostentatiously affirmed the cohesion of noble households, and strengthened their own ideas of social solidarity. Although the commune tried to restrict participation on such occasions, its decrees were ignored. In 1322, the statutes of the Captain of the People allowed no more than twelve young women to accompany a young bride to her new abode;[62] but in 1466 Nannina de' Medici was surrounded by fifty young women and fifty young men, all dressed in the same splendid livery.

Funerals, of course, offered further opportunities to reinforce social groups, whether they were families, professions or fraternities. Just as it was regarded as an absolute obligation on all members of a brotherhood, and often of a guild, to attend funerals, vigils, masses and banquets, so social links inside clans were strengthened in the ceremonial burial of a rich relative. Alms were probably normally given publicly to the poor who attended, and who added their prayers to those of the close relatives of the departed. The amount of alms given emphasized the social rank of the deceased and ensured the popularity of his family. At the funeral of the count of Armagnac, says the Bourgeois of Paris, who was admittedly a scandalizer, "No distribution was made. Four thousand of those present would never have come if they had known, and the count was cursed by those who, just before, had prayed for him".[63]

Yet the giving of alms took on a more precise social significance in funeral banquets; this was probably the legacy of ancient pagan ceremonies. In Flanders, at burials or anniversary masses, at which the tomb was covered with a pall and lit by candles, great families erected a table in the church itself; here the poor were given bread and wine, and portions of meat, peas and butter, if they had received charity tokens called *méreaux*. These *méreaux*, leaden counters bearing the household arms, were manufactured under the control of men who were given contractual responsibility for the management of the property of pious foundations. The tokens were given to the clergy, to religious and charitable establishments (for example, to brotherhoods and leper-hospitals) and especially to members of the family, who were given very varied appellations, some of which clearly demonstrated their membership of the noble lineage (*aeldinghers*). Other names, however, also emphasize dependency (*vrieden, magen, maegschap*), for such distributions also aided indigent relatives whom, very significantly, texts call *den aerme van den bloede*.[64]

Aid to relatives and dependants was given not only on special occasions, but also in individual acts of charity which we can often find in wills. So in 1413, Dino Rapondi, a Lucchese merchant established in Paris, left "one hundred and sixty Paris pounds, to be distributed as his ten heirs think fit, to help to marry poor virgins among his relatives". Similarly, in 1430, Pietro Centurione, a noble and a merchant of Genoa, willed that his clothes, his arms, the silver vessels and furniture in his house, should all be sold. The proceeds of the sale were to be invested in the *Casa di San Giorgio*, and the interest from these public bonds was to be used on the one hand to employ a chaplain and to say a daily mass to the memory of Centurione, and on the other hand to give alms to the poor and dowries to young maidens, provided that they were all *de albergo de Centurionibus et de stirpe Bechignonis.*[65] As a final example of a practice which was probably quite customary in Genoa, Filippo Doria (son of the late Antonio) also decided, in 1451, that the money produced by the sale of his clothes would be invested in bonds of the *Casa di San Giorgio*, and that half the interest would be used to succour "the poor of the *albergo* of Doria", the other half going to monks, nuns and "to poor noble maidens".[66]

Aid for the poor or for the dependants of a clan was often controlled and administered on a regular, almost official basis by the *albergo* as a whole. Indeed, this aid fund was one of the group's fundamental institutions, one of the elements which ensured the cohesion of all the members and, obviously, maintained the prestige of the clan's leaders and a degree of total community. A clan looked after its poor, its invalids, all those in need. This mutual assistance, which was also at this time the concern of brotherhoods and guilds, was practised constantly by the great families. Of course, we cannot discover every foundation of this type; in general, they are very difficult to trace, for there are very few texts, even incidental documents, which refer to the private functions of *alberghi*. However, money was often invested in public bonds, and the normally well-kept records of these bonds have for the most part survived. In 1379, the register of those participating in a compulsory loan raised by the commune lists £144 under the heading *Pauperes albergi illorum de Jacheriis.*[67] By that date the Iacheriis *albergo* was one of the sparsest and weakest of the city, so this entry probably reveals a previous investment; moreover, the clerk who noted the ownership of the £144 added the detail: *cum obligatione quod iam dictas Lb. 144 nullo tempore vendi, alienari seu obligari (possint) in perpetuum.* This was a blocked investment, the annual income from which might be used only for specific alms.

The practice of such investments became very widespread. The Genoese *alberghi* invested their common resources in this way, making voluntary or enforced purchases of public bonds. Thus they became shareholders in the various *Mutui*, then in the large *Compere* then, after the 1407 consolidation, in the *Casa di San Giorgio*. The books of the *Casa* contain a scrupulous record of investments, sometimes even detailing how the annual interest was to be used. Random sampling of the four enormous books of the *Colonne di San Giorgio* reveals the fact that in 1456 most of the Genoese *alberghi* owned a certain number of shares collectively. For example, the Lercarii *albergo* (register of Sarzano, *compagna*): £200; the Ardimenti *albergo* (Porta Nuova, *compagna*): £75. Sometimes the donor arranged a *moltiplicato*, in which only a proportion of the interest was spent every year, the rest being added to the capital. In 1456 the endowment made by Domenico Lercario for the poor of his *albergo* rose to £3,964 (Sarzano, *compagna*); a different entry shows that in that year the *pauperes puelle ex nobilius de Auria* had a capital of £1,569 (Porta register) and the poor of Cibo £215 (Borgo). Indeed, a number of very detailed dispositions clearly show the care taken by the responsible members of the clan in the administration of this communal wealth and the distribution of relief.

Poor relief was not always restricted to mere alms. In 1456 the sum of £600 was entered among the San Giorgio bonds (Borgo register) with the reference: *Domus pauperum prope monasterium Santa Maria de Carnio gubernata per dominis de Albergo de Ardimentis*; so, here, a family clan secured board and lodging for its poor out of its own resources, after the fashion of the brotherhoods. In a quite different domain, the Pallavicini devoted a portion of the income from their investments of £1,794 *ad manutenendum pauperes studentes qui studerunt extra Januam in legibus et medicinis* (Borgo register). Above all, the entries show, as we have already seen, that the great noble households were especially concerned with endowing their daughters. In 1456, again, the Pallavicini possessed a further £750, the income from which was used to marry off the poor maidens of the *albergo*, but only if they chose their husbands from Genoa and went to live in that city.[68] This was also true of the powerful Spinola di Luccoli *albergo*; in 1456 they were already credited in the Sarzano register[69] with the appreciable sum of £5,381, and in 1572, as a result of *moltiplicati* and individual contributions, they held the enormous sum of £79,000; to this, moreover, were added other *colonne* (shares) which were held in the names of individual members but were in fact destined for charitable works. The interest was mainly used to endow the poor maidens of the *albergo*, on condition that they themselves, their fathers, brothers or mothers, were domiciled in Genoa.[70] The constant concern to give dowries to young girls, and thus ensure an early marriage, is, we know, a result of one of the main preoccupations of aristocratic fathers, who often lacked money and therefore delayed the marriage of their daughters. The internal charity of a clan certainly strengthened the ties between its members, but it also ensured for the clan more considered, and therefore more effective marital unions, producing the essential and populous band of dependants. The residential condition which we have met twice is also significant here.

The very late date of our last information (1572) shows that this social cohesion, which represents a sort of total community, existed well beyond the 'medieval' period, at least for some powerful *alberghi* of really noble origins.

Political communities

For all the above reasons, family clans were organized into strong political communities which were more or less independent of princely or municipal authorities. The independence of the powerful rural lineages which remained out of reach of the agents and magistrates of the state was practically complete; the obvious examples are the great *consorterie* of central Italy, in the very *contadi* of powerful commercial cities. 'Feudal' noble lineages exercised economic rights, total jurisdiction and wide administrative rights over men, and the right to levy troops, and these powers were not always decisively broken by the territorial expansion of communes. The history of struggles for influence between cities and the great families of their *contadi* is probably much more complex than writers have hitherto shown; communes always encountered strong resistance, and they often lost.

In the region of Genoa, in the Quattrocento, there were still large fiefs which were completely independent from, and sometimes even hostile to, the city; for example the fiefs of the Fieschi, and especially of the Malaspina, on the Riviera di Levante. Even families which were perfectly well integrated into Genoese circles, which owned opulent houses in the city and had a hand in all the trade of the port and of banking, which regularly sat in the Council of Elders, were supreme in their fiefs on the Rivieras or in the Apennines, and this was so for many years. True, the noble lineages of Spinola, Doria, Lomellini and many others paid the homage of vassals to the commune in respect of particular fiefs, and when they found themselves in difficulty they asked the commune to arbitrate in their favour, as for example when there was disagreement between themselves and their subjects the peasants over the payment of taxes; but these nobles administered their own fiefs, giving justice and enforcing their peace in their own ways. In August 1466, in Genoa, the noble members of the *albergo* of Spinola di Luccoli, the smallest branch of the Spinola but the richest in fiefs, appointed two prosecutors to repress the troubles which were disturbing the peace on their estates.[71] In June 1465, in the presence of the nobles of the *albergo*, the three chiefs delegated their power to three commissioners, all Spinola di Luccoli. They were to make enquiries concerning the request of three of their subjects who lived on their fief at Rocco, that a conviction should be set aside; this conviction had been pronounced by one Borromeo de Alexandria, doctor of law, who was referred to on this occasion as "the representative of the whole noble *albergo* of Spinola di Luccoli".[72] Thus criminal and collective justice was administered in the name of the whole clan as a community. Throughout the Quattrocento, justice was given in this way in all the fiefs of the Ligurian Apennines; this obviously strengthened the feeling of belonging to a real political community.

The real political influence of Genoese family clans is fully confirmed by the fact that the commune requested the most powerful *alberghi* to ratify peace treaties and alliances, either collectively or by the consent of several members. In 1452, the Spinola di Luccoli ratified an agreement with Milan[73] and, in 1467, a pact with the duchess of Milan, Ferdinand of Sicily and Florence.[74] Here we can clearly see the nature and limitations of the commune as a sovereign state. We are far from ratification by the solemn oath of several hundreds or thousands of citizens; agreements were negotiated and signed by the doge with the assistance of the Elders representing the commune, and confirmed by the most powerful *alberghi* in the name of all their members, of their community.

The situation in Liguria is doubtless exceptional; but in Montferrat, in the fourteenth century and probably much later, several feudal lineages such as Montiglio and Rosignano still formed powerful *consortili* which united nobles claiming common blood; they drew up statutes, met regularly in council, and perpetuated the strict application of all their seignorial privileges.[75]

We must question whether we really know the true history of the Tuscan mountains. The struggles between Pisa and the Ripafratta clan are a perfect illustration of the strength of resistance of this noble *consorteria*, even at quite a late period. The Ripafratta held a court known as the *Corte dei Cattani* (or *curia cattanorum*),[76] as were those of several other seignorial clans. This court had jurisdiction over the *homines* or *fideles* of the lineage. Attempts by the city of Pisa to interfere, through its *curia maleficiorum*, provoked strong reactions, and in 1282 the commune itself, as arbitrator, confirmed the rights of the nobles. Twenty-three witnesses all asserted that the *homines* were in the jurisdiction of the nobles, who had exercised that jurisdiction from time immemorial through their officers, notaries, camerlengos, commissioners, wardens and arbiters. Above all, the same document refers clearly to a *communitas fidelium* which thus constituted a political body in itself, under the control of the nobles.[77] It appears that the political communities of clans were not destroyed by the actions of the city, but that they were gradually eroded by the slow emancipation of the peasants (which the city of Pisa certainly encouraged), who then formed their own political community, their *communitas*. It is important to note that this emancipation, which came very late, was restricted – for criminal justice was still the prerogative of the nobles' court – and occurred under the control of the nobles: the earliest statutes of rural communes were not the unilateral fruits of revolt; rather, they were drawn up in the manner of contracts.[78] The peasants were asserting their own political community in the face of whole lineages, who as a result lost part of their dependencies, at least from the juridical point of view.

The political cohesion of the nobles, which was their heritage from feudal times, and which remained fairly strong in the rural areas of Italy, was also sometimes to be found in commercial towns, where in theory municipal institutions were supreme. This occurred in varying degrees of secrecy or openness depending on the relative strengths of the contenders. It might also happen indirectly, through other political institutions. In Tuscany the great families very soon ceased to send representatives to the various councils and magistratures; but they continued for many years to send them to quarters, *sestieri* or other small districts where they exercised enormous influence. The result of this was that later still communes prescribed other political institutions, such as the guilds of the Florentine *popolo*. But this reform seems to have been neither generalized nor permanent; it was probably not completely successful because family clans could still have great influence on public life in Tuscany through all kinds of secret agreements, and especially in 'parties', whose real structure, extent and methods of action are still a mystery to historians.

Any detailed study of the realities of political life in Italian cities at the end of the Middle Ages will always show, decisively, that the great families held the reins of power and monopolized a large proportion of public offices. In Padua, for example, in 1420, members of only 149 families were elected to the various magistratures, and half the posts were obtained by members of only forty-two of these families; in Verona, as late as 1495, the Council consisted of 140 citizens from seventy-nine families, thirteen of which held one-third of the seats between them. In Florence itself, in 1434, Cosimo de' Medici granted the status of *popolani* to old, friendly families of magnates; this gave them access to every office. In the district of San Giovanni, in 1440, only twenty-five family clans received between them 65 per cent of the votes in elections for the signoria and the various councils, and 80 per cent in the elections for the gonfalonier of justice. If we examine methods of election to the emergency councils, the *balie*, we come to similar conclusions: again in San Giovanni, in 1438, five members of the *balia* were Medici; five other families each had three delegates and ten families had two each. John Gage, in presenting these figures, is moved to remark: "Throughout the period the 'popular' government of Florence was so only in name".[79]

It is very significant that cities apparently built communal palaces only long after the commune itself had been established. Giovanni Villani tells us that the palace in Florence was built in 1250, when an early 'popular' government was formed, in order to bolster up the actions of the *popolo*, for *prima non avea palagio di comune in Firenze, anzi stava la signoria ora in una parte della città et ora in altra,*[80] that is, in the quarters which were under the influence of the great families, who thus shared power between them. Genoa did not erect any such buildings until even later, during the fourteenth century (beginning in 1291); until then, meetings of magistrates were held in the *curiae* of the main noble families of the time, in turn; so meetings often took place in a family's *loggia*, beneath its arcades. Several times between 1260 and 1270 such meetings were held under the arcades of Oberto Doria's palace.[81]

At least up to the end of the Quattrocento, in Genoa, membership of the Council of Elders and of all the attendant or marginal bodies of magistrates depended far more on traditional than on other criteria. We lack detailed documents relating to these institutions, so it seems impossible to discern the precise means of election to these bodies; we can only study lists of members to see how they were distributed. We see first that there were equal numbers of *nobili* and *popolani*; in the case of the former, the sole basis was that of the family, and lists certainly show the massive and regular presence of representatives of the greatest families. As for the *popolani*, half, the merchant class, were appointed by geographical districts over which one or more great family groups had control; and it is not even certain that the artisan class, who supplied only a quarter of the members of the various councils, were elected on a guild basis.

The highly complicated arrangements governing the apportionment of the various taxes in Genoa supply enough interesting details for us to imagine the workings of the representative institutions in the city. The officers charged to determine men's wealth and to assess their tax were appointed by lottery; but in the case of the nobles, contributions were prepared *secundum colorem et familiarum vicissitudines*; in the case of the *popolani*, these officers had regard to 'colours' or factions, to the distinction between 'merchant' and 'artisan', and then they acted *habitis solitis consyderationibus a compagnas* (the *compagne* were the city's eight large districts).[82] Among the thirty-six officers thus appointed, the three *alberghi* of Doria, Spinola and Grimaldi each had to have five assessors.[83] In order to estimate a family's wealth these officers summoned the heads of *conestagie* (subdivisions of the *compagne*), for the *popolani*, or two members of each noble *albergo*; these were all to *conquirere qui sunt ex familiis suis*. Even when there was no electoral procedure, which would probably have applied in other aspects of life, this rule sums up the administrative and fiscal status of any member of an *albergo* vis-à-vis the commune-state. Whether a man was a leader, an ordinary relative, or a dependant, of a clan, he had no individuality as a citizen of the commune, but existed only as a member of the family group. He had no need to recognize any of the magistrates of the commune, but rather his clan's representatives, for he was entirely in their hands. This is a striking affirmation of another aspect of the self-government of clans, of their 'political' autonomy.

Thus, in Genoa, the political power of clans was maintained much longer than in other Italian cities; noble *alberghi* continued to command half of all public offices, and after 1528 and the incorporation of the great families of the *popolani* into the twenty-eight *alberghi* of the *nobili*[84] they enjoyed an absolute monopoly of these offices, to which only members of a clan could aspire.

By the fifteenth century, this situation seems to have been quite unusual in Italy; but in many German cities lineages of great families still held all the offices and all the positions of responsibility. In Metz, the *commun* formed their own *paraige* in 1367, after which time magistrates were appointed only by the members of the six *paraiges*, who were called *citains*; the other inhabitants, either *bourgeois* or *forains*, were not represented.[85]

Even in France, royal power was long powerless to break the great families' monopoly on public offices; Beaumanoir, who was bailiff of Vermandois and of Senlis, stated this clearly in the 1250s:

> We see several fine towns where poor and ordinary men take no part in the administration, where the rich have all the power because they are feared by the common people for their wealth or for their blood. So it happens that some are mayors or jurats or tax collectors, and in the following year they elect their brothers or nephews or other close relatives, so that after ten or twelve years all the rich men have all the administrative offices in our fine towns.[86]

It nearly always became necessary to appoint one or more leaders to be responsible for the management of common wealth, the maintenance of internal peace – very fragile in these groups which were often very large – and the control of relatives and dependants. They might have powers limited to specific ventures, in which case they were merely administrators, or procurators. Such were the captain who was elected in Genoa by seventeen members of the Spinola di Luccoli *albergo*,[87] or those appointed by sixteen heads of family bearing the name of Fornario to administer the property of their *albergo*.[88] In 1449, four different *alberghi* – Marini, Lomellini, Mari and Pansani – each elected two of their own members to settle a dispute between themselves and the Grimaldi de Oliva *albergo*.[89]

Normally, however, veritable chiefs asserted themselves. They were either patriarchs, the eldest of the main branches of clans, or the richest, whose prestige obviously caused their primacy; or they were actually elected for one or more years by the assembled leaders of their respective clans, and entrusted with great power. So we find, in cities, the rural tradition of great 'feudal' lineages; for example, the members of the *consorterie* of the Pisa region all assembled and elected *consules* and *rectores*, at first in undefined numbers, but later they appointed a single *consul* to settle disputes between the nobles themselves or between the nobles and their peasants. These private magistrates also collected quit-rents and tolls, and received an annual salary of sixty sous.[90] The *consortili* of Montferrat also elected a *podestà* and a *consiglio di credenza*.[91]

These elected consuls or councils evidently reveal a much closer political cohesion; power could not come solely from personal prestige, from ancestry or from commercial success: it was truly delegated by a political community in the name of all its members. In the Quattrocento, most of the Genoese *alberghi* elected 'governors' in this way; they acted on every occasion in the name of their *alberghi*, represented them against the commune, and managed all their common property of whatever kind. They were at once ambassadors, administrators and even judges. It seems, moreover, to have been of prime importance that justice was carried out in this way; the document which was drawn up in the presence of a notary when sixteen heads of family in the Pinu *albergo* met in the little village of Castagnola in the mountains of the Riviera di Levante states clearly that "It is above all right to ensure harmony among all the members of the *albergo*, concerning their persons or their wealth, that they may, by common recourse, settle any disputes which may arise, and avoid the suits and expense which are often caused between us by enmity and affrays". Two men were chosen each year to settle all disputes and all those present undertook to accept their judgment, under pain of a fine of between four and twenty-five florins, and they agreed not to turn to any other magistrate.[92]

No detailed information is available concerning the political life of lineages in the German cities of the Empire and their administration, but we should note that in Metz the six *paraiges* met to appoint their representatives to the various magistratures of the city; they were convoked by and deliberated under the chairmanship of their heads of household.[93]

The political community of family clans is clearly shown in their judicial powers, the recruitment of men-at-arms, their collective responsibility for taxes and administration by individual, elected magistrates, who were entrusted with the maintenance of internal order; this, at least, is true of certain cities in Italy and Germany – cities where it is most easily perceived, and where it probably also remained stronger than elsewhere.

Spiritual communities

Ties of blood, dependence or neighbourhood, mutual help, especially military, in conflicts and vendettas, and daily intercourse, all definitely created a spirit of community inside family clans which was further reinforced by a devotional cohesion, by attendance at the same services, and by a common creed.

A clan would have its own church, owned and supported by the lineage. This was a relic of 'feudal' times, when large families provided themselves with one or more churches, and with one or more monasteries.

The seizure of churches by lay lords was not carried out solely in the cause of profit, in the desire to confiscate tithes and donations; it was also perhaps due to a distinctly felt need to unite relatives and friends, rich nobles and dependants, in one faith, a single religious community. In early times parishes originated around the oratories which were built on the lands of the lords, around the chapels of their castles; and the prestige of a noble house asserted itself first in its chapel, then in its convent. This was true for princes as well as for ordinary lineages. Patronage of a religious institution was one of the elements of power and social cohesion.

The emancipation of these churches and convents, which thereafter became parish churches or reformed convents, often linked to new religious orders, was not simply the result of a transformation of customs or of the religious life itself: it marked some loss of power on the part of great family communities in the face of the increasing influence of other bodies.

This emancipation occurred only much later in regions where noble households retained their power and cohesion with greater ease. Thus, around Pisa and Lucca, the Ripafratta family were the patrons of the church and monastery of Lupocava (or Rupocava), which were built about 1214. This patronage was almost the symbol of the spiritual unity of this *consorteria.* In 1242 the judgement of an arbitrator still recognized the family's right to confirm the election of the new abbot. At the same period, several *consorterie* in this area between Pisa and Lucca still claimed to be patrons of rural monasteries: for example, the Duodi, the Gaetani and the Gusmani (in San Vito sull'Arno).[94] It seems that the celebrated 'Gregorian reform' of the eleventh century had little effect on lay patronage here, and had little success in encouraging the emancipation of churches and monasteries from lay hands.

In the cities of the West, and especially in Italy, the influence of the families was still being felt much later, discreetly or triumphantly, tacitly or in institutionalized form. The church of a quarter, the parish church of the local inhabitants, would often benefit from the liberality and protection of the rich clansmen living close by, the masters of households – the *loggia.* Such a church would be part of the social group; the leaders would be buried there, and they would embellish it with frescoes or statues. This was so practically throughout Italy and even in the whole of the West. Obviously, it is difficult to ascertain how far parish priests or clergy were among the dependants of these Tuscan *consorterie,* or of great urban families in general; but we can easily imagine that there were at least close links between the clergy and the local lords, and that worship and religious festivals also helped to strengthen the cohesion of family groups and their hold over entire parishes.

The family tombs of the great Tuscan or Lombard families stood in the chancels or side-chapels of their parish or conventual churches, in a clear assertion of the spiritual cohesion of family clans in their worship, and of their influence over priests or monks. Francesco Sassetti recalled in his will that he had commissioned a marble tomb for his father, Tomaso. He wanted this tomb, where he too was to be buried, to be endowed with the income from his locksmith's shop for the saying of masses. The tomb was destined for the church of Santa Maria Novella, where the family had its arms and a picture near the high altar, but these were removed by the monks. Francesco's instructions to his sons are clear: "If you are ever in a position of authority, you must repair and replace everything"; failing this, Francesco wished his monument to be placed in the church of Santa Trinità, where he hoped that his son would become the incumbent. In any case, he wrote, "I charge you not to fail to concern yourselves in this matter, for it involves the honour of our house and the proof of our antiquity".[95] Thus the presence of a family mausoleum inside a church or convent is not fortuitous; it reveals at least an agreement with the clergy and even, in most cases, a clan's position of authority and tutelage.

When we look for evidence of *gentilizie* churches, we find once more that the search is easiest in Genoa, where *alberghi* asserted themselves so strongly that they became recognized institutions. Some family clans were content with their own oratory, or with a side-chapel in a church; these were the smaller households which had been enfeebled with the passage of time, becoming poor and lacking dependants; they had to come to terms with their neighbours, and shared square, *loggia* and church. In 1459 the four Genoese *alberghi* of Marini, Lomellini (the Piazza Banchi branch), Mari and Pansani, who all lived round the Piazza di Banchi, laid claim to common control of a recently built chapel in the church of San Pietro in Banchi; they gathered in the *loggia* of the church and declared their opposition to the claims of another clan, the Grimaldi de Oliva.[96]

In contrast, the most powerful *alberghi* possessed real *gentilizie* churches, each reserved for one group and all its dependants. Here, the leaders of clans had a right of patronage which was recognized by the pope. These churches were often built at a very early period, sometimes in the eleventh century, and were subsequently elevated into parish churches. Originally each was in the hands of a great family, and these families' *de facto* privileges were solemnly recalled and confirmed later – never before the fifteenth century – by pontifical privileges. This was the case with the *gentilizie* church of San Matteo, in the heart of the Doria quarter of Genoa. The history of the foundation and patronage of this church is a perfect illustration of the hold of Genoese family clans over the churches of the city and of the Riviera. Among their fiefs the Doria counted the patronage of the monastery of San Fruttuoso, which was built on the sheer bank of the great Capo di Monte promontory. The abbey soon became powerful, and was their first basilica.

About 1125, a monk from San Fruttuoso became prior of the new church of San Matteo, which was apparently newly built; this monk was a Doria – Martino Doria. The installation of this prior was certainly, as was proper, in the gift of the abbot of San Fruttuoso, but the *jus patronatus* and the *jus presentandi* of the Doria clan were still preserved. From that time the new church, with its square and its cloister, seems to have been the centre of the spiritual and even social life of the Doria who lived in Genoa. Here again the solidarity of a clan inside the city seems only to have been one aspect of the still very lively traditions of a noble lineage which was strongly established in the countryside, and an extension of these into a quarter of the city.

In 1235 the church of San Matteo was mentioned as a parish church. The Doria held it securely in their pockets; in 1413, two bulls of the antipope John XXIII conceded patronage to Francesco Doria "and to his house" in perpetuity, with the right to elect the prior.[97] In 1436, Giorgio Doria installed a chaplain in San Matteo, in the name of his family, charging him to say mass every day and to hold in the church *alia divina offitia tam diurne quam nocte.*[98] In the case of the Doria, this spiritual community extended also to their country seats just outside the town: the same chaplain had just been 'elected' by the *albergo* to be the incumbent of San Erasmo in Campi, beyond Genoa, where their rural residences were crowded in close proximity.[98] Moreover, in 1432, the prior of San Matteo had founded the church of San Illarione (also sometimes known as San Vito), in Albaro, an area close to Genoa where the Doria owned several houses.[99]

Mattia-Moresco refers to five other *gentilizie* churches in Genoa, apart from San Matteo;[100] and there were probably far more. Each was virtually the private parish of a *gens*, of a clan. The areas served by these churches were not geographically defined, as was the case in other parishes in the city. Every member of the family group, even if circumstances had caused him to leave the quarter and reside elsewhere, was still attached to this parish and had to attend services and celebrate feast days there. So, in Genoa, a pattern of *gentilizie* parishes, for the nobles and their dependants, grew up alongside the ordinary system of 'popular' parishes. The *gentilizie* churches, which were built on the properties of clans, often on ancient fiefs, maintained with funds managed by clan governors and served by priests who were elected by the relatives together or appointed by a few responsible individuals – these churches were a decisive factor in strengthening the social cohesion of groups; the squares, *loggie* or cloisters of these churches encouraged group assembly or chance meetings at every moment of daily life. Feelings of belonging to a united spiritual community stemmed from attendance at Sunday services and at baptisms, marriages and funerals. Common prayers even created a sort of clan cult apart from normal Christian worship: on the one hand, there was the cult of their patron saint (Matthew, for the Doria, and they venerated him with a fervour that cannot be perceived through any documents); on the other hand, and more especially, there was the cult of dead heroes. *Gentilizie* churches sheltered the dead, the chiefs, and those who had borne high the name of the clan, who were revered by all relatives and friends. The great number of tombstones shows that it was customary to bury the dead inside the church, even at a very late period, and the placing of tombs (whether in chancel or nave, or outside the church in the cloister) reveals a certain hierarchy of honour. As San Fruttuoso shelters the early admirals, so the town church of San Matteo in Genoa contains the remains of the great Doria statesmen; Andreà Doria lies in the crypt.

In the same way the Fieschi clan had their first burial basilica in Lavagna, in the very heart of their fiefs on the Riviera di Levante; later they built and maintained another *gentilizie* basilica, at the gates of Genoa, on the hill overlooking the sea, near their large palace on the outskirts of the city. This was the church of Santa Maria di Carignano, which was probably less well integrated into the atmosphere and fabric of the city than was San Matteo, for the Fieschi clan remained more distant and reserved, vis-à-vis Genoa, than the Doria.

Communities which united men of the same *albergo*, family clans which were descended from lineages or formed from more artificial associations, clans of masters and dependants or of men of greatly differing professions and stations – communities which united these men for worship, meetings and prayer are not exceptional or even original in the West. They can be found in other, very different groups, especially in confraternities, which were extremely common in Christendom throughout town and countryside. It is possible that when, in many countries, these family-based spiritual communities were losing their cohesion and their strength, men sought more artificial links to replace the old ones, away from ties of blood and name, away even from neighbourhood ties. In these confraternities a common creed was the surest of links; but it is surely striking to note, although it was very late – in the sixteenth century – and probably only in a few regions, that there was some return to the family ideal. This occurred through a paucity of recruits, and through the systematic admission of brothers and sons, who tended to make these once more open groups into family circles, as in Cáceres, in Estremadura.[101]

Thus we can imagine a sort of conflict or competition, as in political life, between spiritual groups which were essentially families, clans of relatives and dependants, claiming common names, ancestors, heroes and saints, and religious groups which were united by worship but formed more artificially, through neighbourhood links or, later, by their common profession.

Family clans certainly constituted a clearly felt and experienced social reality in numerous western cities. They were established in well-defined quarters, they brought together dependants who were protected or succoured by their superiors, and their members were all united by daily intercourse on their squares, in their *loggie*, churches or cloisters, and by prayer and the cult of dead saints and heroes. There is no doubt that membership of a clan characterized the activities and attitudes of men far more than any other necessarily more abstract notion of status, category, 'class' or even, I believe, of profession.

Notes

[1]Aubenas, R., in *Etudes d'histoire à la Mémoire de Noël Didier*, 1960.

[2]On this point, see the very detailed study of Yver, J., *Égalité entre héritiers et exclusion des enfants dotés: Essai de géographie coutumière*, Paris, 1966. In the fifteenth century in Franche-Comté the wills of nobles often still provided for equal distribution among all the children (sometimes even including daughters), and even among all the grand-children or nephews and nieces. Apparently the only method of moderating this was to give the daughters large dowries, to send several children (both sons and daughters) to become religious, and to reserve the main piece of land for the eldest son. See Pernot, A., "La noblesse", 20–26.

[3]Grand, R., "Quelques survivances régionales d'une communauté de famille ou de clan dans la pratique coutumière (XIe–XIVe siècle), surtout en France et en Suisse romande", in *R.H.D.F.E.*, 1952, 178–194; Partsch, G., *Das Mitwirkungsrecht der Familiengemeinschaft im alteren wallischer Recht (Laudatio parentum et hospicium)*, Geneva, 1955.

[4]Faletti, L., "Le retrait lignager en droit coutumier français", Thesis (Law), Paris, 1923; Ourliac, P., "Le retrait lignager dans le sud-ouest de la France", in *R.H.D.F.E.*, 1952; more generally, see Lafon, J., *Régimes matrimoniaux et mutations sociales. Les époux bordelais (1450–1550)*, Paris, 1972; Hilaire, J., "Vie en commun, famille et esprit communautaire", in *R.H.D.F.E.*, 1973.

[5]Pernot, A., "La noblesse franc-comtoise d'après les testaments (1350-1500)", 34–37.

[6]Poisson, C., "La justice à Mantes au XVe siècle", unpublished dissertation, University of Paris X, 1972, 66.

[7]Herlihy, D., in *Economy, society and government in medieval Italy*, 1969, 173–184.

[8]Herlihy, D., in *Economy, society and government in medieval Italy*, 1969, 183, notes 17, 19, 20; see also Herlihy, D., "Mapping households in medieval Italy", in *The Catholic Historical Review*, 1972, 1–22.

[9]Brattö, O., *Liber estimationum*.

[10]These percentages are of 99, 111, 65 and 45 landowners listed, respectively; other buildings adjoined public streets or squares, communal buildings, or other buildings of the same owners, who had been dispossessed.

[11]This is confirmed, moreover, for the dispossessed themselves, by the many towers or palaces which were kept in common; each head of family administered a share, which was sometimes extremely small (see above, p. 195).

[12]Rotelli, C., *L'economia agraria di Chieri attraverso i catasti dei secoli XIV–XVI*, Milan, 1967, 13–14.

[13]Robin, F., "Sestri Levante", 197–198.

[14]Aubenas, R., in *Etudes d'histoire à la mémoire de Noël Didier*, 1960.

[15]For this see Robin, F., "Sestri Levante", 201–202.

[16]*A.S.G.*, Antiche Finanze, Sala 42/65, B, Gabella possessionum, No. 576, anno 1447, out of 94 and 86 entries, respectively.

[17]Russell, J.C., "Recent advances in medieval demography", in *Speculum*, 1965, 89.

[18]Herlihy, D., *Medieval and Renaissance Pistoia*, 61.

[19]Returns made in an enquiry organized by Jeanne of Évreux at the beginning of the fourteenth century, in the eastern part of the Cotentin, show that numbers of women varied considerably from one village to another. See Lhérault, C., "Société et démographie de la vicomté de Saint-Lendelin à partir d'assiettes de Jeanne d'Évreux (1328–1338)", unpublished dissertation, University of Paris X, 1971. Numbers of women (here, girls rather than widows, apparently) varied, according to parish, from 1 per cent of all those listed as responsible for hearths to 16 per cent and even, in one exceptional case, to 19 per cent.

[20]These differences of interpretation from the same records, the *Libri focorum*, stem from the difficulty of identifying with certainty female Christian names; some were the same as those of the men. See Herlihy, D., *Medieval and Renaissance Pistoia*, 116 and 117, note 42.

[21]See Klapisch, C., in *Annales E.S.C.*, 1969.

[22]Robin, F., "Sestri Levante", 194–196.

[23]Cristiani, E., *Nobiltà e popolo*, 128.

[24]Lupo Gentile, M., in *Giornale storico e letterario della Liguria*, 1905, 10.

[25]Lupo Gentile, in *Giornale storico e letterario della Liguria*, 1905, 44.

[26]Lupo Gentile, in *Giornale storico e letterario della Liguria*, 1905, 23.

[27]Herlihy, D., *Pisa in the early Renaissance, A Study of urban Growth*, Yale U.P., 1958, 120–121.

[28]Herlihy, D., *Pisa*, 118.

[29]Gerbet, M.C., "Les confréries religieuses à Cácares de 1467 à 1523", in *Mélanges de la Casa de Velazquez*, vii, 1971, 75–113, especially 87, 100.

[30]Gerbert, M.C., in *Mélanges de la Casa de Velazquez*, 1971, 82.

[31]This is the very interesting thesis which has been elaborated for Germany by Mitterauer, M., *Zollfreiheit und Marktbereich*, 1969.

[32]Lupo Gentile, M., in *Giornale storico e letterario della Liguria*, 1905, 24, 28.

[33]Cristiani, E., *Nobiltà e popolo*, 130, 131: *Domus illorum de Stateris in qua tenetur statere nobilium de Stateris.*

[34]Heers, J., *L'Apennin ligure et la mer*, Congrès international d'histoire maritime, 1969.

[35]Heers, J., *Gênes*, 123–124.

[36]Lopez, R.S., "Aux origines du capitalisme génois", in *Annales E.S.C.*, 1937.

[37]These warehouses are not easy to identify. Texts referring to the sale or leasing of houses sometimes mention the *fondaco* of a family; this word recalls the caravanserais of Moslem countries, and I had imagined that in each case it meant one of these great warehouses (see Heers, J., *L'Apennin*, 9). However, Mattia-Moresco ("Le parrochie gentilizie genovesi", in *Rivista italiana per le scienze giuridiche*, 1901, fasc. 1, 2, pp. 8, 11) identifies the *fondaco* with the whole of a quarter dominated by a great family, the *domoculta*; nevertheless in all the texts I have seen the *fondaco* never refers to one of these great families.

[38]Bigwood, G., and Grunzweig, A., *Le livre de comptes des Gallerani*, Paris, 1962, ii, 54, 70–72.

[39]Chomel, V., "Communautés rurales et 'casane' lombardes en Dauphiné", in *Bibliothèque de l'École des chartes*, 1951–1952, 225–247, especially 228–234; Fournial, E., *Les villes et l'économie d'échanges en Forez aux XIIIe et XIVe siècles*, Paris, 1967, 252; Patrone, A.M., *Le Casane astigiane in Savoia*, Turin, 1959, 64.

[40]Patrone, A.M., *Le Casane*, 59–62.

[41]Chomel, V., "Communautés rurales", 233, 244.

[42]Casini, B., "Patrimonio ed attività del Fondaco del Taglio di Simone di Lotto da Sancasciano e fratelli", in *Studi in onore di A. Fanfani*, Milan, 1962, ii, 227–298.

[43]Petrucci, A., *Il libro*, 13.

[44]But at the onset of the death of Giovanni, all commonly-held property was divided between the two brothers. It is notable that the division was made, not by any judge of the commune, but by the two other brothers, the churchmen.

[45]Warburg, A., *Gesammelte Schriften*, i, 140–144.

[46]Bonvisi, F., "Les Bonvisi, marchands banquiers à Lyon au XVIe siècle", in *Annales E.S.C.*, 1971, 1234–1269, especially 1235–1237.

[47]Lane, F.C., "Family partnerships and joint ventures in the Venetian Republic", in *Journal of economic history*, iv, 1944, 178–196, reprinted in *Venice and history*, Baltimore, 1966, 36–55.

[48]For these societies, see Heers, J., *Gênes*, 200–204.

[49]See above, pp. 151–152.

[50]Heers, J., *Gênes*, 544–549.

[51]*A.S.G.*, Antiche Finanze, Sala 41/103, B, Avariarum, No. 536; these percentages are out of 91, 58 and 68, respectively.

[52]Robin, F., "Sestri Levante", 174.

[53]*A.S.G.*, Antiche Finanze, Sala 41, Gabella possessionum, anno 1447. The spread of estimated wealth of the Doria is as follows:

Less than £10: one entry (£9).
£10–£20: 5 entries (£11, £11, £13, £16, £17).
£20–£50: 4 entries (£34, £37, £45, £45).
£50–£100: 7 entries (£68, £68, £70, £72, £75, £77, £84).
£100–£200: 32 entries (£100, £100, £103, £104, £107, £109, £115, £115, £115, £115, £128, £135, £145, £145, £145, £145, £145, £145, £145, £150, £150, £156, £156, £164, £168, £173, £173, £173, £185, £185, £196, £196).
£200–£300: 12 entries (£201, £225, £231, £231, £238, £250, £288, £288, £288, £289, £291, £296).
£300–£400: 5 entries (£300, £305, £322, £343, £346).
£400–£500: 7 entries (£400, £402, £403, £431, £445, £460, £461).
£500–£1,000: 17 entries (£510, £520, £590, £623, £670, £693, £714, £724, £726, £765, £819, £823, £840, £925, £980, £980).
Over £1,000: 6 entries (£1,003, £1,008, £1,036, £1,108, £1,114, £2,638).

[54]See Figure 5, p. 224.

[55]*A.S.G.*, Antiche Finanze, Sala 41, Avariarum, anno 1479.

[56]*A.S.G.*, Antiche Finanze, Sala 42/46, B, Focagiorum, anno 1465, No. 612.

[57]Heers, J., *Feux, jeux et joutes dans les sociétés d'Occident à la fin du Moyen Age*, Montréal and Paris, 1971, 114–118.

[58]See Montaigne, *Journal de voyage*, 253–255.

[59]See above, pp. 79–81.

[60]*Annali genovesi*, ed. C. Imperiale di Sant'Angelo, Rome, 1923, iii, 26; quoted by Poleggi, E., *Le Contrade*, 18.

[61]Perosa, A., ed., *Giovanni Rucellai ed il suo zibaldone*; i: *Il zibaldone quaresimale*, London, 1960, 28–32.

[62]Herlihy, D., in *Economy, society and government in medieval Italy*, 1969, 183, note 19.

[63]*A Parisian Journal*, 1405–1449, translated from the anonymous *Journal d'un Bourgeois de Paris* by Janet Shirley, Oxford, 1968, year 1418.

[64]Béthune, J. de, *Les méreaux des familles brugeoises*, Bruges, 1890, pp. xi–xiii, xxv–xxvi.

[65]*A.S.G.*, Manoscritti, No. LXXIV, A, 3 June 1430. The Bechignoni were one of the groups which came together to form the Centurioni *albergo*.

[66]*A.S.G.*, Archivio Secreto, Confinium, Filza 4 (1443–1467), 7 September 1451.

[67]*A.S.G.*, Compere e mutui, No. 1857, Mutuum Impositum 1379, a loan contracted in 1378; this information was provided by John Day.

[68]For all this, see *A.S.G.*, San Giorgio, Cartularii delle Colonne, 1456.

[69]*A.S.G.*, San Giorgio, Colonne.

[70]*A.S.G.*, Manoscritti 529, Spinola di Luchulo (a collection of wills and dispositions for the *moltiplicati* of San Giorgio); this manuscript gives a long list of beneficiaries.

[71]*A.S.G.*, Notaio Giacomo de Recco, filza 1, parte 2, No. 65, 2 August 1466.

[72]*A.S.G.*, Notaio de Cairo Andreà, filza 20, No. 153, 6 June 1465.

[73]*A.S.G.*, Notaio de Fazio Antonio, filza 14, parte 2, Nos. 39 and 40.

[74]*A.S.G.*, Notaio de Recco Giocomo, filza 1, parte 2, No. 123, 17 February 1467.

[75]Bozzola, A., in *Bollettino storico-bibliografico subalpino*, 1923, 223.

[76]It should be noted that one of the most powerful *alberghi* in Genoa bore the name Cattaneo.

[77]For all this, see Lupo Gentile, M., in *Giornale storico e letterario della Liguria*, 1905, 29, 34, 35.

[78]Lupo Gentile, M., in *Giornale storico e letterario della Liguria*, 1905, 45. The *maior et sanior pars nobilium de Ripafratta* allowed the procurators of the *popolo* and of the church of San Bartolomeo the right to judge and sentence men in respect of all offences affecting the internal life of the community; fines were given to the Church. See Lupo Gentile, 47–49.

[79]Gage, J., *Life in Italy at the time of the Medici*, London, 1968, 19–20.

[80]Villani, G., *Cronica*.

[81]Costamagna, G., *Cartolari notarili genovesi*, Rome, 1961, ii; quoted by Poleggi, E., in *Urbanistica*, xlii–xliii, 18.

[82]*A.S.G.*, Documenti tornati da Parigi, xx, off. Monetae, fol 61 v°, 9 October 1455.

[83]The *albergo* which appointed a single collector one year elected two the following year.

[84]See above, p. 83; Heers, J., *Gênes*, 610; and especially Ascheri, A., *Notizie*.

[85]Schneider, J., *La ville*, 141ff.

[86]Beaumanoir, P. de, *Coutumes de Beauvaisis*, ed. Salmon, Paris, 1899–1900, 2 vols.

[87]*A.S.G.*, Notaio Loggia Giovanni, filza 1, No. 257, 17 August 1451.

[88]*A.S.G.*, Notaio de Fazio Antonio, filza 16, No. 520, 27 January 1456.

[89]*A.S.G.*, Notaio Risso Baromeo, filza 1, parte 2, No. 63, 2 January 1449; there is another example of this kind of agreement between the Nigro and the Mari of Piazza Banchi: see *A.S.G.*, Notaio Duracino Tommaso, filza 7, parte 2, 11 January 1464.

[90]Lupo Gentile, M., in *Giornale storico e letterario della Liguria*, 1905, 28.

[91]Bozzola, A., in *Bollettino storico-bibliografico subalpino*, 1923, 223.

[92]*A.S.G.*, Notaio Foglietta Oberto junior, filza 5, parte 2, No. 199, 17 September 1459.

[93]Schneider, J., *La ville*, 147.

[94]Lupo Gentile, M., in *Giornale storico e letterario della Liguria*, 1905, 30, 31.

[95]Warburg, A., *Gesammelte Schriften*, i.

[96]*A.S.G.*, Notaio Risso Baromeo, filza 1, No. 63, 3 May 1449.

[97]D'Oria, J., *La chiesa di San Matteo in Genova descritta ed illustrata*, Genoa, 1860, 140.

[98]*A.S.G.*, Notaio de Bagnara Bartolomeo, filza 13, parte 2, 5 November 1456.

[99]D'Oria, J., *La chiesa*, 129.

[100]Mattia-Moresco, in *Rivista italiana per le scienze giuridiche*, 1901, 5f.; San Pancrazio (Calvo and Pallavicino), San Luca (Spinola and Grimaldi), San Torpete (Cattaneo della Volta); San Paolo (Camilla), Santa Maria di Carignano (Fieschi, then Sauli). These *gentilizie* churches can certainly be found in most Italian cities, at least in the original establishment of parishes, when urban expansion was just beginning to take place. In Venice, with very few exceptions, the forty-five or so parishes created in the ninth and tenth centuries were established by great families, who each owned and protected a new church. See Pavan, E., "Maisons, urbanisme et structures", 25–30. See also Tassini, G., *Curiosità veneziane ovvero origini delle denominazioni stradali in Venezia*, Venice, 1887.

[101]Gerbet, M. C., in *Mélanges de la Casa de Velazquez*, 1971, 91–93.

Conclusion

All the foregoing information, although probably sketchy and unequal, shows beyond doubt that there were in the Middle Ages social groups based on the family in very many European cities, and that they were entrenched in varying degrees, according to time and place. These clans were very large, uniting an enormous number of people, evoking tribes rather than simple families, rather even than extended families. The social structures which have been observed were profoundly different from our own and were in general different from structures throughout the 'modern' period; in order to study them, therefore, the historian must resolutely shun modern patterns.

It therefore seems certain that men very often took an active part in collective life, in the economic and social activities of real, tangible groups. This implies a cohesion which was universally felt in every aspect of daily life, and which affected men's attitudes. We can easily accept that membership of one of these clans resulted in the definite involvement of a person in its economic, social and spiritual life; membership also afforded effective protection against enemies or adversity in times of difficulty.

Yet, of course, family clans did not reign supreme; they were merely one type among the many social groups which united men in the towns or countryside of the West, in the Middle Ages. Other groups, bodies or orders such as confraternities, guilds, parties, and communities of peasants or shepherds, also had a very important place in western society. If we are to acquire a reasonable idea of the structure and realities of social life we must not neglect the roles of all these varied groups inside well-defined circles: their effects on a certain number of individuals, their rivalries and alliances, their constant intervention in political and professional life, the multifarious allegiances of men of different stations. If we are to study individuals, we must also examine all these social alliances so that we may be better prepared to look at individual or collective attitudes and ways of thinking.

This essay, concerning a single type of social group, can therefore only supply limited information, and there is a need for similar studies of other groups. Yet on many points the conclusions of this restricted essay are not insignificant. First, we are able to modify, and even to refute in their main points, two theses which are at present generally accepted by many writers, or unfortunately used as solid and incontrovertible bases for future research. The two theses which can be abandoned after the examination of family clans are, I believe, firstly, that there was a large gulf between towns and the country areas around them, so that urban civilization and society are seen as profoundly new and original; secondly, that inside towns in the last two or three centuries of the Middle Ages, human relations were governed essentially by antagonism, by 'class conflict' in the modern sense of that expression.

Links between city and countryside have long been emphasized by many historians who have clearly shown, for most of the West, that the aristocracy, often called 'bourgeois' or 'commercial', was frequently only an office-holding aristocracy which, moreover, owned large estates both in the towns themselves and in the surrounding countryside. As detailed and specific research on the origins or rather the evolution of large cities builds up, we see increasingly clearly that the schema invented by Engels and subsequently presented in very different ways by numerous writers attracted by this invention, can be applied only to a few geographical areas or a few individual cases; this schema, which despite calls for caution has been accepted for thirty years, was fanciful; at the very least, it was an excessive generalization.

With few exceptions, towns possessed only limited social originality; their inhabitants often came from the countryside. Initially, the richest owed their wealth to the ownership and exploitation of estates; the most influential exercised power through their authority over the peasants in their jurisdiction.

This new standpoint is confirmed in many ways by the study of family clans. The great families of the urban aristocracy nearly always claimed rural origins and noble descent, looking to particular fiefs in particular villages. Genealogies of this kind were not pure inventions; far from it. Noble lineages, with power over castles, estates and men, often established themselves in cities and built private fortresses there, retaining authority and jurisdiction over their dependants. Above all, social structures in cities perpetuated those of the fiefs, for clans remained as powerful as before, with many heads of families, allies, protégés and dependants; their organization remained the same, so that the family clans of the towns mirrored those of the countryside. Throughout the Middle Ages these numerous and cohesive groups still kept close ties with the areas where they had been formed, where they had estates and castles, and raised armies; where, too, they retained peasant clienteles.

Wherever we can most easily perceive clan politics, it seems that the most powerful clans tried, by making all kinds of new alliances, to unite under the same name men who owned fiefs and important merchants or bankers. This was well established in certain Italian cities in the fourteenth and fifteenth centuries, and provides proof of the constant involvement in city life by rural nobles; it also shows that a large proportion of urban wealth and power came from the countryside.

The existence of family clans which united large numbers of individuals of very varied stations and levels of wealth, which joined leaders and dependants into one total community where their interests were in common, must, I believe, significantly change our ideas of the structures and relationships of forces inside medieval cities. Above all, men belonged to their tribes, some expecting increased power therefrom, others looking for protection and support. Here, then, is a striking and incontrovertible example of social groups which had their own ways of life, and which were kept in close cohesion by many different links, especially by actual cohabitation inside cities. Thus men's efforts were directed towards a common purpose, and they were conscious of a continuing spiritual community. These groups included great aristocrats, who owned land, or had military or political designs, rich merchants or bankers, small traders, men of little substance, freedmen and even paupers.

Obviously, this contradicts any systematic division of society into socio-economic 'classes' with clear and distinct levels of wealth. Equally, it contradicts the idea of a constant struggle between such 'classes' in pursuit of material interests or political power. These ideas of 'class struggle' have become a commonplace in many popularizations, but they seem to me to be the result of unjustifiable extrapolation, or even the fruit of fantasy; they show an astonishing perfunctoriness in research, and a high degree of conformism. What is important, I believe, is not to prove that a so-called 'Marxist' theory – more than a hundred years old and constantly revived, exacerbated or modified to such an extent that few writers can still get their bearings in the resulting, indisputable orthodoxy – is once more caught out in one particular. The important thing is to be able to assert that such a naive hypothesis, which amounts to the act of faith of a religion, can lead to no serious historical research; for this 'class' hypothesis completely fails to recognize the extreme diversity of conditions and personalities, and the always very complex nature of medieval social ties and groups. To use a pre-established schema, whatever it may be, and especially a 'Marxist' schema, applied like a creed at every turn on the whole of the past and all western civilizations may be satisfying to those minds which cleave to logic and clarity; but it is erroneous and sterile, and shows a startling lack of real historical curiosity.

These two aspects apart, the study of social groups and more especially, here, of family clans inside cities, also enables us to throw an interesting light on some aspects of contemporary social life and even attitudes. Clearly, historians who study material or spiritual medieval civilizations cannot ignore the numerous and complex family groups and their influence on society and on attitudes. It is in the light of their existence that we should look at town planning and civil architecture, the disconnected nature of cities and the extreme fragmentation of social life, the apparent disorder characterizing the different stages of urban expansion. In this light too we should see the existence of social units which were tightly clustered around a small square or a single street; the extremely composite nature of each quarter and the resulting absence of visible social segregation among citizens; the towers and houses with towers, and the distinctive concept of the urban house (very high, narrow houses, towers or the remains of towers, and lateral stairs). It is impossible to explain all these elements unless we look to the strength and cohesion of family groups, to the large numbers of people of various stations who made up these clans or tribes, and to the constraints exerted by neighbourhood links.

The spiritual community of family clans and their interest in churches, called *gentilizie* in Italy, also lead us to view the assertion by noble clans of the right of patronage over churches as more than just the result of financial interest.

The very notion of the commune, rural or urban, must also be modified or improved. I have noted without much emphasis, for the fact was not directly relevant, that for example in the mountain cantons of Italy noble clans formed a *communitas* to administer a particular fief or fiefs. This commune, under the direction of clan leaders, included all the members of a clan including its *homines* and *fideles*; it was thoroughly family-based, and was governed by *rectores*; it was subject to the judgements of a special court. Peasants were released from this community at quite a late period, separation taking place through a series of individual agreements or negotiated concessions.

Noble clans in towns also had their own administration and justice; this situation lasted for many years, into the Quattrocento in some Italian towns in the case of internal matters over which clans tried to assert their own laws exclusively. Around the eleventh century, when they originated, communes in cities seem to have been alliances between the family clans; moreover, these alliances were very often concluded by contracts like commercial agreements. The communes respected all the powers of heads of clans, limiting their own activities and ambitions to the establishment of a kind of equilibrium between the different family groups (for example over the choice of magistrates) and to the avoidance of conflict. In Italy, this was the role of consuls and then of the *podestà*, who was a sort of supreme judge, above the various factions.

The new communes, which were governed by new aristocracies and established on different bases, asserted themselves only very slowly and probably unequally, even incompletely. It seems that historians, influenced by chroniclers, have greatly exaggerated not only the rise of veritable 'bourgeois' and 'commercial' aristocrats, but also the decisive part played in city administrations by guilds, as well as, above all, the eclipse of the old noble families and their clans. Leaving aside Genoa, which was perhaps a quite exceptional city, we can see that several other Italian cities continued to elect all their magistrates, or a good proportion, on geographical rather than professional bases. Moreover, the establishment of a different kind of political power does not imply a serious or even noticeable weakening of noble clans in the economic, social and spiritual spheres of life. 'Popular' communes had difficulty in establishing their rule, and were normally incapable of preventing armed conflicts – which then took on the form of urban revolts – and, *a fortiori*, vendettas. Despite many attempts, communes could not demolish seignorial towers in cities, and they often failed over an even longer period to break ties of blood and neighbourhood, for the military solidarity and, more, the economic and social cohesion of family clans were extremely strong in most towns up to the end of the Middle Ages and sometimes well after. We must therefore avoid attaching too much importance to institutional novelties or 'reforms'; our attention must rather be directed to the realities of economic and social life which point to a much slower and later development.

In complete contrast, it appears that princely states, being very different in character and having more powerful means at their disposal, were able to wage more effective war on government by noble clans and on their power; this, for example, is the significance of the praises addressed by Joinville to Louis IX, for the king had broken the hold of the *lignages* of rich Parisians on the administration of the city. Princes or kings established more stable, stronger, more independent governments in the hands of genuine officials, or at least controlled by them.

This, with the force of the Roman heritage and the density of urbanization, is probably one of the main reasons why family cohesion, in all its forms, was maintained to a much later period in the cities of Italy, Germany and southern France than in northern France and England. No princely power, not even the pope in Rome, was strong enough to resist the clans in these cities effectively, and the activities of the civic authorities against them were likewise insufficient. In Italy, this situation seems to have come to an end only with the appearance of government by real seignories, tyrants or princes; for example, in Milan and Florence, but not in Genoa. So family clans disappeared, not under the feeble attacks of communes, but in the face of increasing princely authority.

Another factor comes into play here: this is the great imbalance in the available documentation. On the one hand my research has borne most heavily on Italy and especially on Genoa; on the other hand Italian and Genoese archives, especially notarial documents, are much more varied and numerous, published texts are more abundant, and so detailed studies can be more precise. All this justifies, or at least explains, the fact that the examples given refer sometimes exclusively to Italy.

But does this imbalance of information reflect reality? Do family clans appear to have been less powerful away from the cities of Italy and Germany because they actually became weaker there earlier, or because they have remained more elusive? This second possibility should not be totally disregarded; the lack of documents, or rather of specific studies, is by no means convincing. It is probable that detailed research in this area would bring to light, in the towns of north-west Europe, various significant aspects of the maintenance of family solidarity within large-scale urban clans.

Abbreviations used in the notes

Annales E.S.C.	*Annales: économies, sociétés, civilisations*
Annales D.H.	*Annales de démographie historique*
A.R.A.L.S.L.A.	*Atti della reale Accademia lucchese di scienze, lettere ed arti*
A.S.F.	*Archivio di Stato di Firenze*
A.S.G.	*Archivio di Stato di Genova*
A.S.I.	*Archivio storico italiano*
B.P.H.	*Bulletin philologique et historique du Comité des travaux historiques et scientifiques*
M.G.H.S.	*Monumenta Germaniae historica. Scriptores*
R.H.D.F.E.	*Revue historique de droit français et étranger*
R.R.I.S.S.	*Rerum italicarum scriptores. Raccolta degli storici italiani dal cinquencento al millecinquecento*

Index

Note: family names are printed in capital letters